'It took courage for Grant to ad post-traumatic stress disorder (P ___ ... rst opened up to me about the issues he was racing, I wasn't shocked. I was relieved. I knew there was a long road ahead. But like everything Grant took on, I knew this one conversation would lead to him accepting the challenge. I knew he was a strong man, but facing this challenge showed me strength was much more than pulling a train or plane which he had done on many occasions.'

David Sharpe, former Assistant Commissioner,
Australian Federal Police

'A brave, life-affirming book from a brave man. Grant Edwards' book works as a thriller, an adventure story, social history and self-help guide. Anyone struggling with the battle that goes on between our two ears will find comfort and help in Grant's words.'

Gordon Peake, political advisor/academic

'As a foreign diplomat I have had the honour and privilege of seeing Grant working in different nations, cultures, and languages where there are no barriers for his noble dedication: to make the world a better one for us all. He is truly a citizen of the world.'

Fernando de la Cerda Bickford,
Deputy Ambassador, Embassy of Guatemala

'Not only is Grant Edwards a respected leader in law enforcement in both hemispheres, he is also an acclaimed athlete, world record holder and mentor to many across the globe who suffer from the debilitating post-traumatic stress disorder. Grant Edwards is a champion of the highest order and a gentleman to boot. Along with my family, I am proud to call him a friend.'

Harry Mitchell, co-founder, Tartan Warriors

'Anyone who has ever met Grant Edwards is immediately impressed by the physical size of the man – but that's only half the human that he really is. Grant's physical strength is matched by his ability to care for fellow humans. In his career, he has leapt more hurdles than most of us have been forced to, but he's done with seeming ease as he's a natural leader. Leadership, though, carries an unseen burden and Grant has had to deal with that for too long. The mark of the man is opening himself to fully disclose his weaknesses and not everyone has the inner strength to do that. For that is what I am most proud of him for.'

Leigh Diffey, NBC sports broadcaster

THE STRONG MAN

A powerful story of life under fire and
one man's journey back from the brink

GRANT EDWARDS

Australian Federal Police Commander

SIMON &
SCHUSTER

London · New York · Sydney · Toronto · New Delhi

A CBS COMPANY

THE STRONG MAN
First published in Australia in 2019 by
Simon & Schuster (Australia) Pty Limited
Suite 19A, Level 1, Building C, 450 Miller Street, Cammeray, NSW 2062

10 9 8 7 6 5 4 3 2 1

A CBS Company
Sydney New York London Toronto New Delhi
Visit our website at www.simonandschuster.com.au

 A catalogue record for this book is available from the National Library of Australia

Cover design: Luke Causby/Blue Cork
Cover image: Author's own
Typeset by Midland Typesetters, Australia
Printed and bound in Australia by Griffin Press

 The paper this book is printed on is certified against the Forest Stewardship Council® Standards. Griffin Press holds FSC chain of custody certification SGS-COC-005088. FSC promotes environmentally responsible, socially beneficial and economically viable management of the world's forests.

I dedicate The Strong Man *to three even stronger women:
my wife, Kate, and daughters Emilee and Jacinta.
Without your unconditional love, support and courage,
I would not be where I am today. I am blessed to have
you in my life, and even though I've written a book
I can't find the words to describe how much
I love each of you.*

CONTENTS

FOREWORD
ANDREW COLVIN, APM OAM

Strength, courage and resilience come in many forms. Some-times these things are obvious and other times they can pass by almost unnoticed. It would be all too easy to see my colleague Grant Edwards only as 'the Strong Man'. It would be forgivable because to meet Grant you can't help but be captured by his size, strength and imposing figure. Here is a man whose reputation and physical presence announce him to an audience even before he enters the room.

But that is not the Grant Edwards I know. I know a Grant whose courage and strength is not in his incredible sporting prowess, his amazing physical strength, or even his long, varied and very successful policing career. The Grant I have come to know has courage and strength beyond what most can see, and he lays it bare for everyone to see in this compelling and very personal story.

I first met Grant shortly after I joined the Australian Federal Police. 'Met' is probably an understatement as Grant was one of the most imposing human beings I'd ever laid eyes on. I fondly recall going to the Royal Easter Show at the old Sydney Showground and watching Grant take on other man-mountains as part of a World's Strongest Man display. As a young cop, I remember thinking how good it was to see him, and that I was just like him . . . Well, of course I wasn't. My entire 20-year-old body could nearly fit into one of Grant's imposing thighs or arms. But he was an AFP officer, and so was I. I was proud that he was representing the organisation and the profession I had joined, and wherever Grant competed I always paid attention – and he always made us proud.

Over the years that followed, Grant took his strongman achievements to a whole new level – pulling planes, trucks, trains and ships, and at his peak he was recognised by Guinness World Records as the strongest man in the world. Despite those superhuman efforts, Grant's story had a darker side, which he kept secret until much later in his career. He had just been offered the highly sought-after role of AFP Commander for the Americas. It should have been a career-defining moment and a justified reward for years of incredible service, but at that time Grant's life was unravelling, and like many sufferers of PTSD, he had largely been suffering in silence. Grant decided to open up for the first time, sharing his struggles with a handful of trusted colleagues, myself included. What followed was an emotional roller-coaster for Grant as he came to terms with his own struggles while also taking a high-profile role in highlighting the importance of police in our society, and the toll that service can take.

The death of a colleague to suicide in early 2017 rocked our organisation, prompting Grant to share his personal battle with the AFP. He detailed the depths of despair he'd reached when he hit an all-time low and contemplated taking his own life only a few years earlier. This was another example of Grant's courage and selflessness. He was all too aware of the potential consequences of baring his soul to the world and to a workforce that traditionally doesn't tolerate any hint of weakness or vulnerability. It was the measure of the man that he took the unprecedented step of opening up, emailing all 6500 AFP members about his mental health challenges and the steps he was taking to gradually get his life back on track. What follows is just a part of Grant's email to staff, and it in no small way helped set the AFP on an entirely new course in how we deal with mental injury and PTSD in our ranks:

What I did know was that I was broken, and for the first time in my life I acknowledged it. I needed to change, but most importantly I needed help.

I was tired and overwhelmed, but the desire to get healthy overrode my desire to worry about what work or others for that matter would think of me.

I confided in a couple of close mates (colleagues) and they helped me immensely through support and encouragement, and reinforced to me that by acknowledging my problem, and more importantly dealing with it, was the most important aspect.

I've done some pretty tough things in my life, but acknowledging this and seeking help is by far the hardest thing I have ever done.

My purpose for writing this email is to encourage each and every one of you to look after each other. If just one person in the AFP finds this email useful then it's been worth me sending this email.

Mental health in our organisation and to that, our profession, isn't a stigma.

It's a result of the highly demanding, stressful and confronting job we have chosen to do and the burden of wearing the badge.

If you feel you need help. Please seek it.

The Strong Man is timely, coming as it does when most police, first responders and military organisations across the world are struggling to come to grips with the debilitating impact of mental injury on their people.

Grant's story does much more than contrast the life of this powerhouse human with that of a fragile father and husband whose life teetered on the edge at a time when he should have been enjoying his best years. It is the story of a police officer who gave everything he had to the job he loved, and to everything he did. It is not a negative story about policing, but it is a reminder of the toll that a career like policing can take.

Grant's story allows us to celebrate what a career as a police officer can look like. It is unique, but it is not unusual. Grant has enjoyed an amazing journey in the AFP, one that was unimaginable to him growing up. This reminds us of the incredible opportunities and challenges that come with being an Australian police officer. While Grant's career has taken a toll, I know he has never once regretted the decision he made to join the AFP. Policing is a calling, a community service and a great privilege. Grant's career embodies all of that.

This is Grant Edwards' story. It is told from his perspective and reflects his view and thoughts. It is compelling, at times it is frightening, and at times sad. But it is also a wonderfully good read.

It's also clear, amid the ever-present danger and chaos that is part and parcel of a policing career, how important it is to have a loving and supportive family in your corner. Grant is blessed to have Kate, Jacinta and Emilee in his life. I have come to know them well, and they are very special people. Together they have been through the toughest of times, and yet they remain strong for each other. It is my hope that the next chapter in the life of my friend and colleague Grant Edwards, the Strong Man, is the happiest and healthiest of his life. He deserves nothing less.

Thank you, Grant, for your exemplary service, for sharing your story, and for having the courage and strength to tell it.

AJ
Andrew Colvin, APM OAM
AFP Commissioner

INTRODUCTION
NOTHING BUT THE TRUTH

'It's like the day you join you're given a backpack and every day you go to work you add a little pebble. After 10 years the backpack has gotten considerably heavier, but you carry on, as though you are still young and fit. After 20 years the number of pebbles has increased and the backpack is substantially heavier. You can only carry it for some of the time, the rest of the time you have to drag it. After 30 years you can hardly move the backpack. It's so heavy that you are physically, mentally and emotionally drained from having to move it, the pain is just too much and the commitment, motivation and vigour you once possessed have all but been drained from your body . . .'
– Anonymous New York Police Department officer, 2018

I'm often asked by friends to talk to their son, daughter, niece or nephew about their aspirations to join the police force. Of course I tell them, hand on heart, that the day I graduated from the Australian Federal Police (AFP) college in 1985 was one of the greatest moments of my life. And it was – because I wanted to do my bit to serve and protect society. Thirty-four years later I'm still motivated by my pride in the uniform and my goal to give my very best. I tell these fresh-faced kids that, as a long-time member of the force, I believe policing is one of the most rewarding and honourable careers anyone can undertake. It's a chance to do tangible good, and the opportunities in the jobs are boundless. I've been sent to Afghanistan, East Timor, the Americas. I've played my part in fighting illicit drugs, child exploitation and human trafficking, and been involved in other causes to help make our society a better place for everyone, particularly our most vulnerable citizens. It is a noble calling.

In recent years though, I've become painfully aware of the toll a lifetime in policing can have on a person's mental and physical health. Because they're entitled to transparency, I've started to advise would-be recruits that policing is one of the toughest and most emotionally brutal vocations on earth. A police officer must constantly deal with the worst side of humanity, which stands to reason because members of the public only ever call the police when a situation becomes out of their control and they're in danger of being harmed – or worse. The insights police gain into the ugliness of human nature have a profound impact. Even when we're off duty we're in a constant state of hyper-vigilance, waiting for *that* moment when hell is unleashed. However, when we're on the job, we need to put that instinct at the back of our mind because when the situation arises a police officer might have to be a counsellor, a social worker, a psychologist, a medic, a lawyer, a teacher or even a prison warden.

It is my hope that in telling my story I'll help show what motivates men and women to commit to a job where they turn up to work not knowing if they'll return to their loved ones at the end of their shift. Our reality is far removed from what's depicted in high-rating cop shows on television. When a cop is caught in a real life-and-death situation there's no moody background music playing. A police officer can't casually draw their weapon and shoot a fleeing felon in the leg because they'll risk facing a criminal charge for using excessive force. In real-life policing, the good guy doesn't always win; detectives don't punch a suspect in the face, no matter how much they might want to. Most commanding officers will bleed for those who serve under them, rather than engage in passive-aggressive pettiness to undermine them. There are rules and protocols that must be adhered to in car chases to protect the public. And not too many cops would mutter anything like 'Go ahead. Make my day' like Clint Eastwood's alter-ego Dirty Harry Callahan in *Sudden Impact*, challenging a punk to take a shot at him. A real cop would be more focused on ensuring there was no bloodshed.

The challenge commanding officers face is to work out how to properly prepare someone – who more often than not is in their early twenties – to experience human tragedy on a sustained level. It's not easy. How do you brace anyone to anticipate the sights, sounds and smells they'll encounter as a police officer? How would you explain to a raw recruit that over their lifetime they'll experience an average of more than 500 traumatic events?

In our profession we're deeply sceptical about almost everything, because from our first day in the academy we're moulded to distrust what we see and hear; to question everything. Eventually we're left with a 'deficit of distrust', where cynicism becomes so deep it eventually permeates all facets of your life. The lessons of our job make us behave differently to the rest of society. Apart from country cops, very few police officers will live near their workplace. We race our friends to sit in the far corner in restaurants or other unfamiliar places so our backs are covered, and we scan for exit points in cinemas and shopping centres in case of a worst-case scenario. We don't tend to associate with the broader community, preferring instead to mix with like-minded others.

In telling nothing but the truth, I always advise a would-be recruit they'll be judged harshly in the court of public opinion. There are people who'll film your every move in a powder keg situation, then selectively edit and post their footage on social media in a way that condemns the force. The trolls and others who believe our badge represents a repressive authority that aims to curtail civil liberties will never acknowledge that it actually identifies us as the public's protectors. Instead, they'll take delight in nailing you to the cross. The irony is that while a police officer is obliged by oath to present the facts and tell the truth, they'll be condemned because someone has chosen not to disclose the full picture of their actions in a stressed situation. When a police officer is required to appear in court they must expect that their integrity, professionalism and credibility might be questioned at length by an alleged paedophile or an alleged wife-basher's legal counsel, who charge their client a king's ransom to do whatever it takes to ensure their freedom. Sometimes you'll be attacked, ridiculed, patronised and mocked in front of your peers, the jury, the judge, the public gallery and members of the media. Criminals will do their utmost to physically and psychologically intimidate you and your family, telling you what they'd do to your wife, mother or daughter if the opportunity presented itself. Yet, as a trained professional, you never give them the satisfaction of a reaction.

If you're in my line of work, it's not unreasonable to expect to be verbally abused, physically assaulted, spat at, bitten or have urine thrown at you. You will suffer physical injuries like cuts, abrasions, broken bones, torn tendons and sprains. You'll deal with horrendous homicides, rapes, assaults and fatal car and motorbike accidents. You might see bodies that have been decapitated or the terrible impacts of chemical weapons on innocent children in a conflict zone. The Taliban may set out to kill you. You could be exposed to life-threatening diseases like chikungunya, dengue fever, sleep apnoea, chronic inflammation, fibromyalgia or schistosomiasis, all of which can debilitate you for years. You'll witness the devastation of natural disasters. You'll remove children from dysfunctional families and be outraged to see they're covered in welts and sores from living in flea-infested, maggot-riddled homes where the stench and the filth offends your senses. You may be required to be present in an operating theatre while surgeons fight to save the life of a drug courier whose gut is full of illicit drugs worth enough money to buy a two-storey house in an exclusive Sydney suburb. You might attend a scene where the friends of a deceased person were so stoned they used the electric cord from an iron to try to jump-start his heart when he stopped breathing. These terrible realities are the 'pebbles' that police constantly add to the invisible backpack we carry. Over time, you realise the pack is heavy but you soldier on, but you only realise the devastating effect of your journey when the day comes that you're unable to carry the load anymore.

Any young person wanting to join the Federal Police should realise it's guaranteed their hearts will shatter if they're called upon to investigate the horror of toddlers being sexually assaulted. God knows you'll be consumed by a rage that makes your body shake and forces tears from your eyes. You'll seethe when you realise the film posted on the internet feeds the perversions of adults who maintain that their 'love' of a helpless child is no different to that between two consenting adults. You'll be haunted forever by the piercing screams of those babies; the only way they can plead for their abuser to stop. Our profession authorises us to take such a person's liberty from them, and in the most extreme circumstances we may have to use deadly force to quell a volatile situation when all other avenues have been exhausted. However, the law also mandates that we're obliged to render assistance and attempt to save the life of that very same person who wishes to harm or kill us.

Anyone considering joining the police ranks ought to expect to work incessant hours. You'll develop poor sleeping and nutritional habits, and possibly form a reliance on alcohol and medications. Slowly but surely, you'll withdraw from your family and loved ones. You will miss many Christmas celebrations, birthdays, significant family events and your children's milestone moments. You'll hear people groan, 'Oh, work . . . again' after you offer an apology for your non-attendance. You will be away from your family and home for extended periods; you will isolate yourself, become angry and intolerant. Crying and sobbing will become one method of expressing your feelings. Eventually you'll be plagued by exhaustion. And you will attend too many funerals for colleagues either killed in the line of duty or who have died by their own hand. Regardless of how they leave us, a small piece of you will be buried with each of them.

Most of us believe we're tougher than the sights and devastation we're forced to confront. And while I have done my best to protect the community, I didn't know that the traumas of my job had devoured me until, finally, I was left psychologically vulnerable and exposed, suffering what's called a 'complete functional impairment'. For years, my smile was my mask, my laugh yet another disguise. But the relentlessness required for me to preserve my job drained every ounce of energy from me because I lived in fear that my career would be terminated if I revealed to my superiors that I was battling with a mental health issue. This was not a pebble for the backpack, it was a boulder that made it all but impossible for me to breathe. I trusted no one – not my colleagues, my friends or even my family. I became lost in a fog that clouded my head. Soon I was listening to a voice that suggested suicide as a way to end the misery that had consumed me.

Fortunately, I was blessed with a strong wife. Kate is my support and my love. If a young police officer is blessed to have such a partner, one who'll love them despite the hardships policing imposes on both of your lives, they should embrace them tightly and never let go. I'm also grateful that rather than use my mental problems as a reason to ostracise me, my superiors at the AFP provided nothing but support, proving we *are* family.

My feelings are best summed up by William J. Bratton, a former chief of the New York, Los Angeles and Boston Police Departments, who analysed the calling of a police officer while delivering the eulogy at the funeral of an NYPD officer in 2015 that I was honoured to attend on behalf of the AFP. I was moved when I heard him speak because of the truth in his words.

'What makes a police officer? Is it courage? Is it compassion? Is it a calling? It's all of these. All these things make a cop, but the one thing most of all: we keep people safe. It's what we do. Sometimes, it can be hard for people who don't choose a life of service to understand . . . At some point every cop has gotten the question: "Why do you do it?" It certainly isn't for the long hours, the last-minute assignments, the missed holidays. It isn't for the stress, or the anxiety our loved ones feel. It isn't for glory or recognition. No one casually chooses a life that can end up here [death]. We choose it because keeping people safe is worth it. Preventing crime and disorder is worth it. Being part of something that has improved millions of lives every day is worth it. And so, we swear an oath, and make a promise . . .'

I acknowledge there are police officers who've been through far worse experiences than me. And to this day I maintain that joining the AFP was one of the most important and proudest days of my life. I couldn't wait to help take criminals off our streets, and I went to work every day believing I could make a difference by doing something worthwhile for the broader community. Now, thirty-four years since my graduation day, I still hold tightly to that belief because I live it. I'm proud to be a police officer, and given the chance I'd do it all again in a heartbeat. Yes, I have suffered, and I wish I'd known more about the psychological and emotional price of my job, but I gain strength from knowing I've been able to save others from suffering. Fighting crime takes a toll, so it is crucial that law enforcement officers – and their superiors – put in place a structure that can protect them, their family, and the community they're protecting. The strongest response is to not only acknowledge we're all vulnerable, but to do something to address the thoughts that keep us awake at night and cause us to shut down from family and loved ones.

After considering all this, if a young person still wants to pursue a police career, then they are made of the right stuff, and our community will be all the better for their willingness to serve. Regardless of which force they join, I only ask that they take strength from the AFP motto: *Policing for a Safer Australia.* But just as importantly, a police officer should not feel as though they need to take on the world alone or that they should suffer in silence.

Policing is a tough job, but we've learnt the hard way it's one that is done by humans.

1
THE TIES THAT BIND

'I cannot think of any need in childhood as strong
as the need for a father's protection . . .'
– Sigmund Freud, father of psychoanalysis, 1856–1939

'Mothers are all slightly insane . . .'
– J.D. Salinger, American writer, 1919–2010

The last place I expected to find myself when I joined the AFP
was sheltering in a rat-infested bunker in Afghanistan with my
colleague John 'Ben' Cartwright as the Taliban launched an
assault on the Green Village, our compound in Kabul.

The village accommodated almost 2000 contractors, NGOs
and an international police force of which I was the second-in-
command. I'd almost completed my year-long mission with the
AFP's contingent of officers, doing our best to shape the Afghan
police force into a professional and modern unit capable of
maintaining law and order in one of the world's most dangerous
places, when two suicide bombers signalled the beginning of
the attack by blowing holes in the village's perimeter fence to
provide their fellow insurgents with a staging post to storm our
base. The insurgents' quest was simple – they wanted to kill as

many of the 'infidel's as possible, and as I listened to the gunfire being exchanged between the Taliban and our security detail of battle-hardened Gurkha veterans, I kept my Glock 22 service pistol trained on the door and took deep breaths to remain calm, terrified by the image that had formed in my mind of members of the Taliban kicking it open with their guns blazing.

I'd arrived in Afghanistan in 2013 aware of the dangers, but as I crouched in that bunker gripping my Glock for dear life it dawned on me that during my then-thirty years in uniform, this was the first time I'd had to prepare myself for a possible shoot-to-kill scenario. Amid the background explosions, machine-gun fire and the incessant wailing of the siren that let the village's multinational inhabitants know we were under attack, I can vividly recall thinking to myself: 'This can't be happening.'

But if my childhood had braced me for anything in life it was this: Abnormal is normal . . .

I was 9 years old when my father, Ray, left our family to live with his boyfriend. I don't know how long he'd been cheating on my mum, Denise, but he explained to my younger sister Jenelle and me that he was different to other fathers because he liked men. It was obvious he found the conversation awkward so I ended his misery by saying I understood and everything was okay, but it was some time before I fully grasped why our lives had been sent into a tailspin. Later that night, when Mum checked on us, Jenelle, who was only seven, asked only one question before we shut the book on the topic. She wanted to know if Dad was a 'poofy-cat'. While it must've cut Mum deeply, her reaction was to simply nod her head and answer: 'We could say that.'

It was tough. Sydney in 1970 was completely different to today. The mentality then decreed men were men and women thanked God for it. You played cricket in summer, footy in winter. Dinky-di Aussies drove a Holden or a Ford, not the so-called 'Jap crap' that was flooding the market. And real blokes didn't dance. As for homosexuals? Well, no one admitted to knowing a 'limp-wrist' because in such a homophobic society there was the fear of guilt by association.

As the only children at our school who came from a broken home, Jenelle and I were already an oddity. We guarded our family's secret closely because we knew the teasing would be unbearable if the other kids learnt the truth about Dad. School playgrounds in the 1970s were hell for any student who was different from the mainstream – the ramifications of being deemed 'weird' by your schoolmates were dreadful, and the punishment was being shamed and excluded. Due to the fear and the lack of trust that mindset fosters, you'd never dare tell a teacher about problems at home; once you talked about it you lost control of your secret.

So I suffered in silence, hoping things would work themselves out. Yet another damaging aspect of suburbia forty-odd years ago was that the gossip mill ran rampant, and very few people ever worried about the collateral damage of getting something wrong. The neighbours who dissected the possible reasons for my parents' marriage breaking down added to Mum's grief. They concluded that for Ray to leave she must have been unfaithful, because he was such a gentleman. I don't know if the slander was the reason for it, but we left our Housing Commission place at Green Valley in Sydney's western suburbs not long after Dad walked out and lived for a while with Mum's parents at Padstow, some twenty-three kilometres away. Nonetheless, the behaviour of our old neighbours taught me to never form an opinion about someone unless I knew all the facts, a lesson that helped me later in life when I became a cop. The people who tarnished Mum's name didn't know that she was heartbroken. Although in despair, Mum still loved my father deeply despite his betrayal.

Another early life lesson I received is that despite your best attempts to bury secrets they eventually surface. When the truth about Ray Edwards was realised at Padstow Park Public School, I was derided in the playground as 'the poof's son'. It was always said slyly from behind a hand, or by a loudmouth in the middle of a large group, so it was hard to identify the culprits. They were cowards, but it was hurtful all the same. It was a tough time, and whoever said 'sticks and stones may break my bones, but names will never harm me' couldn't have had a father whose leaving his family to live openly as a gay man became the talk of the town. Adding to my angst was being the biggest kid in my year – people often asked Mum why I spoke 'funny' because whenever I opened my mouth I sounded like the child I still was in spite of my size. On my eleventh birthday I stood 1.7 metres tall, or 5 feet seven in the old measurements. I was, however, soft-hearted and didn't like fighting. The only time I snapped was when two older boys teased Jenelle because of her weight, and when I heard them call her names, I saw red.

As young kids, Jenelle and I argued and fought a lot. I resented having to look after her because Mum was working multiple jobs to make ends meet. (Dad meanwhile was working shifts at the Auburn RSL and shaping his new life by investing his energies in the Black Stump restaurant he and his boyfriend had bought.) However, despite our fights, I loved my sister and I tried, just as Mum did, to protect her from a lot of the painful stuff we were exposed to. So before I started throwing punches at the clowns who'd reduced Jenelle to tears I yelled, 'The only one who can pick on my sister here is me!'

The injuries I inflicted were enough for me to be paraded before the headmaster, and I don't remember if I got six of the best but he did read me the riot act. At a deeper level, I suppose those two boys pushed me to breaking point, because compounding the fact that Dad had left us was Mum's drinking, which she had begun to do – and quite heavily – to cope with her catastrophe. The day would come when I'd understand why she needed to 'self-medicate' – to numb her pain – but the effect alcohol had on Mum was deadly, and at home, things quickly became toxic for Jenelle and me. As a young woman Mum had always looked after her health. She'd competed in swimming tournaments against the Olympic champion Lorraine Crapp, and didn't have her first alcoholic drink until she turned 28. But such was the devastation grog wrought on her, she died just eighteen years later at the age of 46 as a result of renal failure. I was 24 when Mum passed away in 1987 and I still have a lot of anger about her death. It's as though she chose to die. She hadn't gone to the dentist to get a poisoned tooth fixed, which made her sick with septicaemia, and nor did she utilise help from Alcoholics Anonymous, despite Jenelle and me urging her to go. But on occasion I can imagine her torment, and I'm overcome by sadness. After all, she lost Dad to a man – perhaps if he'd run into the arms of another woman she might've been able to compete and woo him back, but Dad was lost to her for good once his sexuality smashed its way out of the closet, and she couldn't accept it.

Ray was seen as quite the catch when he and Mum met as work colleagues at the Lowes menswear clothing store in the late 1950s. He was a national ballroom dancing champion, he dressed impeccably and he always smelt pleasantly of cologne. He was also extremely polite, attentive and a great chef, skills he had fine-tuned in the army when he was assigned to the catering corps during his National Service. Given how clumsy he was sometimes, it's understandable that the military armed him with a whisk rather than a gun!

Dad fell for Mum and I know he loved her in his own way, and they married and had us kids. When I think of Mum's sense of humiliation, I feel sad – I don't know if she needed to rebuild her self-esteem, to overcome any 'failure' she may have felt as a woman, but after Dad left she formed several relationships with other men. They were all undesirables who used our place as a dosshouse to booze, take drugs and steal from us, with the exception of a bloke called Garry who was with Mum until she died. Garry is only eleven years older than me and I was impressed as a rugby league-mad kid to realise he'd represented the North Sydney Bears lower-grade teams. He met Mum at the abattoirs where she was working as a bookkeeper and he was one of the company's meat-carters. While he was a drinker, Garry stood out from the others because he treated Jenelle and me as though we were his own children, and he showed us only kindness. A testament to our relationship, we've remained firm friends. He was the exception, though, because included among the unsavoury visitors to our home were older members of the violent Revesby Sharpies gang, some of whom would shoot up heroin in our lounge room.

I vividly remember the afternoon when Brian, a frequent visitor to our place, turned up. He was agitated – I now realise he needed a hit – and as I watched he pulled a needle from his pocket, carefully heaped heroin into a teaspoon, heated it with a lighter until the powder turned into a liquid and poured it into the syringe. As he tied a tourniquet around his arm he chatted away, and then injected himself. Suddenly he stopped talking mid-sentence and slumped back into the lounge, his eyes rolling to the back of his head, the blood-filled syringe hanging from his arm, and for a full ten minutes he was in a catatonic state – quite something for a primary-school-aged kid to see. Like other members of the Sharpies who came through our door, Brian died of a drug overdose.

One day I really discovered what the Sharpies represented. I was eleven and accompanying Jenelle and one of her friends at the Bankstown Ten Pin Bowling alley when a small guy aged in his twenties mumbled something to me that I couldn't understand. When I bent down towards him and asked him what he'd said, he clenched his fist and BANG! He broke my nose. As I reeled back, my hands to my face and the blood flowing, he took off.

Any aspiring Sharpies member, I learnt later, had to belt someone out of the blue – today we call it a coward's punch – and naturally, Mum's friends knew who the candidate was.

At the gang's next meeting he was shocked to be told he'd belted an 11-year-old kid. He insisted that couldn't be right – I looked much older due to my height – but ignorance couldn't save him. The Sharpies may have been bad eggs, but before they addressed the next item on their meeting's agenda my assailant copped a flogging when the gang voted with their fists and boots to reject him. There was a lot I didn't like about the impact the Sharpies had on our lives, but they awakened in me a determination to try to be stronger than the weak men Mum brought through our front door.

Despite her own train-wreck of a life, Mum also took in wayward kids, giving them somewhere to stay and helping them get back on track by helping them put their resumes together and apply for jobs. Mostly though, she gave them hope, and Jenelle and I hold onto that thought tightly because we believe that Mum really was kind at heart. At least eight kids stayed at our place during a four-year period, the first when I was thirteen, a 17-year-old girl named Karen.

Karen shared my bed and while there was nothing sordid about it, some friends who came to my birthday party elevated me to legendary status because their pubescent imaginations ran riot when they learnt about my roommate. I realised my sleeping arrangements weren't the norm when a few of the boys who'd told their parents about Karen and me were forbidden from visiting our house again. I have no doubt Karen was my first love, because my heart broke the evening her new boyfriend knocked on our door to take her out.

The last kid Mum took in was also seventeen – this time a loose cannon of a boy who stole cars. At that time we were living on the Georges River at East Hills, and one day he nicked a motorbike parked near the local train station. I was angry – I understood enough to know it was stupid to steal from people who lived in our neighbourhood. Mum had no idea a stolen motorbike was hidden underneath our house, and I finally took decisive action, worried the police would come looking for it – and I wouldn't have put it past our house guest to blame me for the theft. Late one night I pushed the motorbike to the top of the footbridge that spanned the river and rolled it over the edge to a watery grave.

While our family was dysfunctional, Jenelle and I experienced plenty of love, and not just from Mum. Despite the way in which he left us, Dad continued to be our father. I don't know if he paid maintenance because Mum often complained about things I later discovered weren't true, but he paid for expenses like dental bills and clothes, and he also made time for us. I didn't appreciate that at the time though, because Dad and I were so different we may as well have been speaking different languages.

Jenelle and I stayed with Dad at his place in Auburn once a month, but for me it was torture. Instead of playing footy with my mates, I had to watch Jenelle dance at the Neville Munroe School of Dancing in Lidcombe, and it was death by a million quick-steps. Dad did try to connect with me, though. He attempted to talk to me about about rugby league a few times, although I soon realised he'd read the footy reports in the newspaper in preparation just before Jenelle and I arrived for our weekend with him. The giveaway was that he always made mistakes. The day he tried to initiate a conversation about 'that' Tommy Raudonikis guy who was playing for Penrith on the weekend was the final straw – 'Tom Terrific' played for the Western Suburbs Magpies and their hero was playing *against* Penrith that Sunday. I asked him not to worry about the footy anymore. Whenever he made a mistake about something I was so passionate about, it only highlighted how different we were.

When Mum wasn't drinking she was a loving parent, and it says a lot about her pride that even after a hard night she'd make herself look like a model mum before going to work; so prim and proper. The problem was that over the years it became impossible to disassociate from some of the comments she made while under the influence because they were very hurtful. As a man who is now closer to 60 than 50, I fight hard to push that baggage aside and remember 'Good Mum' – the loving mother who worked at multiple jobs to make ends meet and ensure we never went hungry. Jenelle and I might have been raised in a 'loose' household, but I suspect Mum didn't know half of what the Sharpies and others who drifted in and out of our abodes got up to. But *I* knew, and it wasn't great.

Mum's poor taste in men was a constant curse throughout my childhood. One night when I was ten, one of her boyfriends lost his temper at a unit we lived in at Bardwell Park and bashed her. It was terrifying, and I felt torn as Jenelle and I hid under the bed. With Dad gone I considered myself the man of the house, and while I wanted to protect my mum I was too young to stand up to the thug, let alone fight him. The only thing I could do was protect my little sister as we cried to the sounds of our mother being beaten in the living room. When things calmed down we grabbed Jenelle's purse, full of five cent pieces, and sneaked out to the red Telecom phone box on the corner and phoned Mum's friend, Helen the hairdresser. About half an hour later my Pa, Harry Steele, was banging on the front door. He was armed with a rifle and I'm pretty sure he had the barrel trained on the now-former boyfriend as he packed his bags and left.

My grandfather, Henry aka 'Harry' Steele, was Mum's dad – and my hero. We had great adventures together, from fishing or doing the rounds in the Nelson Tobacco Company's delivery truck he drove for a living. I always felt special when I sat with him and his mates in the pub eating salmon and onion sandwiches for lunch while they drank beer and spun yarns with killer punchlines. Every Friday afternoon he took me to the Woolloomooloo Police Boys' Club, where my uncle (Mum's brother-in-law) Bobby McLaughlin was the second-in-command. As I learnt to play the drums, Pa visited some of his mates at the nearby waterside pubs that were havens for wharfies, union delegates and shady characters. He'd be well under the weather by the time the drum lessons finished and when we'd alight the train at Padstow the station master always made the same quip while he watched me struggle to help Pa off the train: 'Cripes Harry, you're meant to be looking after the kid, not the other way around.'

It wasn't until that night at Bardwell Park that I saw the other side of Pa. He looked dangerous holding that rifle. But rather than feel scared, I was happy – proud even – to see my hero make the thug who'd battered my mother beg for forgiveness. As a young kid I also liked that Pa was the antithesis of my father: Pa was a man's man who drank beer, gambled, smoked and had a great circle of mates who he could call on to help with anything.

During business hours, Pa wore a collared short-sleeved shirt, long shorts, knee-length socks with elastic garters and shiny black shoes. Jenelle and I loved it when, after a few beers, he'd allow us to draw on his legs, with the rule being we couldn't go beyond where his socks ended. In his youth, Pa played rugby league for the Tweed Heads Seagulls, and he could fish too – the only time Dad took me fishing I ended up in the hospital's casualty ward because he'd somehow hooked me; it was a disaster. Pa taught me to paint, make handyman repairs and use a power drill, and even though I cut my finger the first time I used it, he wouldn't let me stop because he thought it was important to finish the job.

Dad might have taught me how to pull a beer at the RSL when I was eight – we went to the club early one Sunday morning while he tapped the kegs and collected the coins from the poker machines – but he wouldn't have been able to change the spark plug in a lawnmower if his life depended upon it. While Dad and Jenelle got on brilliantly because of their shared passions for cooking and dancing, it was Pa who was my hero – I was his shadow. Whether he was selling trays of tomatoes he'd acquired at Paddy's Markets for two dollars at the Lugarno Wharf, or driving the truck, I often wagged days from school to be with him. There was nowhere else in the world I wanted to be.

My Nan, Ada, hailed from Roma in the Darling Downs 400 kilometres west-north-west of Brisbane, famous for being the birthplace of six rugby league internationals, including two all-time greats of different eras, Arthur Beetson and

Darren Lockyer. But as tough as they were, none of the town's football heroes matched Nan's heart and spirit. She was a beautiful person who, at the age of 16 left school to look after her siblings. Realising how tough things were at home, she showered Jenelle and me with the affection we craved. She was also a tough old bird, surviving a heart attack at 56 and going on to live till age 81 when, despite having given up smoking thirty years earlier, emphysema claimed her. Nan was adamant that I had it in me to be something despite the hurdles I needed to overcome. Because we moved so much, the friendships I enjoyed with kids from the neighbourhood were only temporary, but despite this I had no problems making friends. But I realise I didn't invest much effort into many relationships because experience had taught me that people let you down: Dad had left us, Mum was unreliable, the calibre of men who came in and out of my life was so very low – one day, even the actions of my beloved Pa would ultimately crush me. I still smile now though when I remember the day Nan told me she'd had her tea leaves read and was told our family would have a third member in the police force. I felt so proud when she said that would be me. And true to the leaves, I would follow my uncle Graham Steele, a detective sergeant, and my Uncle Bobby, into the force.

Nan was the bright light in my life, but my grandmother had no appreciation for punctuality. Before her death in 1996 she asked if I'd make sure the people who attended her funeral were kept waiting. Everyone smiled on that terribly sad day when the undertakers delayed the service for fifteen minutes to honour Nan's last wish.

While I idolised Pa and Nan, I didn't get on so well with Dad's parents. I remember them as strict. Papa, as we called him, was a Second World War veteran, a very hard man who'd be described as 'old school' nowadays. I never felt comfortable around him even though he was only ever nice to me. Dad was one of five sons and two daughters, and I gauged the relationship between him and his father to be strained, especially after he and Mum divorced. I don't know if Papa and Grandma knew Dad's secret, but if they did they never spoke about it.

Another important influence in my childhood was my uncle Graham Steele, who worked in forensics at Gosford. Before we lost contact because of Mum's behaviour I was quite close to him. He had three sons and I liked that they were tight and did what I considered to be traditional father–son things. Apart from his police duties, my uncle was on the board of the Terrigal rugby league club, which my cousins played for. They were all members of the local surf lifesaving club too. Graham was extremely fit, but I later learnt he was such a keen surfer and paddler because he was in the throes of full-blown PTSD and used exercise to deal with it. When the endorphins weren't enough to give him respite, he relied on the more traditional course of treatment that cops used to bury their pain and hit the bottle. As basically a 'one-man shop' at Gosford he was called out to many fatalities on the F3 freeway and the sights he witnessed took a brutal toll on him.

I don't think anyone could've seen what Graham did and not be affected. I recall piles of photographs he'd taken, and some of the scenes they captured were horrendous. Although he couldn't switch off from his terrible duties, as a kid I was unaware of the hell my uncle endured. I'd look at my cousins' lives and think they were blessed to have a sporty, 'real bloke' for a father who worked in a man's job, and who shared the interests of his sons. That said, I never had any desire to move in with them. Even though I knew my own family was dysfunctional, and even though I was still only a kid, I realised Mum needed me to protect her.

There were occasions when it felt as though I was the adult in our relationship. It seemed I was forever trying to protect Mum from herself, like preventing her from driving when she'd had too much to drink, or stopping her from escalating an argument with a boyfriend. I did all I could to protect Jenelle from Mum's destructive nature too, but it was an exhausting battle. From a young age, I harboured a terrible fear that something would happen to Mum if I wasn't with her. It was a form of anxiety and it crippled my social life as a teenager. It became too hard to go out with my friends – while they'd be skylarking, I was tormented with dread that something bad was happening to Mum because I wasn't at home to watch over her. Perhaps she'd fallen over and hit her head because she'd had too much to drink, or she'd choked on her own vomit. The worry would become too much and I'd return home.

Abnormal? I know it was, but as Ray and Denise Edwards' son, I was shaped to accept my life as normality.

2
LITTLE BOY LOST

'If you are going through hell, keep going . . .'
– Winston Churchill, former British prime minister (1874–1965)

When I was 10, Pa Steele, the man who was my everything, tied some bedsheets together and hanged himself. In the lead-up to his death, my grandfather had suffered a stroke, but no one would tell me how he'd died because they knew it would crush me. I'd find out the truth when I accidentally stumbled across copies of the black and white photographs taken by the police forensics team, which had been left on Nan's desk. Clearly I wasn't supposed to see them, and I can only imagine that in her shock Nan had forgotten to put the prints away after Uncle Graham had given them to her, although I'll never know why he did that. I couldn't stop crying for months, but I couldn't tell anyone that I knew how Pa had died because it would destroy Nan if she knew I'd seen those ghastly photographs.

I felt abandoned, and it had a destructive impact on my life. I lost direction at school, and the decline in my marks was of such a concern that the principal considered dropping me to the D 'for dregs' class. Nothing seemed to make any sense after Pa died, and very little seemed to matter. I also stopped playing sport, denying myself what would have been a great avenue to channel my energies. Mum added to my grief by accidentally backing over the prized Malvern Star bicycle Pa had bought me because he thought I had the physique to become a champion cyclist. It was beyond repair and I found the act of throwing it away extremely tough because I was losing a tangible connection to the person I loved most in the world.

To this day I still carry the hurt his final act caused me, but it wasn't as though Pa hadn't warned us he was capable of such a thing. Before he was moved to a nursing home, I remember him telling Nan in their kitchen that he wouldn't be one of those old codgers who was a burden on their family – and he made good on his promise at only age 57, the age I am now. Despite the pain and suffering his suicide inflicted, I now understand the turmoil behind Pa's final battle. When I returned from my service in Afghanistan, I would find myself contemplating a drastic solution to silence the demons in my own head.

Without Pa's guiding hand, life became tougher. Mum continued to hurtle down her own path of self-destruction and the distance between me and Dad only got wider. While I dreamt of being a football star, he wanted me to try ballroom dancing and to learn to cook. I preferred to watch whatever sport was on the television and I silently wished he and Jenelle would shut up as they laughed and carried on in the kitchen while they prepared the food because it was hard to hear the commentary. I finally stopped going to Dad's place when I turned sixteen and did my own thing instead. I fought incessantly with Jenelle and loathed the school playground, where I was still simply known to some as 'that poof's son'. My life hadn't even really started, but if a counsellor had asked me to write three words that described how I felt they would've been: *Lost. Alone. Heartbroken.*

There was no way I could've known at the time, but a lot of pain was hidden behind Pa's eyes. I remember hearing him say to a mate one Anzac Day that he was still stung by being rejected from joining the army on three occasions during the Second World War because he was deaf in one ear. Perhaps that challenged his sense of manhood, but while a legitimate impairment kept Pa on the home front, many of his mates who enlisted never returned. For all intents and purposes he'd seemed to have moved on. He and Nan enjoyed a loving life together and raised three kids. Apart from the family home at Padstow, Pa built a waterfront place on the Central Coast. And I've never forgotten that he was bold enough to scare a mean bastard out of our lives with a rifle.

Henry Steele, aka 'Harry', was a proud man. And perhaps that pride drove his decision to end his suffering – I have no doubt he couldn't tolerate having strangers rob him of his dignity by doing everything for him after the stroke. Despite the many years that have passed since his death in 1972, I'm still his little mate. Whenever I'm down near the old Paddy's Markets building in Sydney, I remember the great times we shared there and I invariably hear myself saying, 'I miss you, Pa.'

Dysfunctional as things were, our lives went on. I lost count of how many houses we lived in, but it was well over twenty by the time I turned 13. We always lived along the East Hills train line because Mum wanted school to at least be the one constant in her children's lives. Enrolling us at Padstow Park Primary and later the high schools at East Hills meant we'd only ever be a train trip away from our classrooms. Being a struggling single mother, sometimes Mum couldn't afford to buy us pencils for school. I started fourth class without one, thinking I'd find one in the classroom. I didn't, but my teacher, Miss Hurley, sent me to the office to drop off an envelope, and while I was gone she asked my classmates who could spare a pencil. When I returned she handed me a pencil case that had belonged to her with fourteen pencils in it. The gratitude I felt that day is something I've never forgotten, and whenever I've served in places such as East Timor and Afghanistan, I've encouraged my officers to support the local orphanages. And yes, I've made sure the kids all have pens and paper.

It was uncomfortable to know that my classmates realised we were poor, but I was also grateful that most of them shared what they could, and I have Miss Hurley to thank for that. She was my first crush. She was completely different to the teacher I had the previous year, who was quick to dish out punishment. I've long suspected Miss Hurley had a soft spot for me because Mum may have told her a few home truths about my upbringing. She was so dedicated to teaching that when I was laid up for a week with a sprained ankle she'd break her train trip home, dropping off my homework so I wouldn't fall too far behind my classmates. Miss Hurley simply saw me as a kid who was burdened with problems and saw Mum as a single mother struggling to cope, and she was good enough to go the extra yard to help. She could never know what impact her kindnesses had on me, but it was deep.

Jenelle remembers the place we rented in Swan Street, Revesby, with the most fondness because Mum bought an above-ground pool with a diving platform from the Clark rubber factory. I remember it as the place I was most in danger of falling in with the wrong crowd. At that time I hung out with some older guys, a rough bunch, always doing dumb stuff. One day I was dared to steal a packet of cigarettes from the Safeway supermarket near the railway station so they could sell the stolen smokes to drinkers at the pub. I accepted the challenge, and the ease of getting away with it inspired me to chance my luck a few weeks later at the local newsagency. I'd slipped a *Playboy* magazine inside a newspaper but was nabbed when I tried to pay the eight cents for *The Mirror*. The store manager wasn't swayed by my tearful promises I'd never steal again and called the cops. He wanted me charged for shoplifting. I definitely didn't want my mother to know what had happened, and didn't bother about calling Dad, so I contacted Mum's boyfriend, Garry.

It says plenty about Garry's character that, despite having outstanding driving warrants, he didn't hesitate to drive straight to the cop shop to see what he could do to help. The sergeant told me to wait in Garry's car. I felt sick as I waited and waited, for what seemed like hours. I feared the longer Garry remained in there, the more trouble I was in.

When Garry finally returned, he had a stern look on his face. He dramatically shook his head before saying I wasn't going to be charged – *this time* – and proceeded to warn me I'd used up my one free pass. It struck me that Garry spoke from the heart when he advised me to keep out of trouble with the law – that having a police record was a burden because no matter how hard you might try to be a good person, it followed you. His words made a big impact. By the time I found out that the sergeant just wanted to give me the fright of my life, I was on the right path. After that I was too scared to even jay walk – and only a few months later, I even became an unlikely star witness for the cops.

Between five and seven in the morning each day, I sold newspapers on the pedestrian bridge at Revesby railway station. The tips were good – although *The Sydney Morning Herald* and *Daily Telegraph* cost eight cents, most people would just hand over a ten cent piece and say to keep the change. All up I'd make $10 a week, a substantial amount of money for a 12-year-old in 1974. But while most 12-year-olds would spend that on lollies or comics, every cent in our house was used to pay the bills. One morning, I watched as a car screamed down the street and smashed into a light pole opposite the train station. Then two young men casually climbed out and walked towards me. I thought they were going to rob me, but all they wanted to know was the time. I guess I had a cop's instinct even then because I made a mental note of their approximate height, weight and what they were wearing, and called the police. I gave a statement but in the end I wasn't required to attend juvenile court.

Despite the fact that Mum, Jenelle and I always worked, money was always very tight. I wore my summer shorts to school on even the most bitterly cold winter days. Mum was working as a full-time bookkeeper but also worked for a catering company and a real estate agency on weekends, and couldn't afford to keep buying woollen trousers because I grew out of them so quickly. As a kid with nothing, you accept things for what they are, and I'd like to believe my childhood toughened me. There were no free rides at our place – if we kids weren't at school, we were at work. In Year 7 my weekends were spent unloading trucks at the Old City Markets, and before that I sorted potatoes; I also worked after school at the Crawford's Record Store in Revesby, and consequently I knew all the songs by the top bands of that era including Sherbet, Skyhooks, ABBA and Status Quo. During the school holidays I worked at the abattoir where I'd either help Garry cart meat or clean the rooms where the cattle were slaughtered. On other school holidays I stuffed mattresses at the Dunlop factory in Bankstown. Most of my earnings went to Mum, and even the cash I kept ended up in her purse because she'd always find where I'd hidden it.

After years of being constantly bullied about her weight, Jenelle left school at fourteen to work as the chief telephone operator at Woolworths in Revesby. The irony is that Jenelle was the brains of the family, and I wished the last school report card she brought home was mine – she finished first in maths, second in science and third in English! In contrast, my own most important lessons as a kid came via the school of hard knocks, and my teachers were the down to earth knockabouts I worked alongside at the Old City Markets. They were a great bunch of men who looked out for me. One day I sneaked off to play some pinball in the Penny Arcade on George Street and a desperado pulled a knife on me, demanding my money, all of about 65 cents. When I took too long to fish the coins from my pockets he started jabbing me with the point of the blade. I was terrified, and after I handed over my coins I sprinted back to the markets.

When the men heard what had happened, some of them sprinted back towards the pinball parlour, intent on teaching the thug who'd stood over a 12-year-old a lesson he wouldn't forget. My childhood certainly wasn't average by any stretch of the imagination, and while I often yearned for normality, I was learning about the realities of human behaviour in the wider world, and fast.

3
MANHOOD MATTERS

'Try not to become a man of success, but rather
try to become a man of value.'
– Albert Einstein, German-born physicist (1879–1955)

Whenever Mum was in the darkest of her alcohol-induced moods, she'd spew vile comments. She said a lot of terrible things, but the one that cut me the deepest was the taunt: 'If you grow up gay like your *fucking* father, I will kill you!' I was twelve the first time I heard that, and the vitriol in Mum's threat was chilling. I knew as a kid I wasn't gay, but as a teenager I fretted. While some of my mates had girlfriends, a little voice in the back of my head told me romance wasn't worth it, that pain and heartache would only follow, so I steered clear. Nevertheless, constantly hearing Mum's disparaging comments about me and my father had a terrible impact on my confidence. Her fear I'd inherit Dad's sexual orientation meant she drove me relentlessly to be a 'real man'. I played soccer, rugby league, softball and hockey. I took up surf lifesaving at Elouera Beach in Sydney's south. As I grew older I'd try my hand at rugby union, basketball and athletics.

Ironically, while Mum set about hardening me in the tradi-tional Aussie mould of brawn and spilling blood on the footy paddock, Dad wanted to introduce me to ballroom dancing. He had no hope. Back before she knew Dad's secret, for Mum footy was nothing more than a bit of fun. Our household was still 'normal', a happy home even, and for Mum – as well as Jenelle and me – all was well in the world. But once Dad left, Mum used sport to set in me what she saw as the masculine traits that would keep me on the 'straight' path. It didn't matter that her weekends were consumed by ferrying me to sporting events, she viewed sport as something that would teach me to be a man.

When we moved into Pa and Nan's place in 1970, I joined the Padstow United Soccer Club. We were different to the other teams because we were coached and managed by women. Mum managed the team and her friend, Val Adams, coached us. They took on these roles because no one else could be bothered, and while we lost more games than we won, they did a terrific job. Mrs Adams was a feisty character who'd embraced an alternative lifestyle and drove about in a groovy Volkswagen beetle. As someone who was more in tune with flower power than power shots, her coaching style was 'chilled'. Every kid in the team – including her son, Stewart – played in a different position each game in what I guess was an opportunity for us to express or find ourselves. Of course, that approach didn't help when we met teams who'd developed strong playing combinations. They made mince-meat of our ragged defence, and had no problem smothering our attack, but that didn't worry us because we had lots of fun. Mum was a terrific organiser and all the off-field stuff ran like clockwork. At the end of the season she and Mrs Adams both stood down, which was a shame, because the team had provided my mother with an interest that kept her occupied after Dad dropped his bombshell.

Due to my size, Mum was often asked by other parents why I didn't play rugby league. They thought I'd be a natural but as it turned out, they made a mistake by judging this particular book by its cover. The idea of me playing a contact sport was by then in synch with Mum's need for me to embrace my masculinity. So in 1976 I joined the Milperra Colts under-14s. We were hopeless; our opposition used us for tackling practice. When we played our last game of the season against the equally poor Bass Hill, our coach had a brainwave that he thought would help us avoid the wooden spoon. He grabbed me and the two other front rowers and instructed us to chew on garlic cloves, figuring the aroma would be off-putting for our opposition whenever we packed down in a scrum. I felt sick as we chewed on the garlic and we were all gagging as we swallowed the stuff. While our victory in the match ensured Bass Hill finished in last place, I can assure you that despite our coach's claim, our garlic breath had nothing to do with it.

The following year I joined St Christopher's at Panania. We won a few games but the coach pulled the pin after our team copped one too many trouncings. However, I did learn the ramifications for foul play when I was sent off after a minor scuffle with a Greenacre player escalated into a one-sided punch-up. I can't remember why the fight started but my eyes were rolling. It must've looked brutal because the kid's father needed restraining as he attempted to run onto the field to give me a taste of my own medicine. I had to attend the junior league's judiciary at Canterbury Leagues Club and was petrified as I waited to receive a one-week suspension. More disconcerting was that the kid I'd bashed was there. For a few days after the punch-up I revelled in the attention I received as the 'crazy bastard' who'd been sent off for fighting – I thought it made me sound like I was a tough guy to be wary of. But when I saw the fear in this kid's eyes as I walked into the hearing I felt like one of the thugs Mum had gone out with. I felt so small, and never raised my hands on the football field again.

Even though I showed no promise as a rugby league player, my height and weight excited a number of coaches who asked Mum if I'd join their team. At 12 years old I was 6 feet tall (1.82 metres) and surprisingly quick on my feet for a big kid. I suppose they thought I'd bring an X-factor to their under-13s by steamrolling opposing players. I ended up at the East Hills Bulldogs, who played out of Smith Park. They were a proud club, and boasted plenty of characters, most of whom hung out in the Starlight Room at Smith Park, an old tin shed near the train line where, despite the many holes in its roof, people congregated on match day for a beer. One thing the police force and footy teams have in common is that they both have characters who invent killer nicknames. By the end of my first training session at Smith Park our coach, Terry O'Donnell, christened me 'Haystacks' after the American wrestler William Calhoun, who stood 1.95 metres tall and weighed 300 kilos.

Mum was delighted to be dubbed 'Mrs Haystacks'. She considered it an acknowledgement that her son was big and strong, a real man in the making. I played with East Hills until I quit rugby league in 1979, but during my time there our team was considered the best under-16 and 17 team in the state, due to the skills of guys such as Tony Moore, Greg 'the Bully' Hunt and Herb Turvey. Some members would go on to play in the lower grades for Canterbury and the Newtown Jets, but as our worst player I wasn't destined to follow them. I discovered early on that while I enjoyed rugby league, I didn't like hurting people – the feelings I had about belting the Greenacre kid proved that – and as a front-rower that was expected of me because we took the brunt of the body contact.

Unfortunately, the fact that I lacked mongrel in my nature was lost on many of the adults, who only saw a hulking kid with the physique to be a wrecking ball. Their initial cries of encouragement when I joined the team were soon replaced by calls for me to not be a 'cat' and to 'have a go'. The dreaded 'poof's boy' slur re-emerged when some of the parents suggested I shouldn't be in the team based on my 'merits'. Their comments almost crushed the few remaining strands of confidence left in me, and it affected the way I played. Perhaps if I'd played in a different team I might have passed as a 'good' player, but the talent at East Hills was red hot and, try as I might, I just couldn't match the prowess of my teammates. I played on, hoping to somehow find the spark that'd make me the player my body's frame probably deserved, and it didn't hurt that training a couple of times a week and playing of a weekend allowed me to escape my home life.

Dad didn't like the junior footy culture – too much beer and testosterone. I also think that deep down he was probably scared of how the other fathers would treat him because of his 'difference'. On the few occasions he came to a game he always looked awkward, and it didn't help that one day he turned up with a 'man bag' – they were a fad in the mid-1970s. Jenelle recalls I hurled it at him in the mistaken belief it was a woman's handbag. Dad and I both had our reasons to be terrified of people's perceptions. I was always fearful of what people would think about him being gay; and given homophobia was rampant back then it's not being overly dramatic to guess that Dad knew if he crossed the wrong person at a game he could quite easily be targeted for a hate crime. I regret I didn't appreciate at the time how brave his turning up to support me was. It's a pity that as a kid you're often too dumb to see the good in what your parents try to do for you.

Although I'd develop it in later years, in my heart of hearts I knew I didn't have what was needed to realise my dream of making the top grade. But despite not being of the standard of the rest of the squad, I played in every game of our undefeated season in the under-16s. Well, every game except for the grand final against the St George Dragons at Belmore Oval, the tradition-steeped home ground of the Canterbury Bulldogs. Being dropped without an explanation left me feeling shattered and Mum pissed off. I was so hurt I lashed out by getting hammered with a friend.

I was simply copying what I saw the adults in my life do; I'd suffered a disappointment and sought an escape. Although my friend and I were still pretty smashed up the following day, we were thrown on the field for the final ten minutes' play when the premiership title couldn't be lost. I watched on as my teammates celebrated the crowning moment of a great season feeling hollow, as though I wasn't really a part of it. I was actually drinking quite a lot at that stage of my life; I was getting wasted every weekend. After moving from house to flat to apartment to house, we'd dropped anchor in East Hills. There was a lot to like about this – as well as the proximity to school, our new flat above the barber had an unexpected bonus: direct access to the East Hills pub, where I'd have the occasional beer with the licensee Ronnie McLaughlin, a distant relative.

I was sixteen by now and because of my size no one ever questioned my age. It was cool to be able to go to the bar and buy a drink for myself – and sometimes for my mother. One of the people I met at the pub through Bob was the former British light-heavyweight champion boxer, Bunny Johnson, who fought the likes of Tony Mundine and the future world champion Dennis Andries. He knew I was only sixteen, and when he saw me drinking yet another beer he pointed to my glass and cursed it as 'Devil's Drink'. 'That's what happens to men when they drink,' he said. 'They become madmen.'

It took a few months for me to digest the wisdom of his words, and when I turned seventeen I stopped drinking because by then I could see the damage alcohol was doing to Mum.

Before the New South Wales government extended the railway to Campbelltown, East Hills was the last stop on the line and it was a magical place for a kid to grow up. It's surprising that despite being such a small part of Sydney, the East Hills–Panania area has produced a plethora of outstanding achievers since the 1950s, including international cricketers Steve and Mark Waugh, Wayne Holdsworth and Ben Rohrer; Australia's most successful Olympian, Ian Thorpe; Graham Windeatt, who won the 1972 Olympic silver medal for the 1500 metres freestyle; the Wallaby Laurie Monaghan, who had represented East Hills Boys High; and a host of first-grade rugby league players who made their mark at Smith Park. The actor Bryan Brown remains a proud son of the area, and hit singer from the 1950s Col Joye and his brother Kevin Jacobsen, one of the nation's top music promoters, are East Hillians. Others include Paul Abraham, the bass guitarist from The Reels, and the Tierney brothers who left the area to tour as members of Human Nature.

Among the many jobs I had as a schoolkid, I occasionally worked as a roadie for Col Joye, which was exciting. I managed to get that gig because I was a friend of his nephew Dave. Apart from being in the same music class, we also performed in the school's rock band. Dave was on guitar, I played the drums and Richard Lane, now an accomplished opera singer, belted out AC/DC covers. Dave's father Kevin brought the biggest names in the entertainment industry to Australia, and one afternoon I even met the Grammy Award-winning singer Joan Armatrading at their house.

While I haven't been back to East Hills for years, in 2014 I took a close look at my old school in my capacity as an AFP officer. Vandals had scrawled graffiti on the walls of the boys' high school as a show of support for the Islamic terror group, ISIS. In the weeks leading up to the vandalism, the AFP had visited the school after reports a student had travelled to Lebanon with the intention of fighting in Syria for Islamic State before being intercepted by his father.

Besides living on top of the barber shop, at one time we lived two houses down from the George's River footbridge, which connects East Hills to the Naval Estate. It was straight out of the Huckleberry Finn story. The property included a private jetty, which was great for fishing from. It seems crazy now to think that despite seeing the occasional bull shark's fin slicing through the water's surface, I joined my mates in jumping off the bridge. It was great fun, but besides the sharks you needed to be careful of other hazards, including speedboats and waterskiers. I often escaped to the Florida Milk Bar opposite the railway station, an old-fashioned milk bar run by a Greek bloke with a counter crammed with confectionery, and a pinball machine. Like the footy, fishing and bridge jumps, playing pinball in that milk bar was a temporary reprieve from the chaos at home.

As I grew older the pressure was crushing. At night I needed to wear headphones to block out the noise from the pub when I was doing my homework; Mum's drinking was out of control and I had to dodge the Sharpies in our lounge room. I pushed myself to be the best I could be, but I kept my problems to myself – and that's why I was mortified when a slip-up meant my form master knew the truth about my home life. When I returned to school to start Year 10, I was puzzled when I was called to see Mr Wilkie – puzzled *and* terrified because he'd been my maths teacher, and he was tough. However, when I arrived at his office he invited me to sit down and asked me a series of questions about my Christmas holidays.

I played a straight bat to each of his questions, ensuring him all was well with Mum and me, although I was confused about why he cared. That's when he produced a note. The moment I saw it I felt my face turn red. It was a letter I'd written one day when I was pissed off with Mum and it spelt out some damning home truths, including that I intended to leave home because I couldn't stand what was going on anymore. My words were scathing, and I mentally kicked myself for having left it in a textbook I'd handed back on my last day in Year 9. Once I regained my composure and reassured Mr Wilkie all was fine, he handed me the letter and said he and some other teachers were worried about me. Within ten seconds of leaving his office I ripped the note up into little pieces, furious at myself for being so careless. I could look after myself.

4

DAD

'Sometimes the shock would last for a few seconds,
other times it was so long that I blacked out.
When I came round my pants would be soaked
through. I'd passed out and wet myself through
fear – or whatever it was. I have no idea . . .'
– 'James', 32, on gay conversion therapy in Australia

When he was a boy, my father was raped by an older male relative. Apart from having his innocence stolen, in the years that followed Dad went to hell and back in his attempt to become 'normal'. He undertook electric shock treatment, and what he endured could've been taken from the pages of a horror novel. In those days it was believed that a gay man's sexual orientation could be rewired by subjecting him to shocks administered through electrodes implanted directly into the brain. Despite the barbarism of this supposed treatment, and doubts about the veracity of its success, tens of thousands of homosexuals around the world subjected themselves to what was tantamount to torture because they were made to feel by the church, the medical profession and society that their sexuality was a 'disease' that needed to be cured.

In the 1970s Dad paid heavily for his bid to be what was deemed 'normal'. As a result of his brain being fried by a treatment that is now discredited, he lost a lot of his memory. When I think now of Dad's ordeal, and the motive that pushed him to voluntarily subject himself to such torment – to be the stereotypical father and husband for his family's sake – I can't help but think that not only was he extremely courageous, his choice was also an act of devotion to Mum, me and Jenelle.

Dad never told me about what happened to him as a child. I'd always thought he'd been molested by a scout leader but Jenelle discovered he'd suffered at the hands of someone known to our father as an 'uncle'. I understand this man died a while back, but his rape – or rapes – caused terrible anguish for my father and, ultimately, for my mother. Not long after he left us, Dad suffered a nervous breakdown, and when I was eleven, I have a dim memory of going to visit Dad – Mum driving us down a gloomy street in Sydney's eastern suburbs, passing through an avenue of ancient trees on both sides of the road and travelling along a long driveway towards a whitewashed building that resembled a small castle. I can't be sure if we were visiting him at a mental health hospital because he was having more electric shock treatment, or because he was recuperating from over-whelming anxiety and other stresses, but I remember listening to the soap opera star of *Number 96*, Abigail, singing her cover of 'Je t'aime . . . Moi Non Plus' on the car radio. It was a contro-versial version because her heavy breathing during the song was said to have sexual connotations.

Mum's decision to take us to see Dad a year after he left us was a sign of the love she still felt for him. She wanted to ensure Dad was okay and I have no doubt the reason Jenelle and I accompanied her was because she thought seeing his kids would give him a boost. Even though my parents maintained a love-hate relationship for many years and argued whenever they were together – and there were some epic blow-ups – I knew they cared deeply for one another.

The interior of the building looked like something out of post-Industrial Revolution England. Its old-fashioned electric lights made a buzzing noise when they were turned on, which was done by pulling a string that dangled from the ceiling. The dark wooden panels on the walls and the outdated furniture only added to the depressing mood of the place. I hated being there, most of all because when I walked down the hallway, men dressed in white smocks – patients – chased me, trying to grab me, and while I don't know if they were playing a joke I was so terrified I ran for my life. I felt an even greater terror when I saw Dad. He was unable to speak due to his treatment and just stared straight through us when we spoke to him. It was shocking. I'd had some traumatic experiences during my childhood, Pa's suicide the most hurtful of them all, but the sight of my father in that hospital bed was among the worst, and it caused me to have nightmares for several months.

I've since forgotten the nature of those terrible dreams, but I vividly recall the heart-pounding fear they generated. It seems the imaginary backpack handed to police when they join the force was being filled with the pebbles of burden and distress long before I took my oath to serve and protect. Much later in my career, when I returned from serving in Afghanistan and needed professional counselling, I realised my childhood scars hadn't ever healed. After I did a series of psychological tests I was found to be at the 'exceptionally high' end of the spectrum for childhood trauma and I have no doubt that hospital played its part in my mindset because that place was the closest I ever came to a house of horrors. God only knows the fear my father would have felt during the time he received treatment there.

I've since read about what Dad and other men endured as they tried to fit in with a society that condemned homosexuality as immoral, criminal and sinful – and it was brutal. A German psychiatrist named Albert von Schrenck-Notzing was among the first to believe the mind was a weapon in curing homosexuality when in 1899 he surmised it took only forty-five hypnosis treatments, and a few trips to a brothel, to redirect a male patient's sexual desire from men to women. Some of the accepted means at the time to achieve so-called sexual 'normality' were mind-bending, including the contribution by Austrian endocrinologist Eugen Steinach, who identified the role testosterone plays in male sexual drive. However, after discovering what he deemed 'female cells' in the testicles of some goats, he formed the theory that homosexuality was rooted in the testes of some men. As hard as it is to believe, there are suggestions some gay men were castrated during experimental surgery and their testicles replaced by those of a straight man.

While the psychiatrist Sigmund Freud believed a person's conditioning could determine their sexuality, his declaration that homosexuality wasn't a disease was howled down by other medical professionals who revealed they'd found methods to 'cure' anyone attracted to members of the same sex. Some men were lobotomised, but my father's treatment was pioneered by a New Orleans psychiatrist, Robert Galbraith Heath, although I can't understand how he was permitted to give people electric shocks.

Another technique – and it's likely Dad also underwent this – was 'aversion therapy'. A Sydney-based psychiatrist, Dr Neil McConaghy, was a proponent of this practice in the 1960s and 1970s. He also created the homemade penile plethysmograph which measured changes in penis volume when a male responded to erotic prompts: photos of men, women, even swans on a lake. It was described as a kind of 'lie detector' and depending on a patient's response they'd receive an electric shock. Apart from the plethysmograph, McConaghy also used apomorphine, a derivative of morphine, to induce severe nausea whenever a male homosexual patient was shown a photograph of a man. McConaghy documented his findings in the *British Journal of Psychiatry*, but in these more enlightened times I can't understand how or why authorities allowed him to indulge in what I consider was blatant cruelty.

The NSW police played its part in the misery inflicted upon Dad's community when in 1958 its commissioner, Colin Delaney, all but declared war on homosexuality by describing it as 'Australia's greatest menace'. My father was never a public enemy. He wanted to be the best possible father to us, a great husband for my mother, and a good son to his parents. He tried to keep everyone happy – and suffered for it. When Dad realised he couldn't change who he really was, he made it clear to me and Jenelle that he loved us and would always be our father. While Dad and I became closer in his final years, when I was a kid my negative reaction towards him stemmed from confusion and anger, but never hatred. I did, however, make the typical kid's mistake of worrying too much about what other people thought, and was anxious that I'd be ostracised, with people insinuating I'd inherited my father's gayness and dismissing me as a dreaded 'poof'. Stupid.

Dad kept a close eye on us and I remember he'd sometimes take me to a farm on the south coast with a friend of his named Gib, who was a great bloke. Gib drove a milk truck and I loved going with him as he collected the milk from the surrounding dairy farms. Those trips were a reprieve from Mum's turmoil, but once Dad became aware of the life Jenelle and I were living as a consequence of Mum's choices, he took us to New Zealand. I don't remember much about that time, but Jenelle thinks he wanted to get us as far away from our mother's influence as possible. Perhaps he had his breakdown while we were over there, but for some reason we returned to Australia and ended up back with Mum. I remember she was angry with him for a long time, telling people he'd 'kidnapped' us. The gulf between them became greater because they couldn't ever talk without their conversation turning into a savage argument.

Despite that, in 1978 they opened a delicatessen at East Hills together, and Dad ran it as if it was a high-end store in Sydney's exclusive Double Bay. He had grandiose plans, and the window display wouldn't have looked out of place in Italy. It was magnificent. Unfortunately, it was lost on the predominantly working-class folk of East Hills, who didn't have an appetite for exotic delicacies like salami, prosciutto, brie or sun-dried tomatoes; it was 'wog food'. I remember the frustration that choked Dad's voice when he'd complain that the customers only wanted to buy devon and corned beef.

I think Dad's motive for opening the store was because he wanted to be closer to Jenelle and me, and we enjoyed having him around. I know he also wanted to keep an eye on Mum, but despite his good intentions both he and Mum followed the same old destructive path. Their working relationship quickly turned toxic and as a teenager I became skilled in the art of mediating because I was often required to referee their latest argument. Mum dealt with the customers professionally and her book-keeping was precise, but she couldn't resist the temptation to chip Dad about the way he conducted business. A few terse words would escalate into massive blow-ups and there were many occasions when I'd return from school to the sight of Dad angrily throwing boxes in the back of the store.

It didn't last. One year after opening the doors of the East Hills Delicatessen, Dad left to pick up some continental cakes from the supplier and never returned. Mum was so worried she filed a missing person's report with the police. When they eventually found him it was heartbreaking to learn he'd admitted himself to Rydalmere Psychiatric Hospital. The pressure of the business, allied with the conflict with Mum, broke him. He suffered a severe episode of anxiety and depression and was in hospital for quite a few weeks.

Jenelle received special exemption from the Department of Education to help Mum try to salvage the business, but it was a lost cause. Mum discovered Dad wasn't quite as bad a business-man as she liked to portray. It was a devastating blow because besides the business, Mum also lost Dad's friendship. While he always asked us about Mum, he kept his distance after that. That loss hurt Mum because Dad was perhaps one of the few people who might have been able to help her. When my mother wasn't drinking she was a wonderful mum, but I often struggled to separate the person who'd verbally attacked me when she was drunk from the caring and beautiful woman who'd once nurtured me.

To this day, Jenelle wonders how things may have been if that 'uncle' hadn't molested Dad. But over the last two decades there's considerable evidence that shows homosexuality is rooted in an individual's biology and genetics, not a choice, and it's a source of pain to me to know my father was one of thousands of men who felt compelled to put themselves through unspeakable torment to try and fit into a society that, when all is said and done, failed to respect who they were.

After he left Mum, Dad had two long-term relationships – with the guy he left Mum for, a bloke who I didn't take to, and then with Terry, who was with Dad until he passed away in 2015. Terry was an affectionate kind of bloke, very creative; he wrote screenplays, books and other literature. He and Dad stayed together at Terry's parents' house for a while after forming their relationship, and because they were strict Catholics, Terry told them Ray was a mate who needed a place to stay. I have no doubt his parents realised the true story, but it seems as though they coped by believing their son and his house guest – who slept in a separate bedroom – were just buddies. I had no ill-feelings towards Terry, and I acknowledge the love he and my father shared was genuine, and deep. However, if you had seen them together in the coffee shop they ran at Tweed Heads you'd never have picked them as lovers. They were two grumpy old men who constantly bickered!

While my father had no interest in rugby league, he was delighted when I immersed myself in athletics – the throwing events: shot-put, hammer and discus. I was encouraged to take up the sport by my physical education teacher, Peter Hadfield, when I was 17. Peter had represented Australia with great distinction as a decathlete, winning a silver medal at the 1978 Commonwealth Games. It didn't take long for me to decide I preferred athletics over rugby league – throwing a heavy chunk of metal released my pent-up anger from being around Mum. I often threw 'angry' and would finish a competition feeling calm because I was spent of all energy, putting everything I had into each throw. I also ran in the 100-metre sprint at school carnivals, and while I was no Usain Bolt my pace surprised many of my opponents.

Dad appreciated shot-put because the principle was easy for him to understand: you threw the metal ball as far as possible! While I predictably scoffed when Dad suggested I do dancing to help my throwing – he thought I looked too heavy on my feet – I couldn't help but shake my head in disbelief when Scott Martin, the bronze medallist for shot-put and discus champion at the 2006 Melbourne Commonwealth Games, revealed that an important part of his preparation was ballet. Of course, the old man delighted in pointing that out when Martin starred in a series of television commercials for a bank which featured him and his instructor.

One of the few times my parents ever attended a sports event together that I was competing in was the 1982 National

Championships in Brisbane, and I felt a great surge of pride and happiness as they watched on with Jenelle as I gained selection in a junior Australian team. It was a rare and special day for the Edwards family. It meant a lot to have Jenelle in the crowd too, because she was always such a fierce and loyal supporter. While she was never overly keen on sport, her childhood was spent at places such as Smith Park, where she'd watch me compete. While there were so many other things she would have preferred doing, she was always supportive. That was why it meant so much for her to see me fulfil my childhood dream and qualify for a national sporting team. After everything we'd endured, I thought that was a triumph we could share.

Years later, Dad would visit me on two occasions when I served in East Timor, and my wife Kate – aka Lordy – formed a brilliant relationship with him. That was poignant, because just eighteen months after his last visit, he and Terry went down the slippery slope of Alzheimer's disease. At the time, I was serving in Afghanistan and Kate did the lion's share of the work needed to help them. However, I do have a very special memory of Dad, one that wouldn't have happened had it not been for Terry, who took me aside one day and said that Dad would love me to give him a father–son hug sometime because I'd never done it. I don't think Terry understood how tough that was for me because one of the legacies of being the son of a gay man was that I found it difficult to show affection to anyone.

But one memorable day I made the effort. It was a pretty clumsy man-hug – I more or less just patted Dad on the back – but it was at least something. And it mattered.

5
INTO THE WILD

After completing my Higher School Certificate in 1980, I left East Hills Boys High for the final time. I had no idea what the future held, but I was excited about making my own way in the world. I look back on my school days, particularly Years 11 and 12, with fondness because I assumed responsibilities that made my time there meaningful. I was a senior prefect in my final two years of school and as a leadership group we were active in shaping the school's policies. I remember we prefects negotiated with the principal, Mr Franks, to allow students to park their cars on the back oval because it was too hard to get street parking. East Hills was also one of the first schools in Australia to adopt the buddy system where a Year 12 student took a Year 7 kid under their wing to help them become accustomed to life as a high-school student.

I enjoyed my reputation as one of the school's main organisers, and initiated such things as donut drives to raise funds for a variety of student endeavours, which included things like sending the rugby team to a tournament in the country and getting a talented musician to an eisteddfod. We were blessed to have a group of tremendous teachers prepared to go above the call of duty to help us succeed in the Higher School Certificate. They did such things as host study sessions at their homes after school hours. Such was the relationship between the teachers and kids, I bought my first car off Phil Gordon, a teacher who was also our prefect master. It was a sound investment because Mr Gordon was a motor vehicle aficionado. After failing to find my groove as a rugby league player, I found my niche as captain of the school's First XV rugby union team, and enjoyed greater success in rugby because there's a much greater reliance on strength in the scrums and rucks. I also played basketball and represented the school in athletics.

Despite my best efforts, my marks weren't good enough for me to enter university – although I'd eventually attain a degree in Anthropology through the Australian National University as a mature-aged student in the 1990s – but that didn't really matter. I was focused on joining the NSW Police Force, and in those days applicants didn't require a degree in criminology. While some of my mates celebrated the end of their school days by going on holidays, I instead landed two jobs: one as a bouncer at a couple of nightclubs; the other as an instructor at the Oxford Gym in inner-city Sydney, which Dad helped me get because he knew the owner. By the time I moved on from both of those places, I'd learnt plenty about life.

The Sydney nightclub scene in the early 1980s was pretty wild. There were no lockout laws or any onus on publicans to ensure the responsible service of alcohol. So alcohol-fuelled violence was as much a part of the pub scene as live bands. I worked at Juliana's Nightclub in the old Sydney Hilton, where

Sydney's rich and shameless flocked for their night out. Paying an obscene amount for drinks was the price for being spotted by the 'in' crowd. The A-listers and executives who rocked up always attracted a crowd because there'd be people hoping to ride on their coat-tails for free drinks or trying to befriend them for business opportunities. I also met many police officers at Juliana's, from both the NSW force and the AFP. They'd discreetly flash their badge to save the $10 entry fee, an accepted practice back then. The place was always crammed with glamorous women, and one of my main duties was to remove the high-class call-girls who'd try to land rich clients by wearing no underwear and 'flashing the goods', like Sharon Stone in *Basic Instinct*. Those women could throw a great left hook when they were angry, as I quickly learnt.

So, this was my work environment as an 18-year-old, and my first lesson about being a bouncer was knowing how to hold your nerve. I quickly discovered that men with a skinful of grog didn't take kindly to being tapped on the shoulder and ordered to move on because they were making a nuisance of themselves. While most took the hint, there was always that one guy who, despite swaying on his feet like a branch in a strong wind, would clench his fists, grit his teeth and snarl about how he was going to rearrange my face. My view on being a bouncer was that it was a great night's work if you breezed through a shift without having to resort to violence. Rather than throwing a volley of punches, I'd always try to talk the person out the door. On those occasions when words weren't enough, I'd look the aggressor square in the eye and invite him to take his best shot. But when I'd warn him to make sure it counted, doubt would suddenly set in his eyes – and most of the time I'd be relieved to see him walk off into the early morning, because I was no Muhammad Ali.

Apart from Juliana's I also worked for Steve Bowden, the former Newtown rugby league player, probably best remembered for missing the 1981 grand final because he was suspended after a punch-up left Manly's enforcer, Mark Broadhurst, with two blackened eyes. Steve's mother was a friend of my grandmother – as a kid I got my first footy boots via Nan when he passed on a pair of hand-me-downs. Steve was in the early stages of turning Stallions at Hurstville into a multi-million dollar venture when I stood on the door. The unwritten rule was that you never parked your car directly in front of the club's main door; the locals knew it, but sometimes unsuspecting visitors who'd clap their hands with glee at finding a space right out the front had their night ruined when they'd return to find a huge dent in their passenger-side door. Unfortunately, some of the clientele needed to be 'helped' on their way when they refused to leave.

The Oxford Gym in Darlinghurst was a 24-hour operation. It was a complete change of pace because it boasted an eclectic membership. On one exercise machine you'd have one of the many models from Chadwick Models agency who frequented the gym, and on the next you could have a flamboyant gay man dressed as though he was an extra from a Jane Fonda aerobics video. We also had members of the Australian ballet – Julie da Costa worked with us before marrying Daryl Somers of *Hey Hey It's Saturday* fame – and members of the Olympic men's hockey team, the Kookaburras, trained there too. I also met many an 'entrepreneur' who specialised in white powders – and it came as no surprise after I joined the AFP to see some of them at the old St James Court after being arrested and charged with organised crime by the National Crime Authority, which would later become the Australian Criminal Intelligence Commission.

There was a set of rules that applied to the gym, including clients wearing shoes while they trained, wiping the equipment down with a towel after they finished using it, and absolutely no one was allowed to drop the weights during a workout. An unwritten rule was for straight guys to not enter the sauna in the evening – for obvious reasons. I was broad-minded, but it would annoy me that the sauna was used by blokes as a place to have casual sex. It was a public place. I was one of a number of trainers who made a point of warning the new, straight members to steer clear of that area after 8 pm because they might not like what they saw.

A high proportion of the gym's clientele were gay, and 95 per cent of them were great. Indeed, I was well fed while working there because many of the members would bring me home-cooked meals. However, besides the activities that went on in the sauna, I couldn't cop it when someone tried to involve me in a conversation about their latest nocturnal adventures. Even at school I refused to listen to blokes talk about what they got up to with a girl because it always seemed smutty and disrespectful. Such talk didn't interest me. When I made that view clear, it embarrassed some of the gay guys and they would try to make a joke about my displeasure. That was just me – and I refused to change, even though my pulling them up about it put a few noses out of joint.

The Oxford Gym was an amazing place, and for someone who struggled to talk to girls at school, it was always a shock to have a Chadwick model sitting on my desk and pouring her heart out to me about her problems – a cheating boyfriend, no jobs, a bad diet. Sometimes I'd surprise myself by offering sound advice, but whenever I thought about asking any of the girls who sought my counsel out on a date, it always came as a dagger to the heart to be told: 'Oh, you're just like my big brother.' I learnt to simply shrug my shoulders and laugh at the thought that I could lay claim to the largest group of surrogate sisters in Sydney. The truth be known, at school I was a long way from being a ladies man. The first girl I had the gumption to ask out was named Leanne. We met through the school band and hung out together for a while, but I moved too slowly to form a relationship. Lacking the ability to realise if or when a girl was interested in me remained a constant theme in my life.

Working as a bouncer and at the gym gave me a head start for when I'd finally join the police force. From both these jobs I learned the importance of de-escalating a situation by reasoning with a person rather than using violence as the only option. The clientele at the Oxford Gym especially reinforced what I'd picked up during my childhood because of the nature of my parents' lives – that is, to respect everyone, regardless of their background. Nonetheless, as I grew older and found myself in environments where I often saw people ignore their personal beliefs to laugh at jokes that secretly offended them, or others who used their authority to bully the weak, I refused to compromise either my beliefs or my standards. I remembered reading somewhere when I was a kid that the day someone started compromising their morals for the people around them was the day they needed to change the people around them.

6
LIFE'S GAME CHANGER

*'Grant Edwards's strength is he set goals and had the courage
to chase them . . .'*
– Peter Hadfield, Olympian

I dedicate this chapter to my old coach, Roger Green.

My selection in the NSW Schools Athletics team that visited
America in 1981 was backed up by my being named to represent
Australia at an international junior athletics meet in South
Korea the following year. That was *the* defining moment of my
then 19-year-old existence.

I qualified when I finished second to Stuart Ludington
at the 1982 (junior) Nationals in Brisbane with a throw of
17.28 metres. However, it wasn't until I received official notification from the Amateur Athletics Union of Australia confirming
my selection that I felt a surge of pride. As I read the carefully
typed letter of congratulations I was ecstatic. The selection
was the result of hard work and also the belief I could be
successful.

Being selected to compete in shot-put in Korea opened up a
world of possibilities for me. I even dared to dream that maybe

I'd one day compete at the Commonwealth Games and the Olympics like Peter Hadfield. I also felt as though I'd finally broken free from the disappointments that seemed to have become the pattern of my life, and welcomed the honour of wearing the green and gold.

It was heartening to hear the reaction of my Nan when I told her the good news too, because it seemed that I'd justified her belief I'd become 'something'. Mum was over the moon. Even though she wondered why I loved a sport which, unlike tennis or rugby league, didn't make the competitors rich, she still equated sporting success with masculinity. Dad – like Jenelle – celebrated my achievement as a moment to savour.

Selection in the national team was especially gratifying because after Dad left, Mum would often insist that I was 'useless and unworthy' and would never amount to anything. She was under the influence of grog when she said such things but they still cut deep. While Nan countered Mum's attitude by insisting I *would* live a life to be proud of, being subjected to such constant negativity and criticism as a kid made me feel worthless. Being picked for the Australian Junior Development team, however, validated me and, allied with the influence of Peter Hadfield, it changed the course of my life.

Peter is an important figure from my teenage years because I made him my male role model when I was in Year 11. After finishing second in the gruelling decathlon event to the British superstar Daley Thompson at the 1978 Edmonton Common-wealth Games, he was on the verge of competing in the 1980 Olympics at Moscow when he became my teacher. That particular Games became a political hot potato when the USA and other nations boycotted them in response to the Soviet invasion of Afghanistan. While Australians were divided about our team's presence in Russia, I was in Mr Hadfield's corner because he saw something in me – maybe a kid desperate for guidance – and he went out of his way to encourage me to be the best I could possibly be.

I saw in Peter a man who I wanted to be like. He had a positive outlook on life, he was a proven achiever and had other interests. Apart from studying economics at Sydney University, he was also an accomplished guitarist. He was different to the other adult males I knew and his suggestion that I take up athletics was a game changer. We did weights in the school gymnasium during our lunch break, but Mr Hadfield wasn't only helping to build my physical strength. He helped me strive to be mentally tougher by initiating conversations about such things as the traits that made Thompson a powerhouse, or why it was important to remain loyal to your beliefs. It was all nutrition for the soul, and filled a void in my life.

I was doing my Higher School Certificate when Peter competed in Moscow. Tuning in at all hours of the morning to watch him compete in the ten sports that constitute the decathlon – the 100-metre sprint, long jump, shot-put, high jump, the 400 metres, 110-metre hurdles, discus, pole vault, javelin and 1500 metres – didn't really help my marks. However, there was no way I wasn't going to watch him, despite the ungodly hour. What I learnt about being a good man from him was of far greater value than anything I read in a textbook.

While throwing shot-put provided me with some respite from the dramas of home, the footy-crazed people in East

Hills couldn't understand why I enjoyed spending so many lonely hours fine-tuning my technique rather than crash-tackling skinny fullbacks or running into lumbering props. They associated shot-put with that 'thing' everyone was made to do at their primary school sports carnival; some even derided it as 'that event the fat kids do well in'. Instead, I saw a beauty in it. To be a good thrower you needed the strength of a weight lifter; the poise of a ballet dancer and the explosive power of a 100-metre sprinter, because you have to generate so much power in the confines of the 2.1-metre circle you throw from. While purely an amateur sport, I trained like a professional, doing weight training, working incessantly on my technique, doing jumping exercises, short sprints and working overtime on my balance.

My selection into the team was also cause for celebration because it came hot on the heels of the recently opened Australian Institute of Sport (AIS) in Canberra rejecting my application for a scholarship. I was one of 800 to apply, and while only 152 were successful, it seemed to many of us that in its early days the AIS had the short-sighted view that it needed instant success to justify its existence. Likely this was a hangover from the disastrous 1976 Montreal Olympics when Australia finished in 32nd place after failing to win a gold medal for the first time since 1936. This left bruises on Australia's national pride, and was the catalyst for then-prime minister Malcolm Fraser to invest in a national institute for sport, with track and field among the eight founding sports. The view of many athletes, however, myself included, was that unless you were identified by the right people as a future world champion or an Olympic medallist there wasn't a place for you in a taxpayer-funded facility that the bureaucrats desperately wanted to be known globally as the 'medal factory'.

Being overlooked was a blow to my aspirations to represent Australia at a senior level because most of my training was done on my own. I had a wonderful coach in Roger Green, who, like Hadfield, was a positive figure during that period of my life. However, I only trained under him once a week. I believe if I'd been granted a scholarship I could've been anything by making the most of the sporting technology, coaching and world-class training facilities in Canberra. The main advantage a scholarship gave successful candidates was that it provided them with the luxury of being able to focus on their sport. I used the snub to spur me along, but the demands of work and life conspired to restrict my progress. I'm happy the current administration at the institute have seen the light – these days they're more inclined to give untried athletes an opportunity to build their careers, something I think should have been standard policy all those years ago.

I was ecstatic to be part of that 1981 NSW Schools Athletics team because Peter Hadfield was one of the team's managers. As well as competing in a high-school meet in Hawaii, we were also part of an athletics carnival at the University of California, Los Angeles (UCLA). I was thrilled to be given the opportunity to run on the famous Drake Stadium's track in a 100-metre race. It was special because that was where Olympic champions such as Florence Griffith Joyner trained. It also lived up to its reputation as a 'fast' track because I posted my quickest-ever time for the event – 11.87 seconds.

The way our nine-strong team was treated in the lead-up to our two-day competition in South Korea reflected a much simpler or more innocent time in Australian sport. It was nothing like the 'rock star' idolisation the national junior team I co-managed at the 2014 Oceania Championships attracted – I was amazed by the amount of gear a multi-national sportswear company gave to each of those young athletes: enough training clothes, tracksuits, shoes, socks and caps to last them for three lifetimes. On the other hand, my 1982 team was sponsored by a concrete company that only paid for our return airfares. My Nan stitched the coat of arms emblem onto my competition singlet, and my tracksuit pants were so short that she stitched a piece of gold cloth down the outside leg to make them longer. While it did the job, I looked different to the rest of the team. I still have those items though, and I treasure them. They represent achieving my dream to wear the Australian colours. The build-up to Seoul, and the competition itself, was a great time for me. I couldn't imagine how life could possibly get any better.

There was so much happening in my life. Apart from being selected as an Aussie representative, at the time I was also in contention for a fully paid American football scholarship at the University of Hawaii – even though I'd never played the game. It was the opportunity of a lifetime, but I was conflicted because after the university's talent scout recommended I be given my shot they wanted me to travel to Hawaii for meetings two weeks before the athletics team jetted out to South Korea. I agonised over what to do. I didn't want to forgo the chance to represent Australia as a shot-putter, but I certainly did not want to hurt my chance at a college education. It was a relief to be advised over the phone by the person who oversaw the college's football scholarships to do my best in Seoul and then get back to them.

The 1982 Seoul (Junior) International Open was sanctioned by the International Olympic Committee and it was a fore-runner to the first Junior World Athletics Championships, held in Athens, Greece, four years later. South Korea was a hive of activity at the time because they were building venues and the infrastructure needed to host the 1988 Summer Olympics. I was amazed to see the early stages of the construction of the Seoul Olympic Stadium – you could see the lines of the structure were designed to imitate the curves of an elegant porcelain vase from the country's Joseon Dynasty. It was also the first time I'd experienced a high-density city and it was claustrophobic. The streets and shops were always crowded. Sometimes I felt as though I was a big pinball because I seemed to bounce off people whenever I went for a walk.

Going to Seoul did so much to help me develop a greater sense of confidence. While I'd been to America the previous year, Korea was my first foray in a different culture. I was pushed beyond my comfort zone because of, of all things, the Koreans' fascination with my body hair. It drove me crazy – *everyone* seemed to want to know what the hair on my arms and legs felt like. Worse still, the more curious types would try to pull it out! It made me feel awkward, and I'd do everything possible to brush their hands away when I saw them coming towards me with their fingers pinched. When the team manager, a fellow from Victoria named Gary, saw that I was struggling he took me aside and advised me to simply go with the flow. 'That's just the way it is, mate,' he said.

It was a great tip, and one that would serve me well much later on when my career in the AFP sent me to far-flung posts. Any awkward cultural situations I found myself in were made tolerable all because of Gary's seemingly innocuous lesson. Even so, if constantly being the centre of attention on the street wasn't bad enough, the cleaning staff at the Athletes' Village treated me as their daily source of amusement because my bed was four inches too short for my body. Sometimes they'd open the door without notice, stick their heads in and call their friends over to take a peek. They'd giggle at the sight of my feet dangling over the edge of the mattress as though it was the funniest thing they'd ever seen. I followed the team manager's advice, and occasionally added theatrics to the spectacle by wriggling my toes and kicking my feet.

If our team management had a crystal ball I reckon they would've bestowed the honour of leading our team into the stadium to the skinny 5000-metre runner from Ballarat, Steve Moneghetti. 'Mona' would become one of Australia's most celebrated long-distance runners, competing at four Olympics. Apart from being presented with a bronze medal for finishing third in the marathon at the 1997 World Championships in Athens, he also won a swag of Commonwealth Games medals. However, as the bus ferrying Team Australia to the stadium for the opening ceremony battled some heavy traffic in the rain, I was stunned to be told *I* had the job of walking directly behind the two Korean schoolkids who'd carry the *Australia* placard and flag. For someone who had spent most of their life being shunted to the back for school photos due to being the biggest kid in the class, it was a shock. I didn't ask Gary why

I was selected but I embraced the honour as yet another positive sign that my life was taking a different path – and I was happy.

The rain bucketed down that night but I don't think I'd ever walked taller than when we marched into the stadium with 15,000 spectators cheering us on. While the fireworks were cancelled because of the deluge, nothing could dampen my pride in representing my country. I'd fulfilled that dream that had been ignited as a kid when I was captivated by the sight of a national team, resplendent in their blazers at Sydney airport. It was a magic moment despite the rain.

However, during the shot-put competition, it rained so hard it actually hurt. It was as if the Korean sky was pouring down nails and needles. My main concern was to keep the shot dry. I was worried it would slip out of my hand in the monsoonal downpour. My best throw of 15.66 metres in the final allowed me to finish in third place behind the winner, Erik de Bruin, who'd represent the Netherlands at two Olympics before being banned by the IAAF for failing a drug test in 1993. (He was cleared of a drug charge by the Dutch Athletics Federation in 1993 but never appealed against the IAAF ban, apparently for financial reasons.) Admittedly, I was expecting to do better, having thrown over 17 metres earlier in the year. However, the disappointment I initially felt quickly disappeared when I stood on the victory dais and saw the Australian flag flying alongside those of the Netherlands and the United States during the medal presentation. It was special. I was happy to simply make the team and wear the national colours, so winning a medal exceeded my expectations. As I stood with the bronze medal draped around my neck I thought of my Nan, who always believed in me; I wished Pa could've told his many friends about his little mate's big achievement; I even smiled, wondering if Mum and Dad would find something to argue about me medalling. And it pleased me no end to think how happy Jenelle would be to hear the news.

Someone who I wanted to phone was my coach, Roger Green. He was a larger-than-life character known throughout athletics as a jolly giant with a warm and kind heart. As wide as he was tall, Roger quickly became a father-like figure to me. He and his wife Eileen welcomed me into their family and his interest in me built on Peter Hadfield's efforts to guide me in the right direction. Roger was a great mentor to many young people. He was so involved in his athletes' throws he'd stand at the fence during a competition and his hips would twitch as his thrower wound up in the circle, preparing to let rip. I was the first of his athletes to represent Australia and if it was at all possible, I think he was prouder of the achievement than me. Roger was a friend to all, and his death ten years ago was grieved by many in the athletics community.

I also spared a thought for myself that night as I stood on the podium. I told myself to try and remember how I was feeling. I wanted to be conscious of that sense of pride and fulfilment in the days, weeks and months that would follow my return to Australia. I'd achieved something special, and in my heart of hearts I wanted that day to be the moment I left behind the backpack from my childhood that was overflowing with pebbles – and boulders – of despair and trauma. As I saw through the heavy rain the small contingent of Aussie supporters cheering my result I allowed myself to believe good things were possible. Did I cry? Well, it was hard to tell because it was raining so hard I needed to squint when I was presented with my medal.

All of the Australians competing in Seoul punched well above their weight. We won five medals against world-class competition; a phenomenal effort considering we were only a nine-strong team. Moneghetti and Lyndal Garling won gold on the running track; Jenny Ganzevoort, a 3000-metre runner, and the discus thrower Bill Apostolidis finished with silver while I returned to East Hills with my bronze. The true measure of our team's success is noted in the record books because each of us finished in the top six placegetters in our individual events.

That bronze medal still takes pride of place among my collection because it has the iconic Olympic rings engraved on it. The ribbon it hangs from is embroidered with the official Olympic colours, and in its own way it's an impressive work of art. The rings are one of the most vigilantly guarded trademarks in the world, and I understand that the reason why they adorn my medal is because the International Olympic Committee supported Seoul in the lead-up to the 1988 Games by sanctioning a series of practice events. That allowed them to use the official logo. Regardless of the reason, having a medal with that symbol on it is, in my mind, a link to my unfulfilled dream of representing Australia in the world's greatest sporting event.

Long after competing at Seoul, I continued with athletics. But despite winning state titles for hammer and shot-put, competing at the International Law Enforcement Olympics, finishing first in shot-put and discus at the NSW Country Championships and seventh at the National Championships, I just couldn't find the distances that were needed to take that extra step.

But I know I gave it my best.

7
ALOHA HAWAII

'Three of NSW's top young athletes – two footballers and a shotputter – have been lured from Australian sport to play American football. Promising Rugby League lock with Western Suburbs, Brett Gale, Rugby Colt Colin Scotts, and Grant Edwards, the NSW shotput and hammer champion, will take up scholarships with the University of Hawaii . . .'
– The Sun-Herald, 18 July 1982

Mum was at home watching *Good Morning Australia* when the television show featured a segment on an American gridiron coach who was in Sydney looking for athletes with the potential to succeed in college football. The coach, Rich Ellerson, was offering a fully paid scholarship (and the chance to break into the US National Football League – the NFL) at the University of Hawaii for anyone who measured up to what his team needed: tall, husky and fast teenagers capable of being moulded into hard-hitting defensive tacklers. He used Gordon Elliott's top-rating program to spread the word and Mum's ears pricked up as the American spoke about what he described as a once in a lifetime opportunity.

As Mum watched the show I was at the gym in the city as part of my preparations to compete in South Korea. In much the same way as she helped the wayward teenagers who lived with us by identifying possible employment opportunities for them, she seized upon Ellerson's invitation for viewers to contact him. She saw this as her chance to do something good for me. Again, when she was sober, Mum was an extremely loving parent who wanted the best for her children, and she had no problem piquing Ellerson's interest in me: calling to tell him how her 19-year-old son was 1.95 metres (6 feet and 5 inches) tall; weighed 100-plus kilos; could sprint 100 metres in 11.87 seconds; was the state shot-put and hammer champion and captain of his school's First XV rugby team.

I was oblivious to Mum's conversation with Ellerson so when I returned home from training I didn't understand why an American was phoning me to discuss the possibility of an all-expenses-paid college scholarship. I was my usual suspicious self because it sounded too good to be true. My childhood taught me not to trust men, so when Ellerson asked to meet him in his inner-city hotel room to talk more about the opportunity, you can imagine what I thought.

The man who'd soon become known to me as 'Coach' appeared personable enough when he welcomed me in the hotel foyer with a warm handshake and a friendly slap on my shoulder. However, I only relaxed when he finally switched on a Super 8 projector so I could watch my first game of college football because it was . . . *awesome!* The hits were massive, the players resembled giants in their padding and helmets, and the athleticism of the college footballers was out of this world. The American razzamatazz with the cheerleaders and marching bands was a show in itself, and whenever the camera panned on the 40,000-strong crowd I noticed it rode the game's every wave and emotion. I had no knowledge about the rules, but when coach Ellerson asked whether I could do what I'd just watched, I didn't hesitate to reply: 'I'd love to try.' When he arranged to meet both my parents at Mum's place to discuss the scholarship, I knew Dad wouldn't be a problem because he'd said to jump at any opportunity to go to America. However, with Mum's issues with alcohol in mind, I pleaded with her to resist having a drink before the meeting – I didn't want to be embarrassed. In hindsight, that was unfair, because despite all of the problems she'd caused, Mum wanted only the best for me. She wouldn't have sabotaged my chance of securing a break like Hawaii. It was, however, fear that made me say it, and I felt awful when I realised my comment had stung her.

Ellerson explained that the scholarship included airfares, most meals, board and all tuition fees, and was worth a cool $100,000. To put the value into perspective, in 1982 the median price for a house in Sydney was $79,425. Our guest spoke in great detail about the university, explaining that it had great professors who cared about their students and it was popular with students from Japan and other Pacific Rim nations. When he mentioned that Hollywood entertainer Bette Midler was a member of the school's alumni, I smiled as Mum nodded, looking impressed. Ellerson said the university's football team, the Rainbow Warriors, usually needed to look towards Canada and Western Samoa for muscle because most Americans preferred to attend college on the mainland.

Australia was being considered a new frontier for talent thanks to Colin Scotts, a schoolboy rugby star from Sydney's northern beaches. Ellerson was at UCLA to check out a high school prospect when he stumbled across a one-sided rugby match between the 1981 Australian Schoolboys team and their American counterparts. Scotts spearheaded the rout, and the longer Ellerson watched the match, the more he liked what he saw. He thought Aussies could make their mark in college football and convinced his superiors to sign Scotts for the 1982 season, and to also send Ellerson Down Under to source some more talent.

While Ellerson explained the positive impact a college degree could have on my life, it struck me that this was perhaps the first time in many years that we resembled the 'perfect' family. While it's been almost forty years since that meeting, I remember it with fondness – the questions that Mum and Dad asked Ellerson reinforced that, despite their being so different to other parents from that era, they genuinely loved and cared for me. Their concerns weren't about the possibility of Hawaii being a stepping stone into the NFL or the famous people who'd graduated from the university, they only cared about how the university would look after my welfare.

After talking for about an hour, I went with coach Ellerson to East Hills Park, a popular picnic ground on the banks of the Georges River. He measured the track for my 40-metre sprint trial and, after running for the opportunity of a lifetime, I was relieved my performance met with his approval. I had to then jump three times to reach a mark he'd made on a pole before he tested my Achilles tendon's strength. The testing only took ten minutes and I was stunned when he said I'd passed the

71

physical. I expected that, at the very least, he'd want to see if I could catch a ball or tackle. I asked if we needed to go to the gymnasium so he could measure my strength, but Ellerson said that wasn't necessary because the university's strength and conditioning staff would worry about that. As far as he and his bosses were concerned they were effectively taking raw chunks of metal from Australia with the intention of shaping them into what he called 'scalpels'. However, said candidates who struggled with the sprint, jump or Achilles tests would have a line struck through their name.

Before I was granted my scholarship I needed to sit a Standard Aptitude Test (SAT) to see if could handle the college's academic demands. It was a multiple choice exam that took three hours to complete. I was concerned because my Higher School Certificate results weren't good enough for me to be placed in a NSW university. For each minute I sat at my desk I sweated bullets, reading and re-reading every question before I answered it. I was ecstatic finally to be notified that I'd passed and was able to attend the university.

A few weeks after passing coach Ellerson's physical test, I was in the Pan Am Captain's Club at Sydney's International Airport meeting the other Aussie recruits, Scotts and Brett Gale, an 18-year-old who'd already played first grade for the Western Suburbs Magpies. We were met in Hawaii by coach Ellerson and two of the squad's Canadian players, big Jim Mills and Ken Moore, both of whom were man mountains. They towered over me and I remember thinking that I would have hated to have the job of kicking them out of the Ritz Hotel, because both boys looked as though they didn't mind rough-housing. I was shocked by the size of them, however, I wasn't intimidated by the thought of competing against players of a similar size on the football field. That attitude wasn't arrogance, it was simply the legacy of performing well in South Korea and gaining confidence I'd never had before. I was also motivated to succeed because going to Hawaii was the chance to do something no one on either side of my family had done.

After checking into the Hilton Hotel, we watched the squad train. What I remember most about that session was how, when the players smashed into one another during the defensive drills, there was an incredible sound – as though armour was clashing. That distinctive noise instilled in me an immediate respect for the velocity of the collisions in American football, and when I saw these guys had the mettle to pick themselves up knowing they'd be crunched again, I felt great admiration for them. Over lunch with Coach and his wife, Ellerson stressed that we had been handed a rare opportunity and should make the most of it. Our day ended when our two new Canadian mates took us out for a heavy session on the drink. What happened that afternoon remains a blur. Despite thinking it was cool to drink beer in a licensed pub with adults when I was only sixteen, I'd rarely touched alcohol after seeing the damage it did to Mum. Nevertheless, I made the mistake of trying to keep pace with the Canucks. As quickly as our hit 'n' run weekend trip had started, it was over. I was home in Australia again by Monday afternoon, nursing the remnants of the wicked hangover I suffered on the other side of the Pacific.

Four months later I was packing for Hawaii and it should have been the easiest decision of my life – I felt like I'd received a golden ticket. The scholarship offered opportunities I'd never dared to imagine, but despite having so much within my grasp, I was torn. In much the same way as I left my mates during outings to return home to check on Mum because I feared that something bad would happen if I wasn't on hand to care for her, the thought of leaving my mother to move overseas made me feel guilty. She still worked as a bookkeeper, but she was socially isolated. She didn't have a boyfriend, she drank too heavily, her behaviour had turned all of our family members against her and, even though they cared for one another in what I call a 'unique' way, the gulf between Mum and Dad was wider than ever. I'd been the man of the house for so long, I was tormented by thoughts about what might happen when I wasn't around. Would she be found dead in her bed because I wasn't there to save her? I wasn't as worried about Jenelle, because even though she was only 17, she was a very capable and competent young woman. My only concern was that she struggled to deal with Mum. I worried whether their relationship would hold up without me to act as the arbitrator during Mum's alcohol-fuelled rants.

The debate about whether I should stay in East Hills was going on in my mind during the weekend I was in Hawaii and being feted by the university. Had it not been for my father and his partner's intervention, there's every chance I might've followed Brett Gale and rejected the scholarship, although Gale's reason was that he'd signed a contract to play first grade rugby league. Dad's words resonated when he advised me that life was short and I should live it without regret. He convinced me to pack my bags and give it my best shot, reasoning that I wouldn't know what might come of it unless I tried.

8
A TERMITE'S LIFE

'We want to be known for the way we play,
not the way we look...'
– Dick Tomey, coach of the University of Hawaii
and Arizona football teams

The moment I stepped into the Rainbow Warriors' locker room I had a target on my back because I was branded an outsider, something many of the squad's Polynesian and African-American members weren't shy in letting me know. They couldn't fathom how an Aussie with no idea of the rules of gridiron had received an all-expenses-paid scholarship to play alongside them. They weren't happy because, in their words, my good fortune denied a 'brother' his shot. I understood that a college scholarship was a ticket out of poverty and a possible life of crime for kids of all colours and creeds in the United States, so I didn't treat their views as racist. It was about an opportunity denied to someone they knew. However, from one of my first training sessions when I was floored by a cheap shot, I realised that in order for me to prove myself worthy, I had to accept I'd be beaten up at every practice session.

There was a sense of tension about my and Colin's presence for quite a while. There were behind-the-hand comments and more cheap shots on the field, but hearing the squad's indigenous Hawaiians openly describe us as 'Ter-mites' did little to make either of us feel welcome. We thought they were implying we'd white-anted some locals out of a scholarship and both of us agonised over this for a few days until I asked one of the quarterbacks, 'Mate, why do you guys call us "termites"?'

He was dumbfounded, then pointed at Colin, saying, 'One-mite'. Then he pointed at me and said, 'Ter-mites'. The penny *finally* dropped, and I couldn't help but laugh loudly. They'd been saying 'Two mates' as a term of endearment! The 'termites' could, finally, breathe a little easier, but we still needed to remain vigilant. Apart from being targets for the folk who resented our presence, we were also considered fair game for the squad's many pranksters. I fell victim to a joke on one of my first nights on campus when I rushed out of my dorm thinking the university's hurricane siren had sounded after midnight. I joined the throng of mainly Japanese students paying a fortune for their American education at a staging point and then waited, and waited, for someone to guide us to safety. They never came. At training the following day I learnt that one of my teammates could perfectly imitate the siren and he'd often open his window, let rip and laugh as he watched the same Japanese kids fall for it yet again.

There were other opportunities for me to be humiliated, though none compared with the first time I padded up for training. American footballers wear nine pieces of protective padding and putting them on was akin to assembling a piece of IKEA furniture, except there was no instruction booklet. I watched the others and followed their lead as best I could, whacking on the thigh pads, the knee pads and shoulder pads. There was one piece left over, though, and its purpose was lost on me. I scoured the locker room for a friendly face, but no one appeared interested in helping. I studied the shape of the padding and it resembled a very large cricket box. My assumption was confirmed when a quarterback, Tim Lyons, looked at me impatiently and said: 'It protects your manhood, Termite.' I didn't fully believe him because Lyons was a renowned prankster, but I had no choice when the boys started to hustle, yelling: 'Time to go!' and 'Come on, Termite, Coach is in a bad mood, you don't want to be late.'

Against my better judgement, I shoved the thing down the front of my pants and it hurt like hell. I could hardly walk let alone run, and it started to chafe, but I gritted my teeth and soldiered on as best I could. As I joined the team on the line for my first-ever field training session, our coach suddenly stopped barking his instructions mid-sentence when he saw a bulge protruding from the front of my pants. His eyes widened when he looked at my crotch for a second time: 'What the hell do you have in the front of your pants, son?'

'The box, sir,' I replied.

He was flabbergasted. '*The what?* Son, you have put the butt pad somewhere it was never intended to go! It protects your coccyx; you probably know it as the tailbone!' When he saw my face turn bright red he broke into a broad smile and laughed. 'Son, you've been had. Welcome to the Rainbow Warriors!'

With that, the entire squad doubled over in hysterics, but I was relieved because given the pain I was in, I'd doubted whether I would have lasted the session.

As the resentment about two untried Aussies receiving a free ride grew among a few disgruntled members, the training sessions became a battle for survival because both Colin and I were targeted for some nasty hits. We were two faces in a squad of seventy, meaning seven players fought for one position. Some of the guys were aged up to 23, and the difference in their mentality to me and the other 19-year-olds was huge. They were mentally tougher and physically they were more brutal. Most also had the advantage of being galvanised by the cutthroat nature of college football. Their approach whenever we were on the paddock was to never give a sucker an even break. Due to the dog-eat-dog nature of American sport, every guy I trained alongside would do whatever was needed to make the team. There was never any escape from the scrutiny, either. We had twenty-five coaches who watched for any weakness of character that suggested you weren't cut out for what they demanded – machines that were willing to run through brick walls for the good of the team.

I willingly accepted the pressure as part of the life I'd signed on for, but the first time I was floored by a cheap shot it really rattled me. I was poleaxed by a late hit and it knocked me out cold. Testament to the force of the hit, I woke to discover that each of the water pads inside my helmet – which supposedly absorb some of the shock from a collision – had deflated. I had no chance of protecting myself because not long after, when an assistant coach signalled the end of a play by blowing his whistle, I stopped running and a strongly built linebacker launched his 110-kilogram frame at me like a kamikaze pilot when my back was turned. The last thing I remember before blacking out was hearing a bang and then feeling my body jolt violently. When I came to, my teeth were buzzing, my neck muscles felt as though they'd been wrenched out of place and my eyesight was blurry.

As much as I wanted to remain on the ground and recover, I knew I couldn't afford to. I realised every set of eyes on that playing field was fixed on me because everyone wanted to see how I'd react to being smashed. They wanted to see whether the Aussie had the right stuff. It would've been so easy to stay down, but a voice inside my head screamed to get back on my feet and move. When I finally stood up I lurched back into position with jelly-legs that wouldn't follow my brain's instructions to run in a straight line. There was no respite from the hit because as soon as I returned to my place on the field the coach blew his whistle and I was back in the fray: running, blocking, hitting and being hit.

Besides feeling as if I'd been crushed by a bus, the first thing that came to my mind amid the fog inside my skull was that I'd agreed to do a phone interview with a Sydney radio station later that afternoon. The host wanted to talk about my being a kid from Sydney's western suburbs who was living the 'American Dream'. Despite my head spinning and the urge to vomit, I couldn't help but appreciate the irony of the topic at hand.

The training was incredibly tough, but I enjoyed it. We started each practice session as a team doing our stretching and warm-ups together. The head coach, a great man named Dick Tomey, was as determined to forge good men as he was to produce champion footballers. He would talk to the squad about our last game and then throw forward to what we were aiming for in our next match. When Tomey finished speaking, a whistle sounded and we'd run off to do specific training with our groups. Mine was the centres and guards. I'd originally been recruited as a defensive player, but when I arrived in Honolulu it was decided I'd be used in offence as a guard, my role being to protect the quarterback and centre. The centre is the player who snaps the ball between his legs to the quarterback to start each play, and we had to barrel the opposition players who were trying to 'sack' (or tackle) him. Playing as a guard was far more complicated than being on the defensive line. While they needed to learn forty plays, guards needed to memorise 180 offensive variations, and on top of my university studies that was a huge ask. Sometimes the assistant coach pointed to where he wanted us to run and I'd think: 'Brilliant, I'll head straight for that linebacker.' However, when the defensive team saw how we'd lined up they'd change their formation and I'd be lost because I didn't have a good enough understanding of the systems to adapt.

American football is a complex game until you get to know the intricacies, so in my early days I ran blind. All I did whenever I saw a defensive player on my shoulder was hit them and keep going. After a while another whistle sounded and the tacklers would work with us; then as that session progressed we'd be joined in succession by the tight-end, the running back, the quarterback and the wide-receivers. Then 'offence' would scrimmage with 'defence', and that meant we second and third-stringers would be beaten up – *again*.

Each football training session lasted for three hours and was followed by a weights or running session, so those first few weeks were a huge shock to my system. You could lose up to four kilos in some sessions, but the expectation at Hawaii was that each athlete would give everything they had at training. If you didn't, the members of the coaching staff made you accountable. We were 'eased' into the week each Monday by sprinting 100 yards a total of 24 times, finishing with a light weights session. The sprints were divided into three lots of eight and it was expected that each sprint would never be more than two seconds off your best time. That meant if you ran 100 metres in twelve seconds, you'd cop it if it took more than fourteen to cross the finish line – and the coaches didn't miss anything.

As tough as it was, I thrived in that environment. The closest I got to the field of play was when I'd join the squad and charge onto Aloha Stadium to the applause of 42,500 people. We second and third-stringers would be fully kitted up as we went through the pre-match drills before taking our seats on the sideline. There's vision on the internet where I can be seen on the sideline in my No. 57 jumper during Hawaii's match against Nebraska, and it's obvious how much I was enjoying the game.

You only need to watch a match to realise bulk rules in college football, and that view was no better reflected than in the frames of my teammates. Jim Mills, who showed us around town during our whirlwind weekend, was a veritable tank-stopper – standing 6 feet 8 inches and weighing 145 kilos. He could also bench press 182 kilos (400 pounds) *without* training. The man was a beast. He used his strength to great effect as a member of the 1983–84 Indianapolis/Baltimore Colts NFL team before forcing his way into the Canadian Football Hall of Fame.

There were other monsters, too. Beau Babka was the 6 feet 1 inch son of Rink Babka, who won the silver medal for discus at the 1960 Olympics, and was wide enough to be a roundabout at a busy intersection. Samoan-born Jesse Sapolu's hulking 6 feet 4-inch, 125-kilo physique was used with devastating effect for the San Francisco 49ers outfits, which won four Super Bowls. These players set the benchmarks Colin Scotts and I had to meet, and one of the first things I focused on as a university student was bulking up. I landed in Hawaii weighing 103 kilos and by the end of my first season I hit the scales at 114 kilos. Besides the hours spent in the gym I have no doubt the little parcel of pills and tablets that regularly featured in my diet (and that I always thought of as just vitamins) played some part in building me up.

The training was a culture shock for us because what was expected of athletes in Australia compared to college footballers was as different as beer and milk. While it may've been 'only' college sport, the students were immersed in a system that was far superior to the programs of any of Australia's elite football codes during the 1980s. I wasn't the only one who was blown away by what was available to the Rainbow Warriors. When Manly's premiership-winning rugby league coach Bob Fulton and John Peard from the Penrith Panthers visited the university on a fact-finding excursion their jaws dropped at what a bunch of schoolkids had at their disposal.

*

While the football squad is a source of pride for colleges, they're under pressure to have their athletes perform in the classroom as well. I was warned if I failed to maintain a 2.3 grade – the equivalent of a C – I couldn't go near the team until it improved. When my grade for Religion dropped to 2.2, my college advisor told me to see my professor to do a 'make-up' paper. There are two groups of teachers in American universities: those who don't support the influence sport has in their college because they argue it undermines the purity of academia; and those who embrace it because they appreciate that sport funds their salary and provides the finances for their projects and research. These teachers are passionate supporters, and I discovered the lengths some will go to for the team when I visited the professor who oversaw my Religion course.

I was studying a degree in physical education, and the only reason I did Religion was because the college selected my subjects for me to fit around my football training commitments, which started at noon. The extent of my religious education experience was attending one Sunday school lesson when I was about seven; I really had no interest in it. But as my coordinator explained when I tried to get out of it to study anything else, it wasn't as though I wanted to become a priest; it was simply a course that analysed the beliefs of the world's major religions.

After speaking to the professor about the team's last game and our star players, I told him about my dilemma. He told me to go away, do a make-up paper on any topic I'd learnt about and hand it in the following week. I put hours of hard work into the paper because I needed to nail it, but when I handed it

to the professor, he took a quick glance and declared trium-
phantly: 'A-minus'. With the stroke of his pen, my average
rocketed to 2.8, which meant I could train with the team.

That spirit of 'generosity' extended to the exam room.
I remember the day the Hawaiian players called me over to join
them during a test, and I was stunned when one said: 'Termite,
this is Louise, and she was the brainiest kid in our high school.
Sit here because she's going to help us.' I did what I was told
and watched in disbelief as one of them peered over Louise's
shoulder and told the others: 'The answer to question No. 1 is A,
No. 2 is C, No. 3 is A' and so on. I was stunned. In East Hills it
was called cheating, but when I asked if this was allowed, one
of them looked at me strangely before replying: 'Yeah, it's okay,
because she's the smart one.'

On other occasions it felt as though I was a character in one
of the many movies made about college life in the 1980s. I was
grateful to be cast in these scenarios as a jock because apart
from the generous marks for make-up papers and sitting in
exam rooms where it was acceptable to copy from the 'smart
one', we also received royal treatment in the student canteen.
Every Friday night the doors were opened early for the entire
squad to gorge ourselves on great cuts of steak ahead of the
following night's match. It was called the 'protein' meal, and
by the time the other students were permitted into the hall, it
was as though a pride of lions had been let loose. There were
only ever a few scraps of gristle left – and you didn't need to
be studying psychology to realise the others weren't happy
that a small group of their fellow students were receiving
such privileges.

Another experience that could've been written for a movie script was when Hurricane Iwa hammered the island just before Thanksgiving. In today's money it caused US$792 million worth of damage, and all things considered, I probably should've been much more concerned about Iwa than I was. I joined a group of the players at the hurricane party that big Jim Mills and his housemates were hosting. There were about nine of us bunkered down and while the rest of Hawaii braced for the worst, Jim invited us to park our backsides as he switched on *The Mary Tyler Moore Show*. This was the last thing I expected, but I'd noticed Jim had placed a long line of shots of vodka and bottles of beer across the table. With the hurricane bearing down on Hawaii, he explained the drinking game. The rule was simple: you sank a shot whenever someone on the show said: 'Good morning, Mary'. Well, strike me down, every second line was 'Good morning, Mary'. By the time the credits were rolling half an hour later my head was spinning. As I staggered back to my apartment, I must have looked like one of the palm trees swaying wildly in the gale-force winds, yet amazingly I slept like a baby through it all.

Since 1982, many Australians have gone through the University of Hawaii's football program, but none have matched Colin Scotts' feats. With his broad shoulders and tiny waist, Scotts was born to succeed in the NFL, and his positional switch to the tight-end transformed him into the 'Thunder from Down Under' with the Cardinals and Oilers. The Americans loved the little kangaroo hop he'd perform every time he completed a tackle and his legend status quickly grew. One story suggested a highway cop let him off a speeding ticket in return for an autograph. Another claimed he befriended the Brat Packer, Sammy Davis Jnr. As the 'Thunder from Down Under' he joined the likes of Hulk Hogan in the WWF Superstars of Wrestling when an injury ended his football career. And the women loved him. One day as we were walking to the local Burger King we saw an attractive girl struggling to change the tyre of her jalopy. Colin asked if she needed a hand and motioned for me to get started. While I wrestled with a dodgy jack that was smeared with grease, he deftly arranged a date. I might have received a quick 'thank you', but it was Colin who got the phone number. That was par for the course whenever you went out with Colin because, while I was clueless, he was a ladies' man.

The differences between the worlds Colin and I came from were really highlighted the night his parents kindly invited me and three other squad members to join them for dinner on the *Queen Mary II* when it anchored in Hawaii. My childhood conditioning caused me to flinch when Colin announced that the bill came to US$1000, but what really shocked me was that Colin's father, a property developer, didn't bat an eyelid. When I sat at that table enjoying fine dining that was beyond the reach of my own family, my thoughts again turned to Mum.

My concern for her had weighed heavily on my mind for the entire time I was in Hawaii. I knew she'd be drinking too much and neglecting her health in my absence. I'd planned to stay in Hawaii over the Christmas holiday to build up for a big 1983, but I felt compelled to go home and visit Mum. Dad sounded mortified when I told him I was flying back to Sydney to check up on her. He begged me to stay in Honolulu because he knew the sense of duty I felt towards Mum would cost me dearly, and warned it'd be a mistake if I thought Mum would appreciate any sacrifices I might make. Dad knew my college days would be over if I returned home. Deep down I knew he was right, but I was in turmoil. My guilt about Mum's life kept me awake most nights, and ultimately it triumphed, because I booked what turned out to be a one-way flight home.

Perhaps I should have spoken to someone at the university, maybe even coach Tomey, to gain a different perspective about Mum. I might have been a man of 20, but I handled the situation the same way as I did with Dad's homosexuality when I was a 10-year-old primary school kid: I kept it a guarded secret. I still didn't have it in me to talk to anyone about Mum's battle with the bottle because I feared what people would think. It was so bloody stupid, and it cost me dearly. I was a slow learner because the fear of being judged stayed with me well into my fifties, and by then the refusal to share my vulnerability would take an even bigger toll.

Like me, Colin had his tough times as he earnt the Hawaiian team's respect. Even so, I was surprised to read in his biography that he'd been duct-taped to a goalpost by teammates and a dog let loose to urinate on him. Nothing like that happened to me – let's just say my pride wouldn't have allowed it – but I certainly admire Colin's achievements. It was through his efforts that other Australians received their opportunity to play in the NFL, including Darren Bennett, Ben Graham, Sav Rocca, Jesse Williams, Jarryd Hayne and Jordan Mailata.

The postscript to my University of Hawaii adventure came a few years after I joined the AFP when a colleague showed me an interview Colin did for *Playboy* at the height of his fame. My workmate pointed to a particular paragraph before saying, 'I think he's talking about you here, mate.' When I read the passage I felt disappointed. Scotts basically said he went to Hawaii with another Aussie but suggested they weren't tough enough to stick it out. When I read that I glared at his portrait before cursing under my breath: 'You *really* have no bloody idea what you're talking about.' But, then, how could he? I'd told no one about Mum's issues. I'd failed because I couldn't accept that Mum was lost to alcoholism.

My scholarship ended when I returned to Sydney and saw Mum had the sickly, gaunt look of an alcoholic. I was devastated by her demise, it had been so fast. She also made it clear that her decline was because I hadn't been at home. And that was it. Just as Mum had opened the door to something special by phoning coach Ellerson that day, she also had it in her to slam it shut. I don't blame Mum for the end of my scholarship because it was my decision to leave Hawaii. But to this day it remains a great regret.

9
REALISING RESILIENCE

Dad was spot on.

My decision to sacrifice everything on offer in Hawaii didn't mean enough for Mum to change her ways. She continued to drink heavily, and while drunk she reeled off the same old hurtful comments. I quickly reassumed responsibility as the adult in our relationship; nagging her to do such things as go to the doctor or simply to get out of bed. It wasn't a pleasant time and I was bitter. The only contact I'd had with the university was via a New Zealander. He'd phoned to ask if I was returning to Hawaii because he'd get my scholarship if I wasn't. I wished him well, but I had mixed feelings about the way it all ended. Some days I cursed myself for not requesting a few extra weeks off to sort Mum out. On other occasions I was angry a counsellor didn't call to see why I hadn't returned, because they might have made me realise what I was throwing away.

Mostly, I was sorry I'd severed the chance to continue being mentored by Dick Tomey. My football coach was the greatest teacher I had at Hawaii and through him I discovered that football was an opportunity to learn something new every day. Dick's lessons weren't just about strategies that won games;

football the Dick Tomey way was an avenue of teaching players to become good humans. He wanted his players to feel empathy and compassion. He was adamant that good footballers had integrity and good character. It was through my all-too brief involvement with coach Tomey that I realised that football of any code wasn't merely a game, it was a place where young men could be prepared for life.

This was an eye-opener because as a kid my motivation to play football was to receive validation from others that I was worthy, and when that never came I felt hollow. Mum's motivation to make me play in the first place was because she saw it as a vaccination from becoming like Dad. I had junior coaches who didn't really worry about class; they demanded victory at all costs. It was all short-sighted stuff compared to what I was exposed to in Hawaii. Thanks to my time with coach Tomey, I appreciated that football could be bigger than glories and trophies. Dick Tomey was a wonderful human being whose aim was to mould men who'd have the courage of their convictions to act when needed.

Coach Tomey, who passed away in May 2019, aged 80, is considered by respected commentators to be one of American college football's legends. A native of Indiana, he joined the University of Hawaii in 1977 after serving as an assistant coach for the UCLA's team. Within three years of his arrival in Honolulu he'd overhauled the university's football program and as a result of his hard work Hawaii cracked the Associated Press (AP) top twenty ranking for the first time in the school's history.

Tomey introduced a sense of 'humanity' into the art of coaching football. I respected that he wasn't someone who dropped F-bombs for their shock value. He also never gave the impression he was a frustrated drill sergeant who liked to sound tough. Tomey's style was to lift people with positive reinforcement. And as a big-picture personality he could put a game of football into its true perspective. He'd note that while the full-time score was important, the lessons a team gained from a loss were often more beneficial to its health than being blinded to any deficiencies by a crushing victory. When we lost our final game of the season to the No. 3 ranked team in the US after we'd led 37–16 at three-quarter time, you could've heard a pin drop when coach Tomey entered the dressing room to find his players hanging their heads in disappointment. There was no hiding the fact it was a bad result, but that particular result didn't reflect who the Rainbow Warriors really were. Rather than unleash a barrage of negativity and point out the individual plays – and players – that had faltered when it mattered, Coach simply told us to accept the loss and to 'use it'. We were 'to take it', 'to go away and celebrate the match because even though we didn't win, we did all right'.

That approach would resonate with me throughout my policing career, because being a cop and a footballer are synonymous in terms of not wanting to be the person who drops the ball, in being a member of the team and giving 100 per cent. Tomey's feedback that day had a massive impact on me. I'd been involved in junior rugby league teams where coaches treated a setback as though it was the end of the world, but here was a coach instructing his team to celebrate what had been done well and to use the disappointment of defeat to better ourselves. That said, coach Tomey was definitely not a walkover.

I never copped a spray from him, but if you were sloppy, ill-disciplined or didn't give the team your all he didn't hold back. However, it says a lot about him that even on those occasions he didn't let fly with profanities or put-downs. Instead, Coach used it as an opportunity to challenge a player to prove they were better than their last performance. As a senior officer in the AFP, I've tried to replicate his approach: to accept the bad results with the same grace you do the good ones – although admittedly this can sometimes be tough. On those occasions I apply what I learnt from coach Tomey. Instead of dropping my head and hunting out scapegoats, I learn all I possibly can from the setback.

I had no idea of what the word 'resilience' meant when I heard coach Tomey mention it for the first time. I looked for its meaning in the dictionary and discovered that it's the capacity to recover quickly from difficulties; toughness. The more I heard him talk about the relationship between resilience and adversity the more I started to think about the importance of this. However, in the early 1980s I struggled to apply it to my own life because I couldn't see clearly enough to make the connection to my personal life. The resilience I needed to rise above such things as Mum's flaws, Dad leaving us, Pa's suicide, and the Sharpies' influence on our lives, was all developed during my childhood; it's what allowed me to keep functioning as if everything was okay, even when it wasn't. I'd spent my childhood learning from disappointments and that's what hardened my resolve, making it difficult for circumstances or results to beat me. However, I didn't know how to articulate this back then. I thought it was a matter of simply getting on with life.

10
THE HUNGER GAMES

While I was in Honolulu, Mum left East Hills to live with Nan in the place she and Pa had built at Summerland Point near Wyong on the Central Coast. It was a disaster; the hurtful things Mum said when her daily drinking session turned ugly left poor Nan reeling. It devastated her to realise that regardless of how hard she tried, nothing stopped Mum from drinking. Mum eventually left to live on her own because she wanted her 'independence', however, she chose to rent a place that was less than a kilometre away from Nan. It was probably for the best because that allowed my grandmother to keep an eye on her.

Returning home after almost a year away was a crash-landing into reality. Mum's ragged appearance shocked me because she looked like a scarecrow. She was only 44 but appeared much older; her face was gaunt and creased. It was also obvious that the time Nan spent with Mum had taken its toll on my grandmother. The self-described 'tough old bird' from outback Queensland wasn't only tired, she was emotionally hurt, too, by Mum's outbursts.

My time with Mum confirmed I couldn't return to Hawaii because she was incapable of caring for herself. I devised a plan to get her into Alcoholics Anonymous; I wanted Mum to again be the person I knew before Dad left. It was also left to me to care for Mum because no one else wanted the job. Dad had stopped talking to her because she was detrimental to his mental wellbeing, her boyfriends had all gone, and Jenelle had no intention of living with her.

I didn't have a problem with Jenelle's decision because even when we were kids she struggled to cope with Mum. While Jenelle and I didn't speak as much as we should have back then, I was pleased she was quietly making her own way in the world, and I wouldn't have wanted to upset that. She'd left Woolworths to work in the service station opposite the Viking Tavern in Milperra, best known as the scene of the infamous 1984 'Milperra Massacre'. The shootout in the pub's car park between the Comanchero bikies and their rivals the Bandidos left seven people dead and twenty-eight wounded. Thankfully, for Jenelle's sake, the gun battle occurred on a Sunday, because service stations, like other shops in those days, closed on the Sabbath.

Nan really wanted to help Mum, but she lacked the energy that was needed for that uphill battle. Indeed, part of the reason I remained in Australia was to absolve Nan of any responsibility for Mum. Nan was almost 80, and I was adamant she deserved to enjoy her sunset years. Besides a life of hard work, Nan had also overcome the trauma of losing Pa, she'd raised her siblings as a 16-year-old and then, as a mother, her own kids, and she played an important role in rearing Jenelle and me. So, I stepped up . . . but thirty-odd years later it still hurts to concede I was destined to fail because Mum didn't want any help – not from

Nan, and certainly not from me. I was blinded to that at the time because I truly believed I could 'fix' her.

Living with Mum at Summerland Point was nothing like my childhood memories of staying there with Nan and Pa. I remember going up there when Pa was building his waterfront holiday home. It was rough and ready living, but I loved it. We barbecued our dinner every night, our shower was an outdoor one and we slept in tents. However, despite the work that needed to be done to finish the house, Pa always made time for us to go fishing together of a morning. When the house was completed I'd spend as much time as I could there. My childhood holidays with Nan and Pa were a carefree time where the sun seemed to never set. I fished, swam in the pristine waters of Lake Macquarie and played outside until I was called in for dinner. It was paradise.

A lifetime later, at Mum's place, I was as much a sniffer dog as I was her carer. Whenever I found a bottle of Scotch or wine that she'd concealed in the house I'd pour its contents down the drain. My detective work caused many bitter arguments when Mum's desire to slake her thirst was ruined by my 'meddling'. But I thought I was doing the right thing.

Not long after I settled in at Summerland Point, I received a shot at fulfilling my childhood dream of playing top grade rugby league, courtesy of an offer from Penrith Panthers coach John Peard. I befriended 'Peardy' when he travelled to Hawaii to inspect the Rainbow Warriors' gymnasium and also to observe the training programs we footballers followed. We'd kept in touch, and I welcomed his letters because they were always full of good cheer and they kept me up to date with the rugby league news.

There was a time in my life when I would've crawled over broken glass for the invitation to train with the likes of Des Hasler, Royce Simmons and Darryl Brohman, but with everything going on in my life I just couldn't put myself through what would've been needed to secure a contract, including the emotional commitment. I knew it'd be disastrous if I put everything into trialling for the Panthers and failed, especially on the back of giving up my scholarship at Hawaii. Besides that, I'd remained in Australia to look after Mum, not chase a footy deal. I thanked Peardy, but I realised my dream of becoming a footy star had passed me by.

I returned to work at the same city nightclub and gym. While I was diligent in my duties, Hawaii had made me realise I wanted more out of life. My mind often drifted back to Honolulu when I was at work and I'd wonder what inspirational message coach Tomey was imparting to my former teammates. I missed being there, and as Mum continued to resist my efforts to help her I'd curse myself for kissing that life goodbye. However, I couldn't go back and in time I realised the desire I had to do something more substantial could be realised by joining the police force.

I applied for the NSW Police, but unfortunately I celebrated too soon after passing the entrance exam. My application was rejected when I attended the physical as I was deemed 'overweight' by the supervisors. I failed due to the old weight–height ratio many government departments, including the police, had in place until the mid-1980s. According to their calculations the correct weight for a male adult who stood 6 feet 5 inches was 93 kilos. I was gobsmacked when the flabby recruitment officer said I needed to shed 20-odd kilos before I could be sworn in. When I protested, saying I hadn't been that weight since I was 16, the sergeant laughed so hard his belly wobbled like a bowl of jelly. He thought I was telling a joke. 'Well, son,' he said in between guffaws, 'eat like you did when you were 16!'

I rallied from that disappointment and applied for the NSW Fire Brigade, the Aviation Fire Brigade, the NSW Ambulance Service and the Northern Territory Police. However, none of them even acknowledged my applications. It was early in 1983 when I saw a newspaper advertisement calling for people to join the AFP. The 'Feds' as an agency were only five years old and, like most Australians, I knew very little about them except that they were formed after a bomb was detonated outside of the Sydney Hilton Hotel during the 1978 Commonwealth Heads of Government Regional Meeting. I sought out my two uncles for their advice and they weren't very supportive, asking why I wanted to be a glorified 'security guard'. They dismissed the AFP as a serious force, mocking the simple entrance exam and the fact that recruits didn't need to do a physical test. They derided their officers as 'plastics' – as in, they weren't real cops – before suggesting I join them in doing real policing work as a NSW police officer.

Their negative view worked in my favour because unlike now, where the AFP has the pick of the best and brightest police recruits, in 1983 it wasn't being flooded by applicants. Indeed, when I sat for the entrance exam at Newcastle's old Customs House, there was only me and another bloke in the room. The senior sergeant who oversaw the exam explained we'd need to score 75 per cent to be accepted. We had two hours to complete the exam. I crossed my fingers when I handed in my paper and the sergeant promised 'We'll be in touch.'

When I received a call a few weeks later from Senior Sergeant Ed Hadzic, one of the AFP's recruiters, he told me I'd passed the exam but I had to get weighed by my doctor. I knew my GP; we often jogged together. When I jumped on the scales I was pleased to have slimmed down to 111 kilos after peaking at 121 in Hawaii. But when I forwarded that information to Ed, he said under the force's height-to-weight guidelines, I had to be 93 kilos – the same scenario as the NSW cops. I was fuming. I could run 100 metres in just under 12 seconds, I could bench press 135 kilos (300 pounds) and squat 230 kilos (500 pounds) – I was in great physical shape. However, a bureaucrat's rule was holding me back. Ed must've heard my heart break because he said he was sorry, but rules were rules and I needed to whittle the excess kilos off my frame.

Adding to my stress was that Mum and I continued to argue, but there were some raw moments of brutal honesty that gave me an insight into the sadness that had consumed her. Even though many years had passed since Dad had left, she still couldn't understand why he chose a man over her. Another moment that rocked me was discovering she'd had an abortion after Jenelle was born. While she was loath to elaborate on the details, I understood enough to know abortions were a taboo subject in the early 1960s and 70s and Mum wouldn't have had a support group to discuss the guilt she obviously felt. I can only imagine when she turned to alcohol to mask all the pain inside of her she had no idea it would eventually control her life.

My shifts at the nightclubs and gymnasium eventually dried up, but Nan knew the secretary-manager of the local bowling club in Gwandalan and he gave me casual work as a barman. I was rostered on for three shifts a week and while it gave me enough money to pay my bills and live comfortably, the work wasn't stimulating. I was, however, pleased that the advice Dad gave me when he taught me to pour a beer at the Auburn RSL many years earlier served me well: 'Don't have too much froth, the customers will think they've been cheated.'

I met many people at the club, including a nurse named Maree who'd go there to escape the stresses of her job. After going out for a few years, we married in 1989. While the union was blessed with the arrival of our daughter Emily (who calls herself Emilee) in 1993, Maree and I were different people and we eventually followed separate paths. We divorced in 2005 after trying to keep the marriage together for Emilee's sake. Like me, Maree remarried and has also found happiness with her new partner. While our marriage didn't end well, I'm forever grateful Maree helped me cope with Mum when she hit rock bottom. Then, Maree and I were living at St Leonard's in Sydney's northern suburbs because she worked as a social worker up the road at the Royal North Shore hospital, and by then I was working in the drug squad in Sydney. However, when she learnt Mum was having blackouts and couldn't remember things, Maree moved heaven and earth to have her admitted there at the hospital. That was a godsend because apart from allowing Maree to monitor her, Mum received excellent treatment until her death.

My job at the bowling club lasted eighteen months, but I was let go when the club's management introduced a raft of cost-cutting measures to arrest a downturn in trade. It meant I was unemployed for the first time in my life, and I loathed it. I applied unsuccessfully for many jobs and, after receiving as many knockbacks, the demons from my adolescence reappeared. They still hissed I was a failure – they reminded me that after eighteen months I still hadn't lost the weight to join the AFP. They said I wouldn't amount to anything. That sense of worthlessness I had inside me took root and grew. It didn't help that my inability to find work left me with no option but to apply for social welfare. Having to front up to the Commonwealth Employment Service (CES) to lodge the slip that documented the jobs I'd applied for to receive my weekly payment of $76.80 was humiliating – there was a stigma attached to being on the dole.

There were plenty of people at the CES in the same boat, and others who needed a helping hand because of health or life issues, but I resented each of the six months I lined up alongside the 'professional' dole bludgers. They angered me. I'd bite my tongue when I was in the queue, listening to them talk about having no intentions of working. There were blokes who bragged about how they supplemented their dole with cash-in-hand jobs because it allowed them to buy their cigarettes and grog. I'd hear some women say it was better to have as many kids as possible, because that meant more money and benefits from the government. The reason I remained quiet was simple: I was embarrassed to be among their number. I felt pathetic whenever I joined the welfare queue because I imagined the people working behind the counter wondered why such a strapping bloke in the prime of his life couldn't get a job of some description. I just wanted to get in and out of the place as quickly and quietly as possible.

Sometimes when I was at the CES office I'd think about the job I'd had in Hawaii just before returning to Australia. I'd done security work on the set of the popular television series *Magnum, P.I.*, which starred Tom Selleck. He was the unofficial king of Hawaii and hordes of screaming female fans hung around the set, hoping to get a glimpse of their idol. Our instructions were to keep them at arm's length, or at least puckered lips' distance, from him. Selleck's popularity was such that his body double acted as decoy at the end of each day's filming by running the gauntlet. While his Aloha shirt was torn from his torso, the real Selleck slipped through the back gate and headed to the safety of his compound miles away from the madding crowd. A few of us Rainbow Warriors players were assigned the work because the father of our teammate Larry Goas ran the security company that looked after all major events in Hawaii. It was more fun than it was work. On the few occasions when we met Selleck he seemed quite shy, but he was personable and seemed to appreciate the job we were doing. I also learnt to respect his work ethic. What the show's millions of viewers around the world wouldn't have realised was that Selleck – and the other cast members – worked through the considerable heat of the day to shoot scene after scene, and despite his status as one of the world's most popular television stars he did it without any complaint, which was great to see.

Now, I was in Wyong – unemployed, unhappy and unfortunately wishing I was back in Honolulu. I didn't allow myself to simply mope about, though. I threw myself into my role as a member of the Volunteer Bushfire Brigade at nearby Gwandalan because that provided me with a sense of purpose. The suburbs around Summerland Point and Gwandalan were mainly inhabited by elderly people and when I joined in 1983 Bruce, the brigade captain, was ecstatic to have a young, fit and able-bodied bloke on his truck. Bruce and his second-in-command, Wal, were typical country blokes. They were laconic, rough around the edges and loved to drink beer. Indeed, I quickly discovered most of the team enjoyed the amber liquid because there were many occasions when we struggled to assemble a full crew for a call-out because some weren't in a fit state to do their duties.

The majority of the brigade were big-hearted blokes who did exceptional work for the community. Unfortunately, one crew member enjoyed fighting fires so much he was charged by police as an arsonist. He'd start a fire and then rush to the station to hit the siren because in pre-mobile phone days that's how the volunteers were summoned. The fire bug's secret unravelled the day someone questioned why he was always the first to know when – and where – a fire had started.

The Volunteer Bushfire Brigade also provided me with my first experiences of being called out as a first responder to 'fatalities'. The closest paramedics to Gwandalan were 33 kilometres away at Wyong, so until the state government opened a nearby ambulance station, our brigade was the go-to mob whenever there was an accident. There were frequent head-on collisions on the Pacific Highway, and even though we weren't trained to cope with what we saw, our crew of tradies, fishermen, retired businessmen and unemployed battlers turned up to accident scenes only to be confronted by badly mutilated or charred bodies.

My first call-out to a 'fatal' was during Christmas in 1983. I was almost 20 when I attended a crash that had killed a family of three, and it was soul-destroying. The police had called us to douse the flames that engulfed the front of the car, and the senselessness of the deaths, especially at such a special time of the year, left everyone visibly upset. I was shaken by the sight of the family's Christmas presents – especially the kids' toys – in the back of the car. That image left an indelible mark on me because those children should have been happily ripping the wrapping from those gifts – but they were gone. To me it was a cruel loss and I spent quite a few days questioning the fate of that family. But as sombre as it was, attending the accident didn't dampen my desire to become a cop because I was in awe of how professionally the police controlled a horrific scenario.

Almost eighteen months after passing my entrance exam, I was still making regular calls to Ed, still trying to circum-navigate the AFP's height–weight rule. My latest ploy to prove I was fitter and stronger than the majority of the cops again fell on deaf ears. I was still 18 kilos over the official weight limit, and because I struggled to lose it I'd started to wonder if I was meant to become a cop after all.

There was one significant win for me, though. After badger-ing Mum to attend an Alcoholics Anonymous (AA) meeting, I treated the night she finally agreed to go to one as a break-through. Mum didn't participate in the proceedings, choosing instead to sit at the back of the hall with her arms folded. She attended two other meetings and contributed nothing to either of them. After her third meeting Mum said she'd refuse to attend any more, describing it as a waste of her time.

I attended a number of Al-Anon meetings to work out a strategy to tackle Mum's problems. Al-Anon is a fellowship group that provides assistance to anyone with a family member struggling with alcohol. After trying to fight Mum's battle on my own, it meant a lot to speak to people who understood the heartache I was dealing with, and for the first time I opened up comfortably with others about Mum's issues because there was no judgement; we were all in the same boat. The counsellor provided some sound advice when I revealed I poured Mum's liquor down the drain. He said to stop doing that, saying it was a waste of time – and of Mum's money – because she'd just buy more. He suggested I instead confront Mum when she was sober, but that was so difficult. When Mum was dry she understood where I was coming from, even agreeing with me that her drinking was a problem. However, she lost all sense of reason with the first sip of the next drink. When I'd see her down the wine and Scotch until she became incoherent, I imagined the devil had Mum so tightly in his grip she just didn't have the strength to fight him.

11
JOINING THE PLASTICS

After my last call to Ed Hadzic, one of the AFP's recruiters, and being told, yet again, to 'just lose the bloody weight', I received a call from the CES. I'd written on an unemployment form that I'd do voluntary work to earn my dole, and the supervisor told me they needed a foreman at a local work site. I was desperate to do something, but told him I had no idea about the building industry. However, the pen-pusher said of all the people at their disposal I was ideal. Before I gave him an answer I phoned Ed at the AFP – again – with the hairbrained suggestion that I would travel to the Australian Institute of Sport to do a hydrostatic body fat test, where you immerse yourself in water to get the most precise body fat measurements. I was certain that test would prove I was fit enough to become a cop, but I think poor Ed thought I was speaking Swahili. He said the AFP was after officers who were only so big and so wide, and before he ended our conversation he added, *again*, that I should 'just drop the weight'. With that edict ringing in my ears, I phoned the CES to find out when to report at the building site and advised the supervisor I could only commit to three months because I'd been accepted by the AFP, although of course I didn't mention my entry was dependent upon my winning the battle of the scales.

Two days later I was at a women's refuge in Wyong, a sanctuary for victims of domestic violence. Our job was to build an extension to the refuge because there'd been a surge in assaults and more room was needed to accommodate the victims. My crew consisted of a qualified builder, two retired builders, a young bloke who didn't have the full use of his left hand and another guy who'd served time in prison but wanted a fresh start. I was told by the pen-pusher not to tell the others what the place was, but he said if I saw any of the women I could talk to them because it might be useful for my impending career in the force. As it turned out, I did speak to a few of the women, and while I'd seen a lot during my childhood, hearing their stories gave me an even greater perspective on how hard life can be.

One woman had a young daughter with her, and she explained that she'd dug really deep to turn her life around. She was a former drug addict – after being violently abused by her spouse she cleaned up her act for the sake of her child. As this woman spoke I felt so much respect for her courage and tenacity. However, while she detailed the horrors of going cold turkey, I thought of Mum and how she wasn't even trying to give up the grog, despite my pleas – and that made me angry, because this woman proved that with hard work and willpower, addictions could be beaten.

As foreman, my job was to ensure the crew turned up on time and did a full day's work. It mightn't have been what I wanted to do but it was a job, albeit a voluntary work for the dole position, but I felt better about myself because anything was better than lining up with your hand open for welfare payments. And of course I was still determined to fulfil my dream of becoming a cop. After speaking to other residents at the refuge, the more I heard about the violence they'd encountered, the more I wanted to join the police to help prevent anyone from being subjected to such treatment.

In a moment of madness I again phoned Ed from a pay phone near the refuge and said I'd lost the weight. He was happy for me, and in the end he made an appointment for me with the Commonwealth's medical doctor, Dr Dwyer, in three weeks' time. When I hung up the phone, my head was buzzing. It was time to have a real crack at losing the weight. I halved the size of my meals for three days; then I halved them again for the next three days and I halved them yet again three days later. I ran every day and sat in the sauna.

I took a leaf out of coach Tomey's book of philosophy by accepting that the only one who could do anything about my weight was me. And I appreciated the support I was receiving from Ed. While the NSW police quickly forgot about me, Ed was always very encouraging, even asking what he could do to help me take the extra step needed to take my place in the AFP. But there was nothing he could do – it was my responsibility. I was driven to do whatever was necessary because being accepted into the AFP was a big break, and up until that point I hadn't had too many breaks go my way. While starving myself was torturous, whenever I felt my resolve weaken I used the idea of what I *could* become when I made it into the force as my motivation.

By the time I headed down to Sydney to get measured by Dr Dwyer the kilos had poured off me, but I looked as terrible as I felt. As I left for the appointment I grabbed some of Mum's blood pressure tablets, a form of diuretic, and took one during the train trip to Sydney in a last-minute bid to lose every ounce of weight possible. When I reached St James train station I had almost three hours to kill so I watched some old men playing a game of chess on the famous board in Hyde Park with the gigantic plastic pieces, popping another diuretic as one player tried to checkmate his opponent. There was an old set of scales near the chessboard and I heard myself gasp with horror when I jumped on and it read 95.5 kilos. There was nothing more I could do except pop yet another diuretic and make my way towards my appointment at Circular Quay to face the music. I staggered down Elizabeth Street, craving a large glass of ice-cold water with each step. When I reached the doctor's office my throat was so parched I needed a few sips of water just to speak.

The air conditioning in the waiting room provided some relief, but I looked so terrible Dr Dwyer's receptionist asked if I was sick. I'd arrived early for the 1.30 pm appointment and after I'd politely declined her third offer of a glass of water, she apologised that the doctor was running late. I croaked that was fine, but inside I was screaming. I *needed* water.

When the good doctor eventually arrived he was in a jolly mood. 'So, what have we got here?' he asked. 'I have to weigh this fine, strapping young fellow so he can join the Federal Police.' He looked me up and down and declared, 'Well, you're a fine specimen, son.' When I said I needed to weigh 93 kilos, otherwise I wouldn't qualify, his nostrils flared as he retorted:

108

'Son, that's absolute bullshit. I've been fighting against that policy for years. Jump on the scales.'

The scales hit 95.5 kilos. As I awaited my fate, the doctor frantically patted his coat pockets before rushing over to his desk where he rustled papers and searched his drawers. 'I must have lost my glasses,' he muttered. I was going to tell him they were on top of his head, but I kept quiet, not wanting to embarrass him. 'Well son,' he said. 'What's it say?'

So many scenarios flooded into my mind, but how could I tell a lie to follow a calling that demands its members value their integrity above all else? My mind was battered by ethical questions, but just when it seemed as though my head would explode, the doctor's voice jolted me back to reality.

'Well, son, what's it say?'

'I'm a touch over 93, doc,' I said.

He just smiled. 'That's fine, son. I'll sign off on 93.'

I could've hugged him, but we simply shook hands. His parting comment made me grin: if I happened to see a pair of glasses on my way out, they would be his. The receptionist asked again if I wanted water but I thanked her and said no – I had no desire to hang around; besides, I was headed straight to the closest McDonald's. There I hoed into a cheeseburger – it was all I could afford – and gulped down a super-sized cup of cola in record time. Unfortunately I reckon I'd only walked 200 metres before I brought it all back up in full view of horrified mothers, businessmen, school children, office workers and the passing traffic. I was so sick my head throbbed with a massive migraine, and I couldn't shake the feeling of nausea – but I'd made it. I was in. I couldn't have been happier.

It was a tough way to qualify for the force, and while I wouldn't recommend anyone else do what I did to lose weight, to me it all seemed worthwhile when I finally received my official notification that I was to report to the AFP's Academy in Canberra on Sunday 11 August 1985. Interestingly enough, eighteen months later the Feds dropped their weight and height limit because the policy was deemed 'discriminatory'. Maybe Doc Dwyer had convinced the powers-that-be their policy really was 'bullshit'.

12
POLICE ACADEMY

'You are a number!

'You will forget who you are, ladies and gentlemen, because from this moment on you're no longer a person, you are a number, and we're going to do whatever it takes to shape you into what we want!'

With that, none of the recruits who were assigned to Class 5/85 were left in the dark about what we'd signed on for when the college's station sergeant addressed us in the auditorium on our first day on campus. I'd seen some hard cases in sport; tunnel-visioned coaches who'd demand blood from their athletes. But this guy, with his army-like flat-top buzz cut, was something else as he stared with shark-like eyes at the thirty pieces of fresh meat he and his peers needed to mould into police officers. From where I was, his body language and demeanour suggested he enjoyed watching recruits squirm as he informed us about our new place in the world.

He paused for what I imagine was dramatic effect, and when he resumed speaking his voice sounded so loud some of my classmates jumped in their seats. 'IF YOU DON'T LIKE WHAT YOU HAVE BEEN TOLD – THAT YOU ARE ONLY A

NUMBER AND THAT WE'RE GOING TO MAKE YOU INTO
SOMETHING – TAKE YOUR PERSONAL BELONGINGS
AND LEAVE. NOW.'

I had no issue with the rules of engagement. I was exactly
where I wanted to be, and my uncles had advised me to expect
to hear that we were all worthless, the worst recruits to walk
through the doors. They said I would have an easier time of
surviving at the academy if I treated the experience as a game,
because everything was really a test of my morals, beliefs,
patience, intelligence, fitness, resilience and everything else.
Regardless of their 'intel', the college's station sergeant's delivery
had me sitting at attention in my chair because I didn't want
to draw any unnecessary attention to myself. While I had no
intention of leaving, two 'persons' objected and accepted his
invitation to hit the road.

Despite their great advice, neither of my uncles were
impressed by my decision to go ahead and join the AFP. When
they pushed me to find my reason for joining, I explained that
the AFP had shown me loyalty. I pointed out that the NSW
cops didn't want me because of my weight, but the AFP – well,
Ed – had stuck solid. I told them I was a loyal person and I'd
repay their faith. My explanation went over their heads because
they continued to deride the validity of a force that was only
six years old, and called us 'plastics'. The day would come when
we members of the AFP would retaliate to that call from state
cops by calling them 'perspex' – as in, they were twice as thick.

I had joined the fourth incarnation of a federal police force.
In 1917 Prime Minister Billy Hughes formed the first one after
anti-conscription protesters in the small Queensland township

of Warwick pelted him with eggs. Hughes was incensed when the local police officers assigned to protect him refused to arrest his assailants under federal law. When he returned to parliament he drafted legislation to create a Commonwealth Police Force, but it lasted only two years. Subsequent Commonwealth Police forces were raised in in 1927 and 1960.

After the Hilton bombing in 1978, the Commonwealth Police, ACT Police and Narcotics Bureau were amalgamated to form the Australian Federal Police. They were derided by their peers in state forces, but I have enjoyed a ringside seat as the AFP has earned a crack reputation as a result of our officers' professionalism and dedication at a number of global and domestic events. They have excelled in their duties in the aftermath of the 2002 Bali bombings, the 2004 tsunami in South-East Asia, the downing of the Malaysian Airlines Flight 17 in Ukraine, the rescue of the Thai soccer team trapped in a cave, in Timor-Leste, in the Solomon Islands and in an active war zone in Afghanistan. The AFP has excelled in its duty to investigate and disrupt transnational crime, combating organised crime, terrorism and violent extremism, money laundering, cybercrime, child exploitation, drug smuggling and human trafficking. The AFP is also responsible for community policing in the ACT and protective services for the prime minister as well as foreign diplomat missions. Apart from training our partners in the Asia-Pacific region, AFP officers are also assigned to peacekeeping missions across the globe.

I drove the 400 kilometres from Summerland Point to the college in the Australian Capital Territory in a clunky old Torana that leaked oil, couldn't go faster than 80 km/h and had no carpet. There was a gaping hole in the floor that was big enough to see – and hear – the road beneath me through. It was raining while I drove towards my new life, and I had to wind all the windows down, otherwise the windscreen would have kept misting up. Fortunately, the cassette player worked well, and my country and western tapes kept me company during the gruelling seven hours it took me to drive to Canberra. However, I couldn't have been happier, and when I walked through the academy's gates for the very first time, I felt my heart swell with pride. I felt the same sense of confidence I did when I performed well for Australia in Seoul, and I welcomed it like a long lost friend. For the first time in a very long time I saw a bright horizon, and as I walked across the parade ground towards my dormitory accommodation I told myself there was no turning back. I was going to be the best cop possible.

Mum was still up on the coast and while I found it hard to leave, I'd finally accepted the advice of the people from Al-Anon. They'd said all along that I couldn't help Mum if she didn't want it. While I thought I could prove them wrong, I couldn't; in the end they were right. Of course, Mum tried to emotion-ally blackmail me before I left by accusing me of abandoning her; a similar comment had made me abandon my scholarship in Hawaii. But after two exhausting years of doing everything I could to help her, I needed to move on for my own sake. My wake-up call was when she refused to attend the AA meetings – rather than see them as an opportunity to beat her demons, she laughed them off as a waste of time.

The course in Canberra ran for three months and I knew it wouldn't be easy. We needed to learn about the complexities of the law, and that meant understanding an array of subjects that included the *Commonwealth Crimes Act*, aviation regulations, the various state offences and what was required to successfully gain a prosecution. We needed to also prove that we understood the extent of our powers to enforce the law: what we were allowed to do as police officers, and what we weren't. Each recruit understood that the AFP wouldn't tolerate tardiness. We needed to maintain a 75 per cent mark in our exams, and if you equated that to a traditional university's standard, it's the equivalent of a distinction. A recruit also risked dismissal if they weren't physically fit. As for poor behaviour, there was a 'three strikes and you're out' rule; and technically, we were on probation for a year. Knowing how easy it could be to lose the opportunity I'd worked so hard for, I committed myself to striving for excellence.

I celebrated my twenty-third birthday at the academy, making me one of the oldest recruits in the course. I studied with people who were smarter than me, and while I failed some exams I managed to hold my own overall. I had one advantage over most of the others, and that was the street smarts I'd honed due to my home life and the various jobs I'd held. However, the advice my uncles gave me about treating the process as a game gave me an extra edge because I allowed nothing to ruffle my feathers.

It didn't take long for me to appreciate that the college's training staff wanted to galvanise us for life on the mean streets. They tested our patience, at any time of the day or night. One evening I walked past Senior Constable Bill Quade – he was related to Rick Quade, the Sydney Swans AFL team's coach – and he yelled for me to hightail it into his office because he wanted to see me about something. As a recruit you address the instructors by their rank, so when I walked through the door I announced my arrival by saying, 'You wanted to see me, Senior?'

He looked at me blankly and barked, 'Who gave you permission to come into my office?'

I was confused. 'Well, you did, Senior.'

He wasn't buying it and growled, 'No, I didn't – get out of here. NOW!' As I walked out he called after me, 'Constable, get in here NOW!'

I returned and the same scenario played out again, with him demanding to know what gave me the right to waltz into his office, before he dismissed me for a second time. When I was called back for a third dressing down I struggled to hide the smirk on my face. I'd worked out the game he was playing; he wanted to test how far he could push my patience. He was dragging me into an aggravating scenario to see whether I'd lose my temper. Our instructors knew from experience if an officer allowed every annoying situation out on the road to get the better of them, they'd be a mess after their first few weeks, so they used the academy to toughen recruits. While I realised the motivation was to help us develop resilience, a couple of my classmates didn't understand. The end result of them snapping back was that they copped even more unwelcome attention until they learnt to go with the flow.

During this time, I regularly drew upon coach Tomey's lessons, especially the need to accept things out of your control. I remembered how he'd explained that the only way individuals could successfully deal with situations out of their reach was to accept that they're powerless to force change. Whenever the senior officers tested my patience I remembered the guy whose cheap shot knocked me out cold during my first Rainbow Warriors training session. He told me afterwards that as an African-American he intended to punish me as much as he could because I'd taken a 'brother's' place. I replied for him to keep it coming because the day would come when I'd finally understand American football and he'd see it on the field. I drew on that because it was an example of how I'd used a tough challenge to improve, and not retaliate. The academy was the same because while the officers drilled us, we had no alternative but to cop it and learn from it.

Life as a recruit was also all about following a routine, and my time in Hawaii and playing sport went a long way to helping me thrive in a rigid environment. Even though I wasn't an elite athlete, I was into it enough to have a training program and a nutrition program. That meant I'd developed the discipline to do whatever was needed to succeed.

I loved the life. We lived on the college grounds and a group of us woke early and did what was called non-mandatory physical training (PT) before breakfast. Then we'd hit the books. In between learning about the law and such things as the powers of arrest, we marched, ate lunch, trained with firearms, learnt to use handcuffs and batons, did our compulsory PT before dinner, and then studied in our rooms before going to sleep. There were opportunities to have a social life, but I threw myself into study and training. Monday was always a tough day because that was exam day. We also needed to be clear-headed to learn complex procedures, which included briefs of evidence, search warrants and other legal issues. Considering all that was at stake, I rarely went out late on a Friday or Saturday night because I couldn't afford to write off a day of weekend study because of a hangover.

I've never been a party animal, but there were some occasions at the academy when I felt as though I *had* to go out with the group because I was part of the team. I didn't want anyone to think I wasn't a team player by staying in all the time. I went to the Private Bin nightclub (then a Canberra institution) once and it was a turn-off to find it full of drunken Army jerks, hell-bent on picking fights. Nothing happened that night, but while I was there I found myself wishing I was back in my room and preparing for the following Monday's exam. The free time I had was spent either hitting the books or on the phone making sure Mum, and also Maree, were okay.

I was fortunate to be at the academy with a great group. Among them was Peter King – aka 'Duck', as in Peking Duck. Peter was the first person I met at the academy and we soon became such great mates; I was best man at his wedding. While Duck avoided as much physical training as possible, he was blessed with a photographic memory. Another great friend was Bob Wynn, who detested being nicknamed Pooh, after Winnie the Pooh. He was an old-school guy and blessed with a wicked sense of humour. One of the toughest of the group was Christine 'Schmittie' Schmidt, and had I been assigned a female partner I would have wanted it to be her. Not only would Schmittie have had your back, she would've taken out any offender – male or female – if they came at her.

While I had no problem with the discipline or physical demands, I struggled with the academic side of things. Unlike at the University of Hawaii, where footballers got their exam answers from 'the smart one', on the AFP's campus you were on your own – and there were times when I really found things hard. I found it daunting, and whenever I handed in an exam I was filled with a sense of dread. If you failed to achieve the minimum score of 75 per cent, you needed to do better on the remedial tests, otherwise you could be cut after failing three exams. I worked harder than most, and while it wasn't easy I managed to hang in there – sometimes only by my finger-nails. However, I never doubted that I belonged in the force; for me it was a calling, as was leadership, which was something I'd always been interested in. While I'd considered other career options, I seemed destined to become a police officer, despite the hurdles I needed to overcome. It was in my blood.

The moment that my being a police officer became real was midway through the course when we were issued our uniforms and warrant cards. The warrant card is kept in your wallet with your badge and it's what gives a cop their legal authority to maintain law and order. It was a huge moment for all of us, and once we received the cards our training stepped up quite a few levels. We did the same things over and over until they were drilled into us. We hit the books hard and fired our Smith & Wesson 38s at the target range. We were taught to use a billy club and handcuffs. Our self-defence instructor, an expert in the Korean martial art of Hapkido, taught us how to use pressure points to make an aggressive person compliant. The training staff also prepared us as best they could for the reality of policing by doing such things as simulating angry crowds, for instance at protests. They pretended to spit at us, rolled ball bearings under our feet so we'd slip over, and screamed profanities. Unfortunately, I found being sent to protests staged outside many of the consulates in Sydney much worse than what we'd trained for. In the first one I attended we had urine and Molotov cocktails hurled at us. However, on such occasions I was always grateful to the instructors at the academy for their training – even the mind games – because they taught restraint and resilience.

The final part of our training before we signed off was our compulsory attendance at an autopsy. It sounds bizarre, but what the members of Class 5/85 discovered was that deaths in the ACT seemed very rare! We waited a long time for a corpse, and while every death is a tragedy, there was an extra sting on the morning we were supposed to attend the autopsy of a male who'd been killed in a motorbike crash because he was one of 'ours' – a recruit in a more senior class. We were gutted by the loss and told that out of respect for the deceased and his family his autopsy would be performed in private.

A few days later we were called to the morgue to witness an autopsy performed on an elderly woman. While many of my classmates were sick during the procedure, and others needed to sit down to regain their composure, I watched intently as the woman's brain was removed, then her heart, before it was ascertained that she'd suffered a fatal heart attack. I can only imagine the time I spent working as a boy in an abattoir's slaughter room steeled me for the sights that disturbed my classmates.

When the three months were over, we all had reasons to feel proud. I was elated to be named the Dux of Physical Training at our graduation day. It was a great honour, and I offered my uncles a silent vote of thanks when the instructors said what they liked about me was my attitude. They'd noticed I accepted everything they threw at me. There was another reason to feel proud – as someone who didn't do well in the HSC, I'd worked hard academically to complete the course. There were other thoughts that swirled about in my mind as I marched alongside my colleagues in our passing out parade: I'd needed to overcome two years of adversity due to my weight to get to the college; I was still upset about having left Hawaii; and there was, of course, Mum to worry about. However, what I remembered most as the commissioner took our salute was that for much of my life I'd been told I'd never amount to anything – but on that day I'd amounted to something special, a police officer, and no one was prouder than Nan. I still smile all these years later when I remember her happiness as she reminded me that her tea leaves had said she'd one day have a third cop in the family. She always knew it would be me.

With that, our training was done and we were sent on our way to a working life that would take us to places that none of us could possibly anticipate. It's now been thirty-four years since then, and it's quite sobering to think that since 2016 I've been the last man standing from my class of thirty. A few left for high-paying careers in law and the justice system; others were just 'done' after years of giving the job their all; some left to join state police forces. At various times I considered following their path – I almost quit to become a National Parks Wildlife Ranger – but I'm so glad I remained with the AFP, which from humble beginnings has become one of the world's most effective crime-fighting forces.

In recent times I've addressed three classes of recruits, but the days of bawling them out and telling them they're just a number and that we'll smash 'em into what we want them to be are long gone. I'm not overly critical of the old system because it was appropriate for that era – plus it worked for me. However, I also support the fact that the AFP has changed tack. We're now respectful of the individual, and serious about providing every opportunity for members of the force to ensure they're the best they can be.

13
A MAN OF STEELE

'I then aimed at his legs, and he staggered, but he still
tried to aim at me. I then fired the second barrel on
the legs. We were then in the open. He fell,
and cried, "I'm done, I'm done."'
– Sgt Arthur Steele's account of shooting Ned Kelly, 1880

Nan was justified in feeling proud when she hugged me on my graduation day at the AFP's academy. The image of her and Mum attending my passing out parade remains a treasured memory because it was the happiest time we three shared together before Mum's death only two years later. Nan's pride in my achievement stemmed from the fact that she encouraged me to become a police officer when I was a boy. Nan pushed me towards the thin blue line because she believed it was an honourable job, plus she thought my temperament was suited to helping anyone in need of a hand.

Having two uncles in the NSW police only fanned the flames, and growing up I would ask them at family gatherings to tell their stories. At the time, I didn't know that my Uncle Graham was suffering from post-traumatic stress disorder as a result of his job in forensics, and he steered clear of mentioning the horrific sights he'd witnessed as part of his job. Like most cops who are asked about their work, Graham found it easier to dwell on the lighter side of policing: humorous incidents, the peculiar characters he'd met, and why it was worthwhile to safeguard the community. While he only recalled the feel-good stories, they stirred my desire to join him on the front line.

During my final year at school, I'd flirted with the idea of going to Duntroon to become an army officer. At East Hills High School I was a second lieutenant in the cadet corps, a senior prefect and captain of the First XV rugby team – leadership sat well with me. I was also extremely proud of my cadet's uniform, which was made up of jungle greens, shiny black combat boots and the famous felt slouch hat worn by members of the Australian army. I discovered the hard way that not everyone was as respectful as I was of the army legacy on the day I wore it to an Anzac march in the late 1970s.

I wanted to honour my relatives who'd served in both world wars and felt proud as I headed towards the cenotaph in Martin Place in Sydney. It was only a few years after the end of the Vietnam War and, as I discovered, the wounds from such things as conscription and Australia fighting in an 'unpopular' war were still open. When I passed a group of adults they let fly, yelling 'warmonger' and other insults at me. To emphasise his disgust one man stepped forward and spat on my uniform. It was cowardly, because even though I was bigger than most boys of 14, he would've realised I was only a kid. If he really wanted to pick a fairer fight there were plenty of soldiers in town that day. I felt humiliated, but I followed my natural inclination to hold my head high as I walked away. That incident actually prepared me for times ahead when, as a cop, I'd be targeted by protesters outside various consulates in Sydney during the 1980s. They also spat at us, in the misguided assumption that we were symbolic of the repression in the foreign lands they were railing against.

I was deciding between a career with the cops or attending Duntroon to become an army officer when a Department of Defence careers advisor visited our school. In one embarrassing breath he torpedoed my plan when, after glancing at my grades, he bellowed his verdict for the entire form to hear: 'I think Kapooka might be more your speed, son. Duntroon is for the best of the best.' He'd lost me on the spot. Kapooka is the Australian Army Recruit Training Centre where soldiers – aka 'footsloggers' or 'grunts' – march until they wear out the soles on their boots. They're taught to ask drill sergeants 'how high?' when ordered to jump. I decided to dodge that bullet.

I also considered becoming a truck driver, even obtaining my licence when I was old enough. Maybe that idea stemmed back to the times when I went with Dad to the South Coast and his friend Gib let me hitch a ride in his truck while he collected milk from the dairy farms. Regardless, I found something appealing about the idea of being on my own, rolling along the nation's highways and seeing different places. However, I appreciate that the reality of working in the trucking industry is anything but a scenic drive through the countryside because of the pressures to meet insane deadlines.

No matter what alternative career I considered, I always found myself wanting to join the police force. I felt it was in my blood. Indeed, I would find out many years later thanks to my ex-wife that policing really was in my genes. When Maree researched the family tree for Emilee she discovered that, apart from my uncles, my great-great uncle, Arthur 'Lofty' Steele, from Pa's side of the family wrote his place in history when he apprehended the notorious bushranger Ned Kelly at Glenrowan in 1880.

Adding to family lore is Lofty's brother, Hugh – my great-great grandfather – who was also a legend in his own right, having ridden in the damned cavalry charge of Lord Cardigan's Light Brigade in the Crimean war. That was the battle that inspired Alfred, Lord Tennyson to write his poem 'The Charge of The Light Brigade' in 1854:

Half a league, half a league,
Half a league onward,
All in the valley of Death
Rode the six hundred.
'Forward, the Light Brigade!'

Learning about Lofty seemed to explain a lot, because as a schoolkid I found it difficult to stomach my history teachers portraying Kelly as a folk hero. He was described in the text-books as a battler who was treated unfairly by the authorities; a colonial version of Robin Hood. But he was neither. By any definition of the law, Kelly was nothing more than a cold-blooded killer, thug and horse thief. The truth is, he's only remembered because he wore a suit of armour and a steel helmet as he committed his crimes. He was an oddity. It frustrated me that the self-confessed murderer and torturer Mark 'Chopper'

Read, who had part of both his ears cut off while in prison, enjoyed a similar status for the same reasons before he died in 2013.

The more I read about Lofty Steele, the more I'd like to see this Victorian police officer take his rightful place in history. There was no love lost between him and Kelly. The pair knew one another long before Ned and his gang terrorised the north-eastern district of Victoria. As Kelly's criminal deeds became bolder – and bloodier – the erstwhile Sergeant Steele grew even more determined to capture him. In an interview he conducted before his death in 1914, Steele told the journalist Brian W Cookson from Sydney's now defunct *Sunday Times* of their mutual 'vendetta'. He provided insights into his foe's mindset by recalling the threats Kelly made via third parties when he realised Steele was committed to squaring the ledger for the murder of three policemen at Stringybark Creek in the Wombat Ranges. Kelly's inherent callousness allowed him to ignore the pleas from the badly wounded Sergeant Michael Kennedy to be spared so he could see his pregnant wife and their children. The Victorian government responded to the slayings by placing a bounty on the heads of Kelly and his cohorts. My relative, however, was motivated by his tunnel-visioned pursuit of justice – and it appears knowing Steele was hot on his heels kept Kelly awake of a night.

'There was always between Ned Kelly and me a fierce sort of antagonism . . . a vendetta,' Lofty told Cookson. 'We frequently exchanged tidings in the last 12 months of his outlawry and his messages were always in the nature of ferocious threats. The last one was to this effect: "Tell that [$%#&*] Steele that if he is in *this country another month I'll shoot him, make him into soup, and make his [$%#&~*] pals drink it! Tell him he can't escape, and I'll get him if I have to come and pull him out of his hiding place with my bare hands! I'll serve him worse than Kennedy." My reply to the man who brought the message was that he could let Kelly know that I was beginning to believe that, as many people had said, I was the only man in the force he was afraid of and that I was confident I would be the end of him yet . . .'*

Lofty would've known Kennedy, Scanlan and Lonigan realised their lives were in danger when they set out on their patrol after Kelly. These bushrangers were masters of the bush and countryside. Indeed, as he saddled up, poor Constable Scanlan asked a friend to care for his pet dog if he didn't return. He didn't. What affects me when I think about those three men is their fate. Regardless of whether it was 1878 or 2019, the same sort of thing could easily befall any police officer. The risk of death or serious injury isn't always through a gun battle. Even the more mundane side of policing can be dangerous. One night after an all-night surveillance job while I was working in the drug squad in the late 1980s we almost had a head-on collision at Bondi Beach because my colleague fell asleep at the steering wheel through sheer exhaustion.

I've drawn my sidearm only on three occasions in my career – twice in Afghanistan – and while I was fortunate not to have to use it, I can only imagine what those three Victorian cops thought when they were ambushed by Kelly and realised they had no chance of surviving. One officer, Thomas McIntyre, escaped the slaughter by fleeing on Sergeant Kennedy's horse. However, he was said to have been tormented by the events of that terrible day for the rest of his life. He retired from the police force in 1881 at age 35, and it appears as though he suffered from post-traumatic stress disorder. It's good for those who are currently fighting similar battles as a result of their service, to take heart in realising that Constable McIntyre and his wife had eight children; he was described as a pacifist who wrote poetry and died in 1918, aged 72.

Although Sergeant Steele continued with his quest to capture Kelly, he was critical of the police hierarchy. In his final interview he alleged that their Melbourne-centric approach to fighting crime in the rugged bush helped the Kelly gang to remain free. He said the hierarchy persisted with sending young cops from the city who were 'quite unused to the rigours of outdoor life' and were so spooked by the 'Wombat murders' they'd run at the sight of a 'solitary horseman'. Lofty said that before the three police murders he offered to use small parties of 'strong active men well used to the hardships', men who could follow tracks and go without food or sleep and be relied upon to keep their heads in a shootout to capture – or kill – Kelly and his men. But his offer was rejected. The image that inspires me most about Lofty these days is how, on the night of the siege at Glenrowan, he and his men raced the ten miles on horseback from Wangaratta by following the railway line when he assumed the volume of gunfire they heard was Kelly trapped like a rat. According to Lofty's account, his first thought when he joined the attack was that it was 'bungled' because the police were firing on the inn despite the number of hostages Kelly had taken. He even made a point of holding fire to spare innocent blood from being spilt. 'There seemed to be no system, no organisation or direction about the attack,' Lofty recalled. 'A determined rush by a few trusty men would have settled the whole business. This was suggested [by me] but turned down because of the likelihood of lives being lost.'

I have sourced Lofty's statement that was taken straight after the capture of Kelly, and it seems Kelly remained a liar until the bitter end. After he screamed 'I am done', having been shot, he attempted to shoot his nemesis-turned-captor:

'I arrived here with five men about five a.m. My men were then distributed around the hut, and I got to the tree near the back door of the hut. A man then came to the back door, and I asked him to throw up his arms or I would fire on him. The man stooped and ran towards the stables and I fired. He then turned and ran back to the house, and I fired again. I am certain I hit him with the second shot, as he screamed and fell against the door. There was then some hot firing, and the bullets whistled all around me. It was then breaking day. I looked round, and saw a man stalking down. I then saw him present a revolver and fire at the police. I could see the bullets hitting him, and staggering him for a moment, with no further effect. I therefore thought he had armour on, and determined to have a close shot at him. I ran towards him, and when within ten yards of him he saw me, and turned round to fire at me. I then aimed at his legs, and he staggered, but he still tried to aim at me. I then fired the second barrel on the legs. We were then in the open. He fell, and cried, "I'm done, I'm done." I ran up to him then, and he again tried to shoot me, but I caught the revolver and pushed it down.'

While few would be familiar with Sergeant Steele's story, there have been at least ten films glorifying the life and crimes of Ned Kelly. In the 1890s a melodrama, *The Kelly Gang*, was popular in theatres around Australia, and since then there have also been at least eleven plays or musicals written about him. The American country and western singer Johnny Cash wrote and performed a song called 'Ned Kelly', and Slim Dusty dedicated two songs to the man I see as a coward. Kelly's heinous crimes have also been used by advertising executives as the basis for television commercials for breakfast cereal and headache tablets. Kids in the 1940s played with Ned Kelly cap guns; Australian artist Sidney Nolan painted a series of celebrated paintings based on Kelly's armour; and when 'Chopper' Read produced paintings of Kelly, the State Library of Victoria purchased one in 2003. At least 20,000 tourists are said to visit Stringybark Creek every year, but I'd like to think they're paying homage to the slain police officers instead of to Kelly.

I don't understand what motivates authors and artists to elevate Kelly to hero status. In their desire to romanticise a man whose actions match some of the most evil contemporary psychopaths, they reduce the slain police officers to mere footnotes – and to me, the contradiction is breathtaking. I think it's time Australians let Kelly disappear in his unmarked grave and celebrate the remarkable bravery of Sergeant 'Lofty' Steele, Sergeant Kennedy, and Constables Scanlan, Lonigan and McIntyre. Good men, one and all, they gave everything they could.

Rest in peace, brothers.

14
NEW COP ON THE BLOCK

When a recruit finished their course at the academy, they were sent to the 'Bullpen' to find out which department they'd be assigned to. The AFP had a rotation policy that allowed its newest members to learn about the organisation by alternating between the drug squad, the fraud squad, general enquiries, the radio room or wherever else they could be put to use. The Bullpen was a room where, just like a prized bull paraded before the judges at an agricultural show, you stood before a senior inspector, an inspector and a senior sergeant and your answers to their questions determined your posting. But it was an inexact science.

The inspector was adamant I should be on a 'truck' (a paddy wagon) in Canberra because he said it'd be a very brave – or foolish – citizen who'd mess with an officer boasting my dimensions. I wanted to join the drug squad because, apart from the macho image of its detectives as tough go-getters who'd kick down doors to arrest hardened crims, having witnessed people shooting up in our lounge room as a kid galvanised me to do whatever I could to get the junk off the streets to spare other children from similar experiences. However, as I listened to the inspector mount his case, the idea of patrolling Canberra appealed to me.

I thought it was a done deal, but when I received my placement I was stunned. I still don't know why, but I had been assigned to the fraud squad, in Sydney! In the pre-cybercrime days, the 'Fraudies' were considered the AFP's Poindexters. They followed paper trails, their investigations conducted from behind a desk as they brought white-collared criminals to account by painstakingly cross-referencing their bank and tax records. As someone who'd never been overly concerned about crossing the 't's' and dotting the 'i's' I didn't know if I had the temperament required for the role. However, rather than complain I committed myself to giving the job my best. My inspiration was remembering that Al Capone, the 1920s gangster who terrorised Chicago, was imprisoned for tax evasion and not his reign of terror.

As a Fraudie my job was to investigate people involved in such activities as ripping off social welfare or white-collar crime, and these days the unit has its work cut out, working overtime because of the tidal wave of online fraud and identity theft. In 2017 alone, the Australian Competition and Consumer Commission (ACCC) reported that Australians had been swindled out of $340 million by well-organised, tech-savvy criminal gangs through such illicit endeavours as investment scams, dating and romance hoaxes, and false billing for services people hadn't received. It's no surprise these criminals focus their attention on older Australians, but statistics reveal that people from all demographics can be easily hoodwinked. However, what comes as a shock in this digital age is that 40 per cent of these criminal approaches are made the old-fashioned way – over the telephone. The offenders are very switched on and can quickly identify any weaknesses in an individual's character. Then they swoop in, causing devastating financial losses and other distress to the gullible party.

On the job, the first person I arrested was a bloke who'd tail postmen. When he saw a Centrelink cheque dropped off in a letterbox he'd steal it and cash it in. A drug addict, he thought nothing of ripping off money from hard-working taxpayers that was intended to help invalid pensioners, war widows and people in genuine hardship. Bank staff had become suspicious of him, and it didn't take long for us to have him in custody after we looked at the branch's close-circuit vision; this bloke was not a criminal genius. Nevertheless, he was my first 'collar' and as I drilled him, it was still registering with me that I *really* was a cop. After we left the academy we needed to do a series of tasks to be considered a 'competent' police officer, and one of them was to interview and arrest a suspect. As I did my duty and my crim was sweating bullets, I couldn't help but feel I was on my way to earning my title.

The fellow had only stolen a couple of cheques, but I treated it as if it was the biggest fraud case in Australian history – which I'd actually be at the centre of in the 1990s during my second stint in the department. I interviewed him for twice as long as expected for someone charged with his crime. I asked dozens of questions, and he answered them. He admitted he'd stolen the cheques and cashed them at either the bank or a pub. If he cashed them at a pub he used the money to buy alcohol. He'd then sell the grog and use the cash he made to buy drugs for himself. He eventually whinged he was getting a headache; he had nothing else to offer. However, I made it clear I had even more questions for him. By the second hour of my interrogation he was pleading for it to end. 'Honestly officer,' he whined, 'I have nothing more.'

He was sentenced, but the judge in the case helped prepare me for one of the disappointments of police work. He simply slapped the thief over the wrist after hearing that he was remorseful, trying to be a better person and in a methadone program. When some of my older colleagues heard about his plea they dismissed it as the 'usual claptrap'. I appreciated that those officers were hard-bitten, and that their attitude was shaped by their years of experience and their disappoint-ment with the court system. It's understandable, but when I left the academy I was conscious not to allow myself to see 99 per cent of life through the same prism of the one per cent. There have been times when that view has been challenged, especially when dealing with paedophiles, but for the main I've understood that people have their reasons for the decisions they make.

I would also learn there were a number of reasons that the odds suggested my first collar would reoffend. Firstly, he was an unemployed heroin addict, which meant his main source of income was the dole, and that money would only last him for a maximum of two days because he'd spend it all on drugs. Once he'd gone through his money he'd need to find more to feed his habit, so unless he gave up drugs he was likely to resort to criminal activity to pay for his addiction. As I say, people have reasons for committing crime; the key as a police officer is to try and understand why they do it.

Something else I discovered in this unit is that you can't put lawbreakers – even those who commit the same crime – under the one umbrella. One day we arrested a woman who also stole Centrelink cheques. She was on welfare, but resorted to obtaining money by deception because she couldn't survive otherwise with the number kids she had to look after. She wasn't what you'd call a 'bad' person, and was genuinely remorseful. It was also obvious she loved her kids and had used the money to raise them.

In that first year I was moved around and given experience in a number of departments that were all based in Sydney, including general duties. I also filled the role most rookie cops get hurled into, which is attending protests at consulates based in Sydney. And they were something else. People would gather outside the gates to protest, for instance to express their displeasure about what they saw as abuses of human rights, but a gathering of supposedly peaceful protesters could quite quickly disintegrate into an angry mob because people would arrive in an emotive state and it didn't take much – perhaps someone using inflammatory language – for tempers to flare.

In these situations, as I stood in a street often thousands of kilometres away from the situations the protesters were opposed to, I often wondered how their behaviour was helping their cause. One such protest was staged in 1986 at the Polish consulate in Sydney by supporters of the Solidarity trade union movement, founded by Lech Walesa. He had influential supporters; Pope John Paul II had received him in the Vatican and he visited a number of nations as the guest of the International Labour Organization. However, when the Solidarity movement was outlawed by Poland's communist regime in 1981, Walesa and other officials were arrested and martial law was imposed. The nation's leader feared the Soviets would use armed intervention to restore 'order'. News of Walesa's incarceration sparked worldwide protests, which is how I came to join my colleagues in protecting the Polish Consul General and his staff from protesters who had broken through the NSW police cordon. Under Australia's jurisdiction, the state police are responsible for the streets outside of the consulate, and the Feds have the responsibility of looking after the grounds within their fence. A very large, angry crowd had assembled, and while a few of the people who set fire to the Polish flag suffered minor burns, others spat at us or threw plastic bags filled with urine at us. Somehow, we, the AFP and NSW police, represented 'repression' in Poland.

An important ritual of joining the force was getting a nickname. Mine came when I was transferred to the drug squad in Sydney in 1987 as a constable and was christened 'Ticker'. Regardless of which Australian police force an officer serves in, their nickname is almost as important as their real name and rank – sometimes a cop's moniker is so well known in various circles it takes weeks before the individual's new colleagues know their real name! Some nicknames are very creative. For instance, one of my mates was dubbed 'Blisters' because he apparently only appeared once the work was completed; and when I worked in surveillance, each member of the team was called Bruce by the owner of a nondescript Chinese restaurant in Redfern where we'd sometimes eat – we ate there because it was well away from the joints where the city's colourful identities gathered. Our bookings were always made under the codename of 'Bruce', so when they took our orders the staff addressed us as 'Mr Bruce 1', 'Mr Bruce 2', 'Mr Bruce 3', and so on.

I'd love to say I was dubbed Ticker because I displayed great heart for the AFP's rugby team, but my nickname came after a run-in with a rogue known as *Ixodes holocyclus*. The aftermath was a serious concern. I was hospitalised and wired up to all sorts of machines as a gaggle of quacks tried to work out what was wrong with me. I'd gone to the hospital because I thought I was having a heart attack while painting Maree's and my home in Gwandalan. One of the reasons we stayed on the Central Coast was so I could be close to Mum; while I was getting on with my life and career, I still checked in on her. It was always deflating because while things were going well for me, Mum was continuing on her downward spiral. However, one day I began to worry about my own health – whenever I lifted my arm up and down I felt severe pains in my chest. I kept telling myself it couldn't possibly be a heart attack because I was only 23, far too young for *that*. But Maree reasoned we ought to head to the hospital because her experiences as a nurse had taught her it was much better to be safe than sorry.

Within minutes of arriving at the casualty ward the hospital's doctors wired me up to heart monitors and other machines. But while they did a lot of talking, no one asked me how I felt. After about 40 minutes of listening to muffled conversations and hearing the word 'heart' mentioned more times than I cared for, I asked if I was having a heart attack or not. It did nothing to lift my spirits to see them respond by hopelessly shrugging their shoulders. Then a matron marched into my room. She was a large lady, and after scanning my chart and then the monitor, she roared, 'So, what are you doing in here, princess?' She clearly tried not to laugh when I said I thought I might be having a heart attack. 'You're not having a heart attack, princess. Have you been in the bush recently?'

As it turned out I *had* been in the scrub, monitoring a yacht that the AFP's intelligence indicated had been refitted to carry drugs. It was anchored in a secluded cove in Sydney Harbour, surrounded by bushland. We'd watched it for days, and because the drug runners needed to get the mast fixed we figured it would remain there for a while longer. After one particular shift I was making my way to a club to watch one of Jeff Fenech's world title fights with mates when the office contacted me to say the boat had just slipped out of the cove. We contacted Customs and they kept a visual on them over the horizon, and when the yacht returned I was crawling about in the bush, armed with a long telephoto lens and taking plenty of photos. We made a good bust eventually; the boat had a tonne of cocaine on board. But in the days that followed the arrests I didn't feel too well.

When the matron heard I'd been crawling around in the scrub, she told me to lift my arm towards the ceiling. Within seconds she came across the culprit, an *Ixodes holocyclus* – better known as the Australian paralysis tick – engorged from feasting on my blood. This little insect is normally found on native animals; they bury themselves into the flesh of the host and secrete neurotoxins which can cause all sorts of problems, such as making a healthy 23-year-old terrified that he is in the throes of a heart attack.

By the time news of my problem reached my colleagues at work, I was already answering to Ticker. I'm not complaining, however, because I've definitely heard worse!

After spending my first ten years in the AFP working in Sydney and Newcastle in the fraud and drug squads, general enquiries, surveillance and the Family Court, I was transferred to Canberra in July of 1994 to work in the Internal Investigations Division (IID). Known as Professional Standards these days, the department has the responsibility of impartially investigating complaints about officers' behaviour or character. Professional Standards (like the IID) is scrutinised by the Ombudsman, and that means each officer works under enormous pressure to ensure their work is of the highest standard.

My view that selection in Professional Standards should be treated as an honour will come as a surprise to some AFP officers. I say that because there are some in the ranks who perceive Professional Standards as the enemy. They describe its members using the disparaging term 'toe-cutter', as if to imply that they'll do whatever is needed to hang a fellow cop out to dry. Believe me, they aren't assassins. And then there are critics who'll insist that anyone who signs on for Personal Standards does it to climb through the ranks.

Serving in IID did in fact help my career, but I certainly didn't join with that intention. It instead presented an opportunity for me to move to Canberra because I thought the change of scenery would be good for Maree and me. We'd become parents the previous year and we were having problems.

I thought we needed to get away from the Central Coast because there wasn't anything there for either of us. My fear that Mum would succumb to alcoholism came true in 1987 when she died in Royal North Shore Hospital aged only 46. It was such a bloody waste. I found it hard to grieve for her properly because apart from feeling anger towards her, I also needed to fix the problems she'd left behind – including a large debt. I was angry with Mum because she refused to help herself. The way she dealt with a bad tooth is a case in point. Despite my badgering for her to see a dentist and get it checked, she did nothing, and it caused her a number of health problems once it turned septic. I felt torn when I said my final goodbye to Mum because I really didn't know whether I'd helped – or failed – her. I'm still wondering that thirty-two years later, especially when I look at what she's missed: namely the beautiful children Jenelle and I would produce.

Dad and I were back in contact as we'd made peace long before I moved to Canberra. While we still didn't have a traditional father-son relationship, I'd realised he always adored me and that was humbling. Now he's also gone, and there are times when I regret that I sabotaged those weekend visits to his home. I know I acted like a brat by thwarting his attempts to connect with me when he made the effort to do such things as talk about rugby league – a subject he had no interest in.

If I needed to know how some AFP colleagues felt about me being a member of the IID, I found out one evening when I was walking over the road from Canberra's city police station and someone yelled from a window, 'YOU'RE JUST A F---ING DOG!'

The cowardly delivery of this insult took me back to my days in the primary school playground when some kids would yell out 'Poof's boy' while hiding among a crowd of schoolmates. This day, this new insult really struck a nerve. I dropped my bag and, with my arms outstretched, I returned fire. 'COME DOWN AND SAY THAT TO MY FACE!' I shouted.

While the invitation was met with silence, the incident reinforced that I was now working in an unpopular office. But I was proud to serve in it because, rather than being the enemy, I realised its members were in fact proud police officers whose job is to uncover – without bias – the truth when a colleague is accused of misconduct. The reason why I knew I could look any officer in the eye was because my only interest was the truth. I benefited immensely from being buddied up with an exceptional officer named Audrey Fagan. Audrey was an exemplary cop; intelligent, tenacious and principled. She set high standards and I did my best to follow her lead. It was Audrey's job to teach me the ropes, and I learnt a lot from her. She believed the nature of a police officer's job meant they could find themselves in a position where they made a mistake. Her view was to respect the officer who put their hand up and said they'd done the wrong thing, but she looked closely at those who displayed a negative attitude or made excuses that didn't ring true.

Audrey and I became great friends; in fact I became close to most of the people I worked with. It was logical; we worked long hours together and our work was the kind in which people need a strong bond to do well. I'd drifted away from my friends at school when I left for Hawaii and then the Central Coast. It was the days before social media and most people lost touch with their schoolmates because life overran us. I'm happy that I have reconnected with many of them through Facebook and Twitter; many have achieved great things in their life. So cops tended to become the people I associated with after hours, and that's why Maree and I would hang out with Audrey and her then-partner Andrew; we always had a good time together.

I was fortunate to form such a strong friendship with Audrey because the nature of IID meant you couldn't talk to anyone outside of the unit about problems you might be having with a case. Audrey was a never-failing pillar of strength and wisdom, and as was her nature, she went above the call of duty to help me find my feet in a tough gig.

We both worked on a groundbreaking sexual misconduct and bullying investigation in the workplace alongside the future commissioner, Mick Keelty, in 1996. It was unheard of for a police force to undertake such an operation against their own, but the AFP command was determined its workforce would be under-pinned by the values of respect and decency – something the current Commissioner Andrew Colvin has built on. A group of male officers in an area of ACT Policing were accused of treating some female counterparts appallingly. It was amazing to watch Keelty work of a morning when we'd travel with him in his car and he'd conduct his briefing while he drove. Mick had no notes and he wrote nothing down when we replied to his questions, but his recall was exceptional. I believe most people who operate at the same level as someone like Keelty have two common attributes: a photographic memory, and they don't sleep much. By the end of the investigation quite a few officers were punished, and also lost their jobs.

Like Audrey, I respected those officers who, when they were being investigated, would put their hand up and say 'I stuffed up'. It was a sign they recognised there was a problem and were sincere about remedying it. However, the officers who were adamant they hadn't done anything wrong concerned me, especially when the evidence suggested otherwise. They seemed to be the ones who'd repeat the behaviour that had brought them to our attention. One such person was a senior constable who was the subject of numerous complaints from the public about his behaviour. In those days we 'invited' anyone who appeared on our radar into the office for an interview, and when I went outside to meet him, he was on his mobile phone with his back to me. I called his name to let him know I was ready to conduct an interview concerning allegations about his conduct and manner. Incredibly, his response was to hold his hand up dismissively, as though telling me to 'shut up' – it turned out that his seemingly uninterruptible phone call involved the serious business of booking tickets for a concert. When I finally got him into the interview, I levelled the litany of complaints against him, and after hearing his responses I submitted a recommendation that he be given a Section 44(e). That's when the commissioner sacks an officer because he's lost faith in them because of their behaviour in the community. That officer was dismissed.

One of the realities about police work is that the nature of it means officers deal with unscrupulous people all the time. It's prudent to always be on guard, because criminals know how to compromise people who they think have a weakness. Sometimes we need to think creatively – sometimes you have to think like a criminal to catch one – but always within the rules of the law. We needed to think differently when I was in the drug squad in 1987 and had a warrant to search the home of a substantial dealer in Sydney's south-west. This guy was as cunning as a rat, and that was why he'd been one step ahead of the law for so long. He owned a few properties in a cul-de-sac, and that was strategic because it meant he knew who lived there – and who was snooping. It was difficult to get to the property but in order to get him out of his house we orchestrated a gas leak. We had the local gas company on board and they knocked on the doors of the homes in his street telling the occupants they needed to evacuate their houses.

The AFP didn't have its own drug dogs, so Customs brought theirs in, but despite being told by a reliable informant where all the dope was, we found nothing. The dogs went crazy because they picked up the scent of the drugs, but their handler said the stash must've been removed sometime within the last twenty-four hours. When we climbed into the roof cavity we found $370,000 worth of paper notes. It was a massive amount of cash and while a senior constable and I were counting it out, the drug dealer insisted he speak to us. He told the NSW cops on the scene he was willing to tell us everything as long as he didn't have to speak in front of them. We walked around the side of the house and when I realised he was spinning us a lie, I asked him to tell us about the money. His response was: 'What money?'

'You saw it, the money we just took out of your roof,' I said.

'I don't know anything about any money,' he replied with a shrug.

'Hang on,' I pressed. 'You saw the $370,000 we found inside your roof.'

'I don't know anything about any money,' he countered. 'If you found money, do what you want with it.'

With that, I asked whether he was attempting to bribe us and his response was for me and the senior constable to take it to mean what we wanted. We brought charges of bribing a Commonwealth officer, which ultimately were unsuccessful.

I know of some good officers who ruined their careers by having what's best termed as 'improper relationships' with female informants. After I extradited a woman from Cairns to Sydney, I was surprised when she called me one evening to say she wanted to meet me – on my own, in her apartment. She wanted to share some information on the proviso she became a registered informant. I smelt a rat, especially when she insisted for the third time that I turn up on my own. When I went to the address she gave me, it was a penthouse on Park Street in Sydney that overlooked Hyde Park. My gut feeling was not to go up – no doubt the place was tricked up with cameras ready to catch me when she tried something. I turned on my heels and walked straight back to my car at speed.

That's why I believe policing is about listening to the little voice in your head, because your conscience knows what's right, what's wrong, and what to avoid. I met many officers through my IID investigations who found themselves under investigation all because they ignored their gut feeling.

My boss at IID was Superintendent Bob Gray, who I regard as an outstanding police officer. Bob placed a heavy emphasis on finding the truth and investigating every minute detail of a case. He was an old-school member of the fraud squad, and so thorough that he often drove me nuts when I first started working with him. Whenever I thought I'd completed a report he'd look at what I'd handed him and punch holes in it. By the end of the grilling I'd go away to make sure my work was watertight.

Thanks to Bob I learnt the value of leaving no stone unturned when I was assigned to work on a case that involved two officers who'd been accused of murder. We were contacted by the Commonwealth Ombudsman after a strapping young bloke who stood 6 feet 4 inches high went out one night in Canberra, had a drink and a steak with his mates, and was found dead at his home a few hours later. Our initial investigation noted that he'd been taken to hospital when he took ill and whatever was wrong with him had affected his speech. The people we inter- viewed thought he was speaking an unusual foreign language because they couldn't make out what he was saying. We were told he also made gurgling and gargling noises, and his blood pressure rocketed to a dangerous 260/150, high enough to cause a series of serious medical problems including stroke, heart attack, and heart or kidney failure, or even to cause the body's main artery, the aorta, to rupture. When the bloke caused some trouble at the hospital, two AFP officers were despatched and he was 'scheduled' – that is, taken to a mental health facility for treatment. No one there could work out was wrong with him but he was medicated. Upon being discharged, the man went home. When his friends turned up to his place later they found a trail of blood, puddles of vomit and his corpse slumped on the ground.

His aorta had haemorrhaged and the result was catastrophic. However, when the doctor gave his statement at
the coronial inquiry he said that, in his professional opinion,
the patient died because of what he described as the 'brutality'
of the police. Witnesses had reported that when the police
restrained him they were seen to bend him over the boot of their
car to apply the handcuffs. The doctor – who'd by all accounts
recently gained a law degree, thus giving the impression that
he considered himself a legal doctor – said he saw marks on the
man's chest and that formed the basis for his conclusion that
the two officers had acted heavy-handedly. We were advised by
the Ombudsman that as a result of this inquiry the two officers
faced an allegation of murder.

The IID pounded the pavement during this investigation.
Due to Bob's diligence we tracked down and interviewed every
doctor, nurse, orderly and patient who'd been in the hospital
waiting room that night. This meant we travelled to such
far-flung places as Uluru and Christmas Island to speak to the
witnesses. They painted a clear picture of what had happened,
and it didn't support the doctor's allegation of police brutality.
Indeed, the evidence we gathered allowed for the charges that
had been levelled at the two cops to be downgraded from murder
to manslaughter, and upon further evidence they faced the
less serious charge of causing grievous bodily harm. Nonetheless,
these officers – who'd been stood down from all duties – were
devastated to have a cloud of suspicion hanging over them. They
were adamant they hadn't done anything wrong. However,
we hit some brick walls as we tried to collect as many facts
as we could for the case. The dead man's family was livid – they

supported the doctor's allegations, and it didn't help that despite the seriousness of the situation the doctor refused to cooperate, saying it was our problem and not his.

Halfway through the investigation Bob accepted a redundancy, leaving me – a constable holding the brevet rank of sergeant – in charge of the case. The brief he handed over was a couple of hundred pages long. I followed his principles and went down all number of wormholes. While the case involved twelve months of intense work, it was worth the effort. We found that the deceased had a severe blood pressure problem which, while it afflicted many members of his family, he hadn't told anyone about. When the coroner ruled that neither police officer had done anything wrong, the onus of responsibility was ultimately found to fall upon the doctor. The family apologised to us and after thanking us for our efforts they made plans to sue the doctor for what they alleged was 'incompetence'. The relief of the two police officers was obvious. Being cleared of any blame by the coroner lifted the weight of the world off their shoulders.

I served in internal investigations for four years, until I was transferred to Los Angeles. It was double the time most other officers spent in that department, and there were detractors who saw that as a sign that I enjoyed the work. However, to the person who yelled out I was a 'dog' for working in the department, I can honestly say every case was treated the same way. My time in IID taught me to look at things from a different perspective: to see how police could find themselves in a difficult position or, in some cases, how they'd put themselves in that position. One of the reasons police are investigated is because they're often required to make split-second decisions, and in most cases they're forced to do so without knowing, or understanding, the full picture. It's the nature of the job. There are, of course, some officers who are lazy or deliberately undertake their work in a manner that gets them in trouble.

However, I'm proud that as a member of IID I had only one intention: to cut through the layers of innuendo, blame and confusion to find the most important factor, the truth.

One December evening in 1986, I was standing guard at the Cobb and Co Motel, a modest two-storey hotel in Gosford on the NSW Central Coast where my aunt worked as a cleaner. I was waiting for the Australian prime minister, Robert James Lee Hawke – or 'Bob' – to arrive, working a 'protective shift' where we'd sit in an adjoining room to a VIP's accommodation. My job was to protect the 'integrity' of the prime minister's room, which meant I made sure no one went in or out of it when he wasn't there. I was still a member of the drug squad and had been given the job because I lived nearby. The way the shift worked was that as soon as Mr Hawke went to bed, his protective team stood down but stayed close by. Once they stood down it became my responsibility to guard his room. It was meant to be an easy job, but no one had taken into account a wedding party at the motel, which soon became this 24-year-old constable's worst nightmare.

When I noticed guests from the reception run from the dining room to the pool, I thought the hosts had spared no expense on the grog. The group was blitheringly drunk, but I was stunned to see some guests rip their gear off to go skinny dipping in the pool, in full view of the courtyard the prime minister would need to cross to get to his room. At that precise moment I received a message over the radio. The PM was returning from his special duty of the day, which was to open the Mooney Mooney Bridge, a 75-metre-high construction designed to improve the traffic flow on the Pacific Motorway linking the Central Coast to Sydney. His ETA was eighteen minutes. I had the unenviable job of trying to clear the area of the groomsmen, bridesmaids, great-uncles, mates from the husband's footy team and members of the wife's netball team – and none of them gave two hoots about a large policeman yelling for them to get out of the water and, more importantly, to put their clothes back on.

The clock was ticking. Mr Hawke was now only fifteen minutes away, but no one in the pool was responding to my pleas. I was desperate, so when I saw a distinguished looking gentleman leave the reception room and walk towards me I made a quick assessment, noting that he was walking in a straight line and looked old enough to command respect over the group. 'Mate,' I pleaded. 'The prime minister is on his way, and I need this lot to get out of the pool quick smart and get the hell out of here.'

Then I smelt his breath, and realised the distinguished gent was as drunk as the others. He was just an old-timer who knew how to handle his grog. I'm certain the only words that registered with him were 'the prime minister is coming' because he replied, 'Hawkey is coming to *this* place?'

'Yes, mate, and we have to clear the pool now.'

'You're not pulling my leg, are ya? *Hawkey* is coming *here*? Shouldn't he be staying somewhere more flash?'

By now I wanted to scream, but I still held some faint hope this bloke might help. 'Yes mate, he's staying here, and we have to get everyone out of the pool. NOW!'

He nodded, turned to the mob and slurred in a surprisingly loud voice, 'Hey everyone, the PM is coming to our party!' And with that he ripped *his* gear off and, in violation of the hotel's NO BOMBING rule, jumped in, splashing about like an excited child, all the while squealing, 'Hawkey!'

At this time Mr Hawke was at the peak of his popularity. After being elected in 1983 he was at the helm when the crippling El Nino drought finally broke. The recession, which at its peak had an unemployment rate of 10.3 per cent (and I was among that number), had also ended. And when the John Bertrand-skippered *Australia II* created history by becoming the first challenger in 132 years to win the America's Cup, he famously declared that any boss who punished an employee for taking the day off to celebrate was a 'bum'. Hawke rode the nation's good times better than most, and as a result he enjoyed an 'almost mystical bond' with voters. He was seen to embody the age of optimism during that particular period in Australia's history. He was also a parliamentary paradox: besides being a Rhodes scholar, his battle with the bottle was well documented. However, many Aussies admired that he'd set the world record for downing a yard glass of beer in eleven seconds while studying at Oxford University. While a battle with the bottle would be a skeleton in most other politicians' closets, Hawke was quite happy to embrace and exploit his reputation as a 'larrikin'.

He was definitely among friends that night. The mob in the Cobb and Co Motel's swimming pool had already started chanting 'Hawkey, Hawkey, Hawkey'. By now I was openly cursing the sergeant who'd rung me on my day off to say there was a 'straightforward' shift available not too far from where I lived. The more I ordered the wedding guests to get out of the pool and clear the area, the more I was drowned out by their 'Hawkey' chant. The twenty-third prime minister of Australia was now only three minutes away, and short of using brute force, there was no way the drunks could be dispersed in time. I resigned myself to my fate – whatever it may be – as I heard the Commonwealth cars pull up in the driveway.

Bob Hawke and his then-wife Hazel were greeted at the motel by a large group of drunk and naked revellers. They were cheering and laughing; some were dancing. Hawke's security detail stared at me before mouthing a not-too-discreet 'What the hell is going on here?' But all I could do was shrug my shoulders and motion that they'd refused to leave. Mrs Hawke retreated to the VIP suite, but Hawkey revelled in the attention. He sat down near the pool and lit a cigar. 'Hawkey,' said the old-timer. 'Want a beer, mate?'

The PM thanked him for the invitation, but explained that he was off the drink these days. Another likely lad asked the PM for his thoughts on the upcoming Test cricket series against India. Bob didn't miss a beat. 'They've never won a series here before, and they won't this summer. Allan Border will do a good job.'

On it went. I have to admit, I was impressed. Here he was addressing a drunken rabble as though each member was his best mate. A couple of blokes jumped out of the pool to shake his hand. They were both dripping wet, and one was as bare as the day he entered the world. I swung into action. 'Please leave the prime minister alone, sir. Please give Mr Hawke his space.'

It was madness. What struck me about Mr Hawke was his authenticity. There were no minders advising him on what to say, and regardless of which political party people followed, they seemed to realise their nation's leader was the real deal.

In contrast to that night was the time I was assigned to Dr John Hewson's security at the Newcastle Show before he led the Coalition to the ill-fated 1993 election. He just wanted to be John Hewson, but his advisors were insisting that he wear clichéd country apparel for when he was paraded about the showground like a prized bull. Hewson kept protesting that it wasn't him. When he was instructed to take one shirt off because the colour did nothing for his complexion, he replaced it with a checked one. When that didn't suit, his advisors said to try on another one. While Dr Hewson was a gentleman, I think the difference between him and Mr Hawke is that Hawkey would've told the advisors where to shove their country clothes.

I won no friends among the prime minister's security detail that night, but I'll always remember how Bob Hawke, who passed away on the eve of the 2019 Federal election, handled an unexpected situation. It provided me with some extraordinary firsthand insights into why he had the Australian people eating out of his hand. Hawke not only understood them, but he didn't give the slightest hint that he thought he was better than them – even when they were behaving badly. I like to recall that night as when I witnessed democracy at its purest.

15
CARE FOR KIDS

'You'll find in this job that the younger kids will always let you know which parent they want to be with . . . never forget that children don't lie about things like that.'
– Senior Sergeant Rex Bertolli

I had two stints in the Family Law Court. The first was in Sydney from 1986–87, and later in Newcastle from 1992–94 when I was transferred there to work as a member of the AFP's fraud and general crime section. We did anything and everything in Newcastle, which was then the sixth-largest city in Australia. We also covered a lot of ground – our beat stretched from the Central Coast to the Queensland border. Besides working on fraud and the Family Court, we officers from my department could also be assigned to investigate drug-related crime.

It only took my first day in the Family Court to remember what a soul-destroying experience I'd found working there as a young constable. I witnessed many decisions that I didn't think were in the child's best interests, and it often made me wonder what possible chance those kids had in life. When I worked in the courts there was a proliferation of divorces because 'no fault divorce' had been introduced in 1975. It meant anyone filing for divorce didn't need to prove their spouse had done anything wrong, they only needed to cite 'irreconcilable differences'. The relaxation of the law ended the social stigma about failed marriages because people accepted that life was too short to be trapped in a relationship that wasn't working. The opposite view was prevalent in the early 1970s, when my sister and I were the only children at our school who came from a 'broken home' and some people looked down their noses upon learning about our parents' separation.

As former partners spewed venom before a judge, the nature of the Australian family unit as we knew it changed forever. Some people hailed it as an age of liberation, but it was also a traumatic time for many people – particularly the children who struggled to understand why their parents no longer loved one another, and why a judge could decide who they would live with. Personally, I didn't have a problem with the concept of divorce because my childhood home life had 'normalised' it. I'd accepted from a young age that marriages broke down. But something that never failed to shock me at the court was the way some parents would behave in front of their children – and in public. These people had so much hatred they weren't concerned about self-control, and they were also oblivious to the pain they caused their kids as they openly swore and swapped insults in front of stunned bystanders.

I couldn't compare my upbringing to any of the kids at the centre of those custody battles. While many of these children were dragged up in squalor and a hateful environment, Jenelle and I were loved, and while Mum had her moments, we never went without. We always had food to eat, our home was kept clean and Mum was always presentable in public. She also ensured we went to school well-groomed. Dad also cared for us, and if anything, my time in the courts helped me realise my family was actually bound by love. I was reminded of that whenever I was required to separate former spouses who were abusing one another. While Mum and Dad fought, they always put Jenelle and me first, sparing us from exposure to their verbal outbursts. I'm grateful that Mum and Dad maintained their dignity because it saved Jenelle and me extra heartache.

In all states except Western Australia, the Federal Government maintains jurisdiction over family courts. This means the AFP is responsible for enforcing the court's orders across all but one of the nation's states or territories. Sadly, I got to see the ugliest side of family law cases, with some people thinking nothing of using their child as a pawn to inflict even more pain on their former spouse. Sometimes, during my drive home to the Central Coast, I'd think about the terrible things people would do to one another, including telling the judge blatant lies, in their attempt to hold the moral high ground. It was deplorable to see decent people have their character torn apart publicly. That was something I thought a lot about, because my marriage had turned sour during my final year at the Family Law Court.

Maree and I became parents in 1993, and despite our problems we stayed together for the sake of Emilee. However, after over a decade of living separate lives under the one roof we decided to divorce in 2005. Due to my experiences at the court my priority was to spare Emilee from any unnecessary pain, and

I was pleased when Maree agreed that was her intention too. And while there were times when things could've gone down a bad path we both realised it was important to get back on the right track for our daughter's sake.

There'd been more changes to the law when we filed for divorce. Sending couples to court was now the last resort. Instead of leaving it to a judge to decide on such important matters as custody, couples attended a series of compulsory meetings which included counselling, custody and the division of the assets. I was comfortable with that because based on what I'd seen, I didn't want it left to a judge to make those decisions on our behalf. It was good that Maree and I formed resolutions that we both found acceptable.

The high stakes often made these hearings powder kegs, and whenever there was a threat of violence the judges ordered a police presence in their courtroom. Sometimes we were called upon to sit with the couples during their counselling sessions. If a partner became abusive and made threats to their 'ex' or their solicitor, we were required to put the cuffs on them, take them outside and let them calm down.

My colleagues and I generally used that break as an opportunity to advise the person to keep their cool because they weren't helping themselves – or their kids – by behaving aggressively. More often than not it was the husband in handcuffs. They'd explain that their rage was because the world as they knew it had crumbled, and they felt lost. Some had brought that collapse upon themselves, so it was hard to feel any sympathy for them. However, there were others who were stunned to be in the court; they genuinely didn't understand what they'd done wrong, being good providers who'd put their family first. I tried to keep an open mind because my parents' marriage and separation had proved there was always a lot more to a story. Still, I learnt there are deadbeat dads *and* mums. It was impossible sitting through these sessions not to form your own opinions on how the system worked, and it sometimes seemed to fail good people.

Another hard reality was that whichever half of the warring party could afford the top silks had the odds stacked in their favour. Being the first to submit the required legal papers to the court also often went a long way to ensuring the judgement went in that party's favour; it was as though they were rewarded for being quick off the mark. During this period of my police career I encountered some violent and despicable males, and I'm the first to acknowledge that the court was correct in keeping them well away from their children. However, not all fathers who appeared in the Family Court were like that, and there were men who, I believe, despite proving they were the better parent, missed out on custody because of their gender. It was a common complaint in the 1980s and 1990s, with many a disgruntled father calling a talkback radio station to vent their spleen and tell hosts such as John Laws and Ron Casey that they'd been treated harshly and lost everything because the court favoured the mother.

It was a dangerous time, because someone, or a group, took their grievances too far. Between 1980 and 1985 judges and other people involved in the Family Court were targeted in a series of shootings and bombings. It was madness. The judge David Opas was shot outside of his house in 1980 and he died in hospital. Another judge's house was bombed, along with the Parramatta

Family Court, in 1984. Pearl Watson, the wife of judge Ray Watson, was tragically killed the following year when a bomb exploded outside her home. While this all happened before I finished at the academy, it serves as a warning that emotional people are capable of terrible things.

I've been fortunate that life has provided me some great mentors who've had a positive impact on me, both personally and professionally. As a young police officer I was blessed to come under the wing of Senior Sergeant Rex Bertolli, a very wise man. He could see I'd struggled after enforcing my first few warrants. Sometimes a child would be taken from what seemed to be a decent household to live in a residence that was no better than a filthy, stinking dump with dirty crockery and cutlery that'd been in the sink for days, and food rotting on the counter. There was one incident when I had a court order to remove a child, and when I saw the state the poor toddler was in I wanted to vomit. The child had worn a soiled nappy for so long there were maggots inside it, and his skin was covered in welts. I learnt that the only way to handle situations like that was to try and remain emotionally removed because if you allowed it, the misery would swamp you. The idea of being emotionless was a general rule for most cops, and that's why some long-serving officers may appear devoid of all feeling. They've turned off their feelings to avoid being hurt, and as such they become brick walls that nothing penetrates. Only, as they get older, they discover they've been collecting those bloody pebbles . . .

There were times when I couldn't help but wonder how the court came to its decision based on the houses I'd seen, and I may even have suggested that judges ought to make a surprise visit to the home of each parent before making their call. Senior Sergeant Bertolli took me aside one afternoon and offered me some advice, which I subsequently applied to a number of situations: 'Grant,' he said. 'You'll find in this job that the younger kids will always let you know which parent they want to be with. Never forget that children don't lie about things like that.'

He was right. Whether a child was happy or not, they'd always radiate their feelings. Bertolli's words were ringing loudly in my ears a few weeks later when I was sent to relocate an 8-year-old boy from his father's house to his mother's. When I arrived with the warrant and explained to the boy what was happening he burst into tears. He clung to his father and started screaming, 'Dad, I don't want to go back there, it's horrible! PLEASE don't let them take me there!' He also made it clear that he intended to run away from his mother's place.

The father was broken but did all he could not to fall apart in front of his son. It was tough, and even though I wasn't a father at that stage of my life, his pain was obvious as I watched him attempt to comfort the boy. He assured him that everything would be okay and he'd fix their situation. The boy was near hysterical when I took him, and it cut me deeply because I'd dealt with the mother and she wasn't a pleasant person. She'd benefited from getting the paperwork into the court before her former husband, and, like me, a few people who were privy to the case thought she was focused on destroying the father. As the dad gave his boy one final hug I decided to say something because even though I was wearing a police uniform and executing a court order, I wasn't a robot. How couldn't I be moved by what I was witnessing? Something else that motivated me to speak was the Bertolli formula: the child's reaction proved conclusively who he wanted to live with.

I stopped at the door and paused before explaining to the father the process that would start when his son, my policing partner and I left his home. I told him it was our duty to deliver the boy to his mother's front door (in her presence), however, what his son did after we crossed the boundary after delivering him was out of our control. I advised the father that if I was him I'd consider parking my car near the ex-wife's house in case the son decided to run away, because there was nothing we could do to stop him. With that, I went to the mother's house, walked the boy up the footpath and rang the doorbell. When she answered the boy screamed at the top of his voice 'I HATE YOU', leapt off the porch, bolted down the path, pushed his way through the gate and ran for his life. I wanted to make sure the boy hadn't run away, so I called his father, who was parked down the road, to make sure he had his son. Once I knew he did, I hung up and that was it for me – duty done.

The mother's immediate reaction was to hurl abuse at me and my partner, and demand we go and fetch her son. When I advised her that we'd executed our duty, she called us more unflattering names. Her language was vile. I then explained that if she wanted us to take further action she'd need to return to court and obtain another order. She unleashed one last volley of abuse before telling us in no uncertain terms that she couldn't be bothered. In my mind, her decision was the best possible result for the boy.

What I did that day wasn't unethical, because I simply informed that father – and other mothers and fathers since – the processes involved in what we did, and how the system worked. We'd executed the warrant when we delivered the boy to his mother; the boy exercised his choice when he ran away. Had I been reprimanded I would've found it easy to justify my actions to my superiors. My advice for the parent to drive to his or her former partner's house was sound, because if a child did run it was better to have a parent on standby so we didn't risk having to investigate a missing child. And on the occasions when it was clear that a father who'd gained custody wasn't of good character, I provided the mother with the same advice. File this story under the 'complexities' of policing, because I'm quite comfortable with my actions.

Sometimes there were horrendous stories about a parent who'd fought tooth and nail to rescue their son or daughter from miserable conditions. I thought my partners Detective Constables Keir and Ferlazzo were doing the right thing when we were assigned to collect an 18-month-old girl from a farm near the Hunter Valley in 1994. It was the closest thing I'd seen to Ma and Pa Kettle's property. There was a tribe of ten kids, and the entire family was illiterate. They grew their own produce and weren't connected to power, living more like the district's early pioneers in the 1800s than a twentieth-century family.

However, as we discovered, the grandparents and mother were lovely people. While the grandfather boiled a billy over the fire for us to have a cup of tea, Keir and I carefully explained why the child was being taken away. I could see that the other children were loved and cared for; they were well fed, seemed happy and were polite. When the mother handed the baby to us she was crying, and the sadness we witnessed as the grandparents and the infant's siblings said farewell to her was genuine. However, there wasn't any hint of anger, which was a surprise. When we were about to drive off, the family thanked us for being so understanding and the older children presented us with a big box of freshly picked home-grown fruit and vegetables as a sign of the family's gratitude. We told them it wasn't necessary, but the adults insisted we accept the gift.

During 1993 we were called to defuse a few explosive situations. Some ex-husbands would try to demolish what had once been the family home so the wife would only end up with the land value. And some men gave up well-paid jobs and went on unemployment benefits because they didn't want to pay maintenance after their wife moved in with a financially well-off new partner. It was a minefield, but the ones who suffered the most were the children who'd been exposed to the ugliest sides of their parents' characters.

As someone who came from a broken home, and whose first marriage ended in divorce, I know that family law is a huge issue. It doesn't matter what you think about the sanctity of marriage, the fact is it's easy to have a union dissolved and often children are caught in the crossfire. It's because of my experiences in the Family Law Court that I still can't reconcile the fact that while we need a licence to drive a car, anyone can have a child – or that there are people who should never have been allowed that privilege.

Kids deserve better.

16
THE PRICE WASN'T RIGHT

My time working in Newcastle was divided between the Family Law Court, the drug squad and the fraud squad. It was my second stint as a fraudie, having worked in that department when I left the academy in 1985. It was from there that I made my first arrest, the heroin addict who had been caught trying to cash stolen Centrelink cheques at a bank in Sydney. It was far from the AFP's biggest case, but in 1992 my Detective Sergeant Frank 'Wardy' Ward, investigated – and nailed – a very big fish: Australia's biggest social welfare cheat. This person ripped off $1.2 million from taxpayers, but what amazed me most was the person behind it. She certainly didn't look like someone who was capable of masterminding such a crime. Indeed, few criminals I came across matched this person for her coolness, sheer cunning and brazenness . . .

To most outsiders, 76-year-old Ann Lillian Price appeared to have lived a fruitful life. She'd procured an enviable real estate portfolio that earned her almost $100,000 a year in rent – a princely sum in the early 1990s, considering the average annual wage was $22,000. One of Ballina's most popular socialites, Price hosted lavish parties at her waterfront home. She also had a penchant for life's luxuries. Price travelled first class on overseas holidays, owned a Mercedes-Benz and enjoyed shopping sprees for jewellery. Her house contained quality antique pieces, and she dined in fine restaurants with her partner, Kenneth Myles Carruthers. No one had any reason to suspect that the elderly couple were doing anything more than enjoying the rewards of hard work and astute investments.

However, Price had a secret. In 1992 the nation was stunned when our investigations revealed that she'd ripped off over a million dollars from the Federal Government via fraudulent pensions.

Price came to our attention not long after government agencies started to use computers to cross-reference information between departments after the *Data-Matching Act (Assistance and Tax)* was passed by Federal Parliament in 1990. The Act was fiercely debated by politicians and civil libertarians, who expressed concerns about privacy issues because the law allowed the data of all welfare agencies to be more easily cross-referenced with Australian Taxation Office (ATO) records. In time, the *Data-Matching Act* would catch many social welfare cheats, but none were anything like Price. Social welfare departments were vulnerable to fraudulent activity before the computer age, because confirming such things as proof of identity was a nightmare for public servants who needed to cross-check the forests of paper documents that were filed across the nation. Catching a social welfare fraudster who'd applied for pensions in different states was a tough assignment; it entailed a huge commitment of time and resources, and that allowed thieves like Price to profit.

On 6 June 1992, a routine data-matching exercise between social security and veterans affairs isolated three pension recipients who were all born on 13 November 1915. The names entered into the system were Ann L. Price, Ann L. Price-Pontifex and Annie L. Ramsay. The similarities in the names raised suspicion, and the Department of Social Security (DSS) referred the matter to their Fraud Control Unit. The briefing I had with Wardy and DSS investigators Bob Cheshire and Craig Brown took place on 16 March 1992, and the deeper we dug, the more systematic we realised this woman had been. From what we could ascertain, Price had accumulated over ten identities. Our investigations also uncovered that her partner, Carruthers, had fraudulently netted $46,000 by claiming a Veterans Affairs pension and other social security payments by making false statements on his applications. He'd serve 200 hours community service when the law finally caught up with him.

During the early stages of our investigation I was adamant that Price must have a criminal history. I contacted the state police forces for their help, but no Ann Lillian Price appeared in their systems. Nevertheless, we had enough evidence to obtain search warrants, and ten days later Wardy and I were driving 600 kilometres up the Pacific Highway. Our evidence suggested there were at least thirteen aliases now attached to Price's address, and I remember saying to Wardy it'd be terribly embarrassing if we walked in on thirteen grannies in the lounge room knitting cardigans and scarves for their grandchildren.

We knocked on the door of what we believed was Price's main residence. The Mercedes-Benz was parked in the driveway but no one was home. The gardener said Price and Carruthers were in town, so we waited until they returned in their second car, a Mitsubishi Magna. Wardy said because this was my collar I should let Price know the game was up. However, as I was politely introducing myself, Wardy barged forward and shouted, 'Listen, we know what you're up to, just give us what we need!'

Price's surrender was immediate and breathtaking. Without saying a word, she simply turned on her heels and marched towards the study. Wardy followed her, watching as she opened two desk drawers and pulled out her collection of bank passbooks, bank statements and an assortment of credit cards. She also surrendered a Victorian driver's licence. Despite the ill-gotten wealth she'd accumulated, she carried a Campbell's Cash & Carry card to purchase the discounted drinks and food she stored in the large cool room at the rear of their palatial home. Among the evidence we recovered were credit card receipts for expensive jewellery, a receipt from a travel agency for first-class travel amounting to around $8000 and evidence she'd taken at least twelve overseas trips.

When Frank asked Price whether she was going to confess to the fraud, her reply belied her grandmotherly appearance. 'You have everything,' she snarled. 'What more do you want?'

She was hard-bitten, and while she conducted a tape-recorded interview in which she admitted to receiving up to ten social security pensions over twenty-three years, our investigation was interrupted when Carruthers took a turn and requested an ambulance. While Price realised the game was up, he'd wanted to delay the inevitable. We called an ambulance – just to be safe – but the first thing Carruthers did when he arrived at the hospital was phone his lawyer.

Price, however, knew she was caught. 'So, how much of a *lag* am I going to get for this?' she asked.

Her use of the word 'lag' – an old term for doing time – suggested she might be an old jail bird. In our interviews she expressed no remorse for her crimes; instead she was seething. 'How am I going to survive now you've taken all of my money?' she demanded to know.

Price indicated she had a heart condition and requested we spare her the drama of going to the Ballina Police Station to be charged. We decided there was no need for this given her health problem, her age and the fact that she'd complied with the requirements of the summons. Later, however, I discovered that the real reason she didn't want to go to the police station was because she didn't want to be photographed or have her fingerprints taken – she had successfully used the same ploy to avoid having her real identity revealed during an encounter with the Victorian police. Moreover, thanks to an investigative journalist, we'd also learn that apart from being imprisoned previously for forgery and other crimes of deceit, she'd served time in Pentridge Prison for her role in Melbourne's illegal backyard abortion business in the post-war years, a crime that in Victoria at the time was punishable with fifteen years in prison.

When we returned to Newcastle I made further enquiries to the Victorian and South Australian police, requesting that they check whether Ann Lillian Price – or any of her long list of aliases with the corresponding birthdates – had a criminal record. It wasn't long before I received a detailed report from Melbourne that confirmed she was well known to them, having racked up a number of convictions. Ann Price-Pontifex had first come to the notice of Victorian police in 1955 for forging and uttering (that's the passing of a forged document); she was convicted and placed on a three-year good behaviour bond. In 1960 she was charged with larceny and fined 15 pounds, only escaping heavier punishment because the police failed to place her criminal record before the magistrate, so he was unaware of her previous conviction. In 1963 Price was sentenced to two years' imprisonment after being charged with forging and uttering *and* false pretence. In 1971 her pattern of dishonesty continued when she was again charged with forging and uttering after altering the will of one Millie McCormack shortly before the woman's death. She was sentenced in the Melbourne County Court to eight years' imprisonment, with a minimum of four to serve. She successfully appealed the sentence in 1972 and was discharged after entering into a recognisance to be of good behaviour for four years. To try to keep her on the straight and narrow, the court made her pay a $5000 surety. She knew no shame; on the day she was released from prison, Price brazenly applied for – and received – another DSS pension under the alias of Joanne Price. Indeed, when she was sent back behind bars after a counter-appeal by the Crown, she not only retained her position as Governing Director of Pontifex Holdings Pty Ltd, the company that managed her real estate transactions, but the government continued to dutifully make welfare payments to Joanne Price's and Ann L. Ramsay's bank accounts (because *Ann* Price was in prison).

Our forensic investigations into Price's web of welfare deceit ascertained that she collected her first legitimate welfare payment, a widow's pension, under her married name of Ann Price-Pontifex on 11 November 1969 when she was 53. By the time of her arrest she'd received $88,108.20 from that pension. However, records noted she'd been refused a pension a few months earlier when the consulting general practitioner ruled she wasn't entitled to an invalid pension because she wasn't legally blind. Her first taste of welfare fraud was telling the Department she'd paid rent for a property on Hotham Street, St Kilda. However, it wasn't until many years later that it was realised her company, Pontifex Holdings Pty Ltd, owned it. When we were able to piece together her history of dishonesty – and the amounts of money she'd illegally obtained – I needed to sit down.

On 30 July 1970, Price made her first successful application for a fraudulent pension, receiving an invalid blind pension under her maiden name, Ann L. Ramsay. She gave her birthdate as 11 November 1915, and over the next twenty-two years accrued a total of $91,028. Price returned to the social welfare office on 10 August 1972 and assumed the identity of one of her sisters, Joanne Price. It proved to be a windfall because she made another $80,691.

Price realised she was on a good wicket and on 24 January 1974 she applied for an aged pension under the alias of Rudi Cattai, who was born in 1913. We discovered that Cattai was one of the patients Price had looked after when she ran a nursing home in the 1950s. She was obviously an opportunist because when Cattai passed away Price stole her identity, and that made her $87,934.

Price proved how brazen she could be on 17 October 1974 when she applied for an aged pension under the name Millie McCormack, born 1920. What made her decision to do this extraordinary was the fact that Price had been imprisoned three years earlier for attempting to alter McCormack's will in an attempt to seize the woman's estate. Wardy noted that while she may have missed out on the 'grand prize', she still earnt $87,275 from McCormack's name.

In 1975, Price took her mother's maiden name and applied for yet another aged pension under the alias Lillian Ann Wakefield, born 1918. Interestingly, this was the only pension the Department challenged. However, by the time they ceased making payments she'd banked $37,384. It was four years later, 1979, before she tried her luck again. This time she applied for another aged pension as Hazel Dove, born 1913. Ms Dove gave her address as being in the Sydney beachside suburb of Cronulla, and the Department's officers were told she paid rent to her cousin, a Mrs L.Price. The truth was, Ann Price owned the property, so she was paying rent to herself. She received $74,649 as Hazel Dove.

Price purchased another property in Malvern Road, Prahran in Melbourne in 1975, but by April 1981 it was used as her 'mail exchange', where she received correspondence for seven of the fortnightly pension cheques she was receiving. Her cunning knew no bounds; Price indicated on some of her applications that she was paying rent to various people at this address. No one at DSS made the connection.

In 1981, Price moved to the North Coast of NSW, and three years later was granted another widow's pension under the name of Jean Pontifex, born 1921. Price stated on her application that she had lost her husband during the Second World War. Our investigations eventually revealed that Jean was actually Price's twin. 'Jean' said she lived rent free with her sister near

Ballina – it was actually a property Price had purchased in 1982. A total sum of $52,394 was deposited into 'Jean's' account.

Price's appetite for ill-gotten gains was insatiable, and on 3 December 1985, posing as Rudy Cattai, the identity she'd assumed in 1974, Price advised the Department that she was in dire straits and had nowhere to live. She requested emergency rental funds, and not only was 'Rudy' back-paid the amount of money she was 'owed' by the government, she was also granted the emergency rental assistance she'd requested. The reality of Price's financial health was that in December 1983 she sold a property she and Carruthers had jointly owned at Tintenbar, NSW, for a profit of $243,000. As the sole owner of a property at Ocean Shores, she made $236,000 profit over seven years. At the time she lodged her claim for rental assistance, Price had just purchased her waterfront property at Ballina for $98,000.

The DSS located other paperwork that proved she'd requested emergency payments on all of the pensions she was receiving for either a large part of, or in some cases, the entire time she accepted the payments. 'Joanne' Price claimed she was paying rent to a landlord named 'Carruthers', and in 1987 a DSS officer telephoned this Carruthers to verify whether Joanne Price was renting accommodation from him. The male who answered the phone confirmed she was, but said Joanne was away visiting a sick sister. A few days later Price was audacious enough to phone the officer to request rental assistance to help pay Carruthers for her accommodation. The requests for the funds, reserved for people who were close to becoming destitute, was further proof that Price would do anything for her own financial gain.

In 1990, Price received a Department of Veterans Affairs service pension (as an eligible spouse) in the name of Lillian Pontifex, born 1915. Her greed finally brought her undone because this request allowed for the successful cross-matching of the DSS and DVA data, which flagged the likelihood of multiple frauds. However, the amount of money she'd pilfered shocked everyone.

While the majority of Price's wealth was obtained illegally, she possessed an entrepreneur's spirit. But she was also unscrupulous, receiving food vouchers and other benefits a woman of her ill-gotten means didn't need and wasn't entitled to. I know some people have an attitude that taking money from the government isn't a major crime, but it is – and a serious one. Welfare fraud affects many people. In 2018, the government managed to claw back $61 million from 26,300 people who had allegedly defrauded Centrelink. While the Department of Human Services' specialist fraud and compliance teams found some of them made genuine mistakes, there were also those who'd committed acts of deliberate fraud.

I've long maintained that welfare fraud isn't a victimless crime. Hardworking Australians are taxed highly to contribute to social welfare, and the money that's allocated for pensions or unemployment benefits is intended for people in genuine hardship. Welfare thieves are also taking money that could be diverted to mental health, schools, roads, hospitals and law enforcement. When I was unemployed for six months in 1985 I felt humiliated every time I went into the CES office at Wyong because I wanted to work. The reason why I applied for the dole was because, despite sending numerous applications, I couldn't get a job. I had no money and needed a hand. However, I participated in a work for the dole-type scheme because I wanted to feel as though I'd at least done something to earn my money. Whenever I attended the CES I was exposed to the professional dole bludgers. They had no shame, and even though I heard them boast they were doing cash in hand jobs, they thought nothing about getting a government handout. They could've taken a leaf from Mum's book. If my mother was anything, she was a bloody hard worker. As a single mother in the 1970s she had the gumption to work three jobs a week – as a bookkeeper for two companies, and as a cook at a catering business – to make ends meet. As kids Jenelle and I were taught that all work is honourable by working at such places as the markets, selling newspapers or cleaning the slaughterhouse at the abattoirs. However, I'm afraid people of Anne Price's ilk considered people like us to be mugs.

Around this time Price was beginning to slip up, using the wrong name and forgetting other details about her aliases because the list was so long. Her court case became a great joke. First, the judge who was assigned to hear the case in Ballina had to excuse himself because he rented his property from the defendant! The case was transferred to Coffs Harbour, but after numerous adjournments due to Price citing ill health, failing eyesight, problems with her defence lawyers and her dramatic collapse in the courtroom, the trial was rescheduled to be heard by Judge Brian Gallen in the NSW District Court in Sydney. Adding to the circus at Coffs Harbour was the media's interest in the case. I vividly recall the judge's anger when the pack invaded his court to film Price being taken away by paramedics after she collapsed. Few chased the story as hard as Channel 10's *Hinch,* hosted by Derryn Hinch. Its premise was to shine a light on any corrupt behaviour by bureaucrats, the clergy, paedophiles, politicians, law enforcement officers and everyday citizens. With segments such as 'The Shame File', the story of an old lady who'd rorted the government out of a million dollars was tailor-made for them.

The *Hinch* journalist had been chasing Price for weeks. One day during a break in the trial he asked if we could chat but I told him to phone the media unit in Canberra for a comment. The journalist said he wanted an informal chat, because he prided himself on his accuracy and needed to get his head around a few points. He told me it would be an off-the-record conversation; he just needed the correct information. Call me naive, but I agreed to help, although the warning bells should've sounded when he asked whether he could film me talking to him for overlay. When he wired me up with a lapel microphone he insisted it was just so he had a recording for his notes. I said it'd be okay as long as our discussion was off the record. He said he'd look after me, and I'd forgotten about our conversation until later that evening when my phone rang and I copped a rocket from Wardy, who was screaming down the other end of the line. 'WHAT THE HELL ARE YOU DOING GIVING INTERVIEWS?' I was confused, and when I said I hadn't done an interview he yelled, 'WELL, I'M WATCHING IT NOW, GRANT!'

I'd stuffed up; what I had thought had been an off-the-record chat formed part of the story. I copped a roasting from high command as well, but they didn't take any action. What hurt me most of all is that the media attention actually helped Price get a lighter sentence, because Judge Gallen said she'd been made a virtual prisoner in her own home as the journalists hunted the story. It hurt to hear this as Price stood before Judge Gallen on 28 May 1993, having pleaded guilty to ten counts of false pretences and nine counts of defrauding the Commonwealth. In his summing up of the case, his Honour stated that 'greed' was the sole motive behind the colossal fraud and sentenced Price to a maximum of six years in prison with a minimum of two years. The sentence only added weight to my theory that the old convict-day mentality that decrees it's 'okay to screw the government' is entrenched in some elements of the Australian character, although I am not suggesting in any way that his honour, Justice Gallen, subscribed to that view. Adding to the disappointment was the knowledge that the sentence would hardly be a deterrent for other fraudsters.

The government took action to recover some of the money Price stole via the sale of her properties and by seizing monies from her bank accounts. Meanwhile, the Department of Public Prosecutions (DPP) wasn't happy with the sentence and appealed against its leniency. True to form, Price also appealed, but her appeal was dismissed after only one hour of submissions. It wasn't all bad news, however, as the DPP dropped their appeal against her on the same day. I went to the prison to drop off some things that belonged to Price and when I asked the prison officers how she was faring, one of them chuckled and said she was thriving. Price was so highly regarded by the other prisoners because of her criminal history, she was made the 'Top Dog'.

Ann L. Price passed away in 2014 at the fine old age of 99. Her story ought to be a sobering lesson. When cross-examined by the Commonwealth's prosecutor (DPP), Sarah McNaughton, Price blamed the government for 'allowing these loopholes in the first place'.

17
COOL RUNNINGS, SKIPPY STYLE

'The important thing in the Olympic Games is not to
win, but to take part; the important thing in life is
not triumph, but the struggle; the essential thing
is not to have conquered but to have fought well . . .'
– Pierre de Coubertin, Father of the modern Olympics
(1863–1937)

I thought I'd fulfilled my dream to wear the Australian Olympic blazer when a tailor measured me up for one at the induction for the 1992 Winter Games squad selected to compete in the French city of Albertville. When I won my bronze medal in the international shot-put event at Seoul, I treated it as my first step towards becoming an Olympian. I devoted my energies to becoming the best thrower I possibly could, but I just couldn't find the metres that were needed to go to the next level. I thought whatever hope I had of becoming an Olympian had passed me by after I cut back on my athletics commitments when I went to Hawaii and then joined the police force. That's why I was ecstatic to be invited to join Australia's Winter Olympic Squad at the AIS after my four-man bobsleigh team competed in our first international campaign – a tough seven-month slog through North

America and Europe. I listened intently as officials briefed us about our responsibilities and requirements as *Olympians* . . .

A few weeks earlier me and my teammates were in the final stages of what had been an amazing experience. We'd competed against the superpowers of bobsleigh, including Germany, Switzerland, the United States and Canada in a series of World Cup events staged in Canada, France, Switzerland, Germany, Austria, Italy and Norway. We spent almost a month in Canada before our first competition, and that time was used to learn how to bobsled and to acclimatise to the sub-zero temperatures. Once we landed in Europe our time there was a blur. If we weren't competing, we were driving overnight to another event. The events quickly rolled into one and it soon felt as though we were a band on tour. Once we finished a contest we had to pack everything away and head to the next gig. We earned our spurs, though. Each of us were banged up in some horrific crashes, and there were other challenges we endured. We lived out of each other's pockets, and while we were living and competing in some of Europe's most expensive ski fields, it was frustrating to be on a backpacker's budget. I ordered a can of cola at a kiosk in St Moritz but when the woman behind the counter demanded the equivalent of seven Aussie dollars I changed my order to tap water. To save money on accommodation we sometimes shared beds, something I loathed. I had to starve myself to be at the right weight to compete, and that made me feel like a bear with a sore head. However, those tough times were forgotten when the tailor put his tape measure around my chest. The idea that I'd wear an official blazer – complete with the Australian coat of arms and Olympic rings – was too good to be true.

For me, becoming a bobsledder was similar to gaining a football scholarship at the University of Hawaii. It was a bolt from the blue because I didn't go looking for it. I'd been working on a surveillance job as a member of the drug squad, staking out a Sydney hotel, when the big brick-like mobile phone I'd been issued with rang. Someone from HQ was calling to pass on a message that NSW Athletics was trying to contact me. I had no idea what they might want. I was 29 and hadn't been overly active in the shot-put circle. When my shift ended I found out Bobsleigh Australia was looking for candidates with my physical attributes to compete overseas. A few minutes after that call I spoke to John McDonald, whose son Justin formed Bobsleigh Australia, and agreed to go to the AIS in Canberra for testing. I had no idea what to expect.

I was still recovering from a footy-related hamstring injury I'd suffered while playing for the Woy Woy Lions in the Central Coast competition when I joined other hopefuls, including Ted Polglaze, Jason Giobbi and John Trutwin, all of whom would become my teammates, in performing the exercises designed to see if we had the required explosiveness. We found out that, apart from being the head of the association, McDonald would also be our bobsled's driver. He explained that we wouldn't receive any funding from the Federal government because we hadn't qualified for the Olympics, so if we wanted our shot at competing in Albertville we'd need to foot our own airfares and some meals. As I recall, McDonald's father – a multi-millionare – paid for most of our accommodation, which was extremely generous because the price of rooms in places such as St Moritz during peak season would've put the trip out of most of the team's reach. He also advised us that the campaign would last from September 1991 to March 1992 – seven months. Among the nations we'd compete in were Canada, France, Austria, Germany and Switzerland. I'm not suggesting I wouldn't have agreed to be a part of McDonald's plan had he not tossed up Albertville as a lure, but there was no stopping me once he did. I'd accrued enough leave through overtime and holidays to take the extended time off that was needed. Emilee hadn't been born when I was offered this opportunity, so I had no inner conflict about going. My marriage was beset by problems and Maree and I were doing our own things. Nevertheless, she didn't support my decision to give a 'stupid idea' a go. But the chance to represent Australia at the Olympics was too powerful to resist, and there was no stopping me once work rubber-stamped my leave.

We assembled in South Australia to take our baby steps. There was no way we could prepare ourselves for what would be the white-knuckled terror of our first ride – Australia doesn't have a bobsled track. We were very restricted in what we could do. It's laughable to think that the closest we came to a bobsled before our first race in Calgary was jumping into an oversized billycart and sprinting along a stretch of Adelaide's old Grand Prix track. It helped us learn how to enter the sled correctly, but nothing could brace us for the scarier side of bobsleigh: hitting speeds of 130 kilometres an hour, the terrible crashes and crushing g-forces.

When I applied for extended leave from work, I was unaware of the tumultuous state Australian bobsledding was in. I was surprised because in what was essentially a minor sport in our footy-obsessed nation, the rift ran deep. It's a little-known fact that Australia competed at the 1988 Calgary Olympics, where the Jamaican bobsledders not only won over the world with their courageous efforts but also inspired the 1993 Disney movie *Cool Runnings*. The driving force behind Australia's Olympic debut was Sydneysider Adrian Di Piazza. And while we'd been his opponents in 1991, he deserves recognition as a trailblazer. His efforts to form the Australian Bobsleigh Foundation in 1985 allowed our nation to become a fully-fledged member of the International Bobsleigh and Skeleton Federation, which meant we could compete at major competitions. However, 1991 brought great challenges, allowing McDonald to form a rival organisation and compete for a place at Albertville. Di Piazza responded by recruiting the Olympic sprinter Paul Narracott, who famously defeated Carl Lewis – the American superstar who'd finish his Olympic career with nine track and field gold medals – in a 1984 60-metre indoor race in Japan. He also signed former decathlete Stuart Andrews.

While I don't mind conceding he'd attracted the superior athletes, Di Piazza and his team couldn't match the financial clout of Team McDonald. The gulf was no better reflected than by the sleds at each team's disposal. McDonald invested $60,000 in our two- and four-manner from the famous Dresden factory that had made Messerschmitts for Germany's Luftwaffe in the Second World War. These East German-made sleds were highly sought after due to their revolutionary carbon-fibre, cigar-shaped design and other technologies that shaved invaluable seconds off the clock in a sport where results are decided by a thousandth of a second. The star-studded American team we competed against consisted of the two-time 400-metre

Olympic hurdles champion, Edwin Moses; Willie Gault, the 1983 world championship 4 × 100-metre relay gold medallist, who also played in the NFL; Minnesota Vikings football star Herschel Walker; and Renaldo Nehemiah, the 110-metre hurdles champion and a San Francisco 49ers Super Bowl winner. What I appreciated from watching them was that, while those men could physically blow any crew off the track, their sleds didn't match their athletic ability. The American experiment proved that not even the strongest, fastest and most skilled teams in the world can compensate for a well-designed sled. Through McDonald's efforts – and substantial funds – we enjoyed a distinct advantage on the clock over teams who'd otherwise prove to be of a similar standard to us.

We'd picked an amazing time to launch our assault. Bob-sledding at that time was impacted in a positive way by the geopolitical changes that had swept through eastern and central Europe in the early 1990s. Communism's grip appeared to be loosening, starting with the demolition of the Berlin Wall in 1989. After the wall, which separated West and East Germany, was pulled down by citizens from both sides of the great divide, Germany's 1991 bobsleigh teams competed as a united team for the first time since the end of the Second World War – and they set the pace. The Soviet Union had all but disbanded after countries from behind the 'Iron Curtain' received their inde-pendence, allowing Latvia, for instance, to compete under its own flag. All this meant we were making our run for the Olympics when many quality teams were chasing the same goal. We weren't daunted; the only people who'd placed any expecta-tions on us to perform were *us*.

The time we stood at the top of Calgary's famous Bobsleigh, Luge and Skeleton Park to prepare for our first run is seared into my memory. Running up and down the old race track as we'd jump in our giant billy cart in flat-as-a-tack Adelaide was a distant memory. We'd watched bobsledding videos and read training manuals, but nothing could've prepared us for our moment of truth. For reality to bite, we needed to stand on top of that track with a 121.48-metre vertical drop from start to finish and see, hear and even feel the energy of our opponents as they jumped into a sled and rocketed down the ice.

On the surface my teammates seemed fine, cracking jokes and laughing, but such were my nerves that my knees were sending SOS signals as they knocked together. In the sense that I'm not an adrenaline junkie, I wasn't a natural bobsledder. I've never had the inclination to parachute, bungee jump or paraglide, being perfectly happy for my two size 13s to be planted firmly on the ground. Even now, you won't find me pushing to the front of the queue to get on a roller-coaster with my daughter, Jacinta. I like slow, steady – and safe. However, there could be no turning back that night in Calgary, and I took many deep breaths to calm myself down because the build-up to that first run in Canada was, at that point of my life, my scariest moment. Given that, it's not unfair to ask why I'd place myself in such a precarious position. It was all about the Olympics. I was so badly bitten by the bug that I was about to take a great leap of faith in my life. I wasn't joking when, terrified, I shouted to the boys before our first run to reach the finish line in one piece.

In my mind's eye I can still see myself at the top of the track, dressed in a body-hugging green-and-gold lycra outfit decorated with spiderwebs and wondering what on earth I was doing! The knots in my stomach tightened as what I was about to attempt dawned on me. I was a long way out of my comfort zone. I started drawing long, deep breaths to calm myself and allow me focus on what I needed to do. I thought about the processes and procedures. We'd done a walkthrough of the course earlier that day to familiarise ourselves with the track. I was the team's brakeman, which meant I sat at the back of the bobsled and applied the brake when we finished our run. It was crucial I kept count of the corners – there were fourteen at Calgary – to know exactly where we were during the race and when to drop anchor. It was important that I applied the brakes at exactly the right time for a number of reasons, one being not to rip up the track. The brakes resembled two big steel rakes and were attached to arms on either side of the sled. They were applied by pulling them out like oars and digging them into the track as hard as possible. Because the bobsled had a combined weight of 640 kilos and was travelling at speed, it took a mighty effort to bring it to a halt. The timing was vital. If the brakes were applied too early, both the officials and my teammates would have good reason to be angry with me. The officials would turn on the brakeman if he hit the brakes while still on the track because it chewed up the ice, causing the event to halt while the damage was repaired; the teammates would shoot daggers because they'd need to push the sled uphill to get it onto the exit track, something that was considered unnecessary hard work.

I vividly recall the moment we were given the green light to start our first 'real' run. There was a collective surge of energy as each team member pushed the bobsled as fast and hard as possible. It was magnificent. Bobsledders only have 50 metres of track – or six seconds – to push off before they jump into the sled, and each second counts – the speed and gravity that's generated at the start of the race determines how fast the team will travel. You go flat out, then the leap into the 'bob' must be controlled. This is for a few reasons. First, the spikes on the soles of your shoes that grip the ice are like needles, and there are hundreds of them, so it's important not to kick your feet out and gouge a teammate. Second, once you're seated it's crucial to bring your heart rate down by taking deep breaths and remaining still. It's also drilled into all bobsledders to not make any sudden movement during the run because it doesn't take much to tip the bobsled off balance and crash – something we discovered on a couple of occasions.

It was smooth sailing until we hit the third corner; then we were off and flying. I've never forgotten the sound of the wind roaring past my ears and the screech of the sled's four runners (or blades) cutting the ice from the starting line to the finish as we hit 130 kilometres an hour, the noise intensifying the sense of drama and danger. I didn't dare do anything except keep my head down and count each corner so I knew when to pull us to a halt. I'd also been pre-warned by experienced competitors that, as the person at the back of the bobsled, I should be braced to take the full brunt of some crushing g-forces. It felt as though I was trying to bench press a piano. However, I didn't allow anything to distract me as I continued counting the corners. I made no sudden movements, I fought the g-forces, and I waited for the correct moment to hit the brakes. I was surprised that the faster we hurtled our way towards the finish line, the more

I loved what we were doing. When I climbed out of the bobsled I was still shaking, albeit with excitement and exhilaration. While my teammates and I would share some white-knuckled moments during our campaign, all of my doubts and fears had been exorcised in that first run. It was now full steam ahead.

We Australians were embraced by the bobsledding fraternity. The Europeans considered us a novelty because they traditionally equated Aussies with such sports as surfing and rugby. The Canadians were among the many who went out of their way to make us feel welcome, and their generosity in lending us tools or even spare parts for emergency repairs dug us out of a few holes. Another great supporter was Albert II, Prince of Monaco. The Prince had competed in the bobsleigh at five Olympics, and he threw his royal clout behind us. He was an extremely popular figure on the circuit and whenever we saw him with his team there were never any vice-regal formalities. We'd simply chirp, 'Good morning, Bert.' Each member of his crew was from his personal protection detail, and they were built like monsters. But if their facial expressions were an indicator, they loathed our attitude, perhaps because our greeting may have seemed disrespectful. Of course, we were simply being Australians, and to his credit Bert would always reply with a cheery, 'And how are my Skippies today?'

While competing on the 1991 World Cup circuit was a rewarding time, it was also a challenging one. I needed to be strict about what I ate because I had to keep my weight under 112 kilos to fit into the sled. As a result I was always 'hangry': constantly angry because I was so hungry. While the European and North American teams travelled between venues in a luxury coach and boasted gear stewards, mechanics and other support staff who looked after their athletes' every whim, we did all our own heavy lifting. After competing we did the repairs, stowed our gear away and carried the sleds to and from the track. Team members who weren't racing prepared the four runners for competition, which took the better part of two nights because we had to wet and dry polish them to ensure they were smooth enough to minimise the friction with the ice when we raced.

It was all part of the fun, but it came at a price. Sometimes our physical training – particularly stretching and flexibility work – took a back seat to our chores. Contesting the World Cup on the smell of an oily rag meant we never recovered from being beaten up on the track. While our opponents were sleeping or getting massages, we were travelling overnight to the next venue. I drove the team van most of the time and once we arrived at our desti-nation we didn't immediately head to our rooms to sleep. Instead, with the help of our coach, Doru Frîncu, who'd competed for Romania at the 1980 Lake Placid Games, we unloaded the gear, carted the sleds to a secure location and completed what seemed to be a never-ending list of running repairs and other duties. Fortunately, we were a tight-knit group, and everyone accepted their responsibilities without complaint. Team morale was important because, as I mentioned, there were occasions when we slept two to a bed to save money. I made sure I bunked with our sled's driver, Jason Giobbi. While he was as strong as an ox, and became an Olympian, Giobbi was five foot nothing, meaning I could stretch out as I slept. There were definitely times when living on top of each other was tough, but our camaraderie remained solid because everyone pulled their weight.

While there were only six of us, I think the toughest test was never having our own space. I was always in the car with someone; we shared beds, and trained, ate, competed, travelled and even socialised together. Fortunately, our team spirit, and the belief in what we were doing, was solid. That allowed us to soldier on. As the oldest member of the group, I'd be called upon to help my teammates with a lot of problems. I did my best to help them, but I felt the same claustrophobia they were fighting.

My worst crash occurred during a training session at St Moritz, when the four-man sled that McDonald and I were in toppled over onto its side. McDonald couldn't get under the cowling (the front of the sled where the driver sits), which prevented me from sliding myself further into the capsule to protect my shoulder. To get some relief I placed my helmet on the track, giving myself the leverage needed to lift my shoulder off the ice because it was getting badly burnt. However, the friction made my helmet heat up and it felt as though my head was going to burst into flames! I remember thinking I could get by without a shoulder but not without my head, so I gritted my teeth as the shoulder took the full brunt. At most tracks the organisers have staff stationed at different points of the run, and when they see a crew in trouble their job is to throw a rope across to stop the bobsled's momentum. For whatever reason, there wasn't anyone on duty that day, so we were consigned to a painful journey. When we finally came to a halt it felt as though my shoulder was stuffed, even though there was some movement. The doctor who examined me believed it had been dislocated in the crash but had somehow managed to pop itself back in place before the finish line.

Our team had good reason to toast the success we enjoyed during the German leg of our campaign. When we set out on our quest the AOC assured us we'd compete at Albertville if we finished at least one World Cup meet in the top 16 – and we did! Looking back, however, there should've been a greater sense of foreboding when, after the news of our result reached home, we were advised – with only one meet remaining – that we needed another top-16 performance to seal the deal. The goalposts had been moved mid-match, but as we celebrated into the early morning we figured the AOC would do the right thing. We didn't tick the second box, but like the rest of my crew members I was walking on air when we received notification to attend the AOC team induction at the AIS. I couldn't see why they'd waste our time if we weren't going to Albertville.

That time in Canberra was such a great experience. Apart from the thrill of being measured for my Olympic blazer, I had the added excitement of joining my team to film the commercials that Channel Nine planned to run during their coverage. While my memory is hazy, one spiel went along the lines of: 'G'day, we're bobsledding's Thunder from Down Under, and you're watching Channel Nine's Wide World of Sports coverage of the Albertville Winter Olympics. See ya on the ice, Australia!'

When the AOC's management selected me as the 'talent' for a mock media conference conducted by respected sports journalists Ian Hanson and Alan Clarkson, I thought it was yet another sure-fire sign I was on the plane. I didn't know it at the time, but its purpose was to show all team members why it was important to expect the unexpected if the media's spotlight shone on them.

After congratulating me on my selection, both reporters made me squirm. They asked some tough questions, the killer one being how I felt, as an AFP officer, knowing an opponent had tested positive to steroids. A hundred thoughts raced through my mind as I searched for the *right* answer, although in hindsight it should've been as easy as saying, 'It'd be very disappointing if it's true.' However, with every set of eyes in the room fixed on me, I was confused about whether I'd be seen to be speaking as an athlete or a police officer, and that was an important distinction because cops were discouraged from publicly expressing personal opinions. We simply told journos to call the media unit in Canberra. As a result, my initial response was muddled. Finally, I offered a half-hearted shrug of my shoulders, knowing I could've done much better. From that experience I learnt the importance of always having something ready for the media, even if it was a 'nothing to say' comment. Regardless of this public grilling, the induction was huge for me. It seemed as though I'd finally done it: *Grant Edwards, Australian Olympian* had a nice ring to it.

I set myself up for a major disappointment by forgetting that good cops take nothing for granted. While my teammates and I thought we'd paid our dues to compete at Albertville, we'd been set up for a crash that would hurt more than anything we'd copped while screaming down the track at breakneck speed. When Australia's 23-strong team marched into the Theatre des Ceremonies on 8 February 1992, our four-man bobsleigh team was at home watching the opening ceremony on television. We'd been advised via a letter from the AOC after the induction in Canberra that they thought we wouldn't be competitive enough to do Australia proud. That made us angry, of course. Mexico, Jamaica, Latvia, the Virgin Islands and Chinese Taipei were all supported by their Olympic bodies to *compete*. But what really still burns is that the AOC ignored the message from Pierre de Coubertin, the father of the modern Olympics, stressing that the Games weren't about winning, but taking part. While the AOC has since adopted a policy to provide as many people as possible with the opportunity to compete because it enriches their lives, in 1992 the committee appeared fixated on perceptions. Fortunately, Narracott and Glenn Turner were selected to compete in the two-man event and, despite being former rivals (they were on Di Piazza's squad), we cheered them on as they finished in twenty-eighth place out of a field of forty-six.

Two years later I tried out for the 1994 Lillehammer Games squad, but by then life had overtaken my Olympic dream. It was too hard to get the time off work because I'd chewed through most of my leave. I was also transferring to Internal Investigations, and you couldn't really leave cases 'hanging'. An even more pressing – and joyous – reason for me missing out in 1994 was that my first daughter, Emilee, had been born the year before. The births of both my girls, Emilee and Jacinta, are the two proudest moments of my life. A surge of incredible emotion overwhelmed me each time. My outlook on life changed forever the moment I laid eyes on them for the first time. All that mattered was these precious little beings who needed me, and I was determined to protect and nurture them. One of the cool things I did with Emilee was taking her to the University of Newcastle when she was a newborn. I'd just started my anthropology degree and

I took her to tutorials. Fortunately, the lecturer loved having Emilee about the group. Indeed, she'd even tell the class that we were going to study in the fresh air outside because 'I don't want all you people coughing on her'.

It's still disappointing to realise that my dream of becoming an Olympian wasn't meant to be, although I take immense pride in being a member of a team that *qualified* for Albertville.

18
A FILTHY BUSINESS

*'Despite rising rates of seizure at the border . . . the
drug trade is increasing as supply grows to meet ever
increasing demand.'*
– Australia's Minister for Immigration and Border Protection,
Scott Morrison, 2014

I learnt there is no honour among drug users one night in 1991
when I was called to Brunswick Heads on the New South Wales
North Coast. Ostensibly, a drug courier had been tortured to
death by his bosses. He hadn't; he had been with 'friends'. But
when he overdosed, instead of phoning an ambulance and risk
getting in trouble with the police, his mates ripped an electric
cord from their iron and plugged it into the power point. They
then took the end where the exposed wires dangled and placed
it directly over his heart in an attempt to jump-start it. The bloke
didn't stand a chance, but his associates justified their actions by
saying they'd seen electric jolts used to bring people back to life
on television shows.

The only reason they weren't all electrocuted was because
lying on the floor meant the victim was earthed. Had he been
in a chair it's likely we'd have been investigating several deaths.

What angered me was that the person who'd overdosed might have survived if one of his mates had called triple-zero. But, as I found to be the way with drug addicts, they rarely think of anything other than themselves or their next hit. Common sense seems to go out the window. I remember reading an intelligence report from the United States in the late 1980s saying that a bloke had injected a cocaine solution down his urethra in an attempt to improve his sexual performance. He suffered from a prolonged erection – it lasted for days – and when it subsided, the blood that flooded into his body caused blood clots in his hands, feet, back and chest. About ten days later, the gangrene had spread to the extent that nine of his fingers and both legs needed to be amputated. His penis eventually fell off. There was a suggestion that perhaps an impurity had caused the problem, but I'd simply suggest it isn't an intelligent thing to try.

Some elements of working in the drug squad are disgusting. The stories that follow are indeed unsavoury, but treat them as cautionary tales. Hopefully they'll provide some insights into how police officers who are fighting the war on drugs can sometimes find themselves elbow deep in shit, literally.

One of the many ways drugs enter a country is via 'mules'. People who are recruited to smuggle contraband across international borders often do so by ingesting pellets of illegal substances such as heroin and cocaine that have been packed tightly into condoms. The typical drug mule can swallow anywhere between 80 and 125 capsules, which can weigh up to 1.25 kilos. The mules take incontinence medication before and during the flight, and once they reach their destination they swallow laxatives to help the pellets pass through their digestive system. And in no time at all the drugs hit the street.

I'd like to think if people knew more about how their 'blow' or 'smack' was delivered they'd have second thoughts about the source of their highs. But mules' actions aren't without risk to themselves. Apart from the threat of being caught by Customs and convicted to a long prison sentence, they're also in danger of suffering a terrible death from heart or respiratory failure should any of the ingested pellets rupture. A mule stands to make no more than between $3000 and $4000 for risking their life and freedom, a mere pittance compared to the earnings of drug lords, who make a thousand times that once all of the drugs have been sold.

If you think there is some sort of adventure in trying to smuggle drugs, consider this story from the US. It proves how little the life of a mule means to the drug cartels; what happened in 1995 to a 21-year-old from Colombia was nothing short of disgraceful. I heard about this case because I continued to receive the latest intelligence from the drug squad, even though I'd transferred to the Internal Investigation Department. Their reports are disturbing because they document the real currency of the drug trade: human life. The man, who'd just secured a job on a cruise liner, was enticed to make some extra cash by smuggling heroin into Miami, but the drug-filled capsules he'd stuffed into his belly started to leak and he died of an overdose. However, his contact wasn't going to let the drugs go to waste. The autopsy on the mule's body showed that the supplier had used a 12-inch knife to gut the man's corpse and retrieve the bags of white powder so he could still supply his clients. The body was dumped on the street. The authorities were able to ascertain that the young Colombian was a mule because the contact had failed to retrieve two pellets that were lodged in his oesophagus.

When I started at the academy in 1985 my entire class was asked to state our career goals and aspirations. I declared that I wanted to become a detective sergeant in the drug squad and play a part in the war on drugs. I thought I could help make a difference. I was given my shot, having two stints in the squad from 1987 to 1989 (and after serving in the organised crime unit) and from 1990 to 1992. We enjoyed some good wins, but that invisible backpack of mine was filled with the pebbles that would weigh me down when I was no longer the mentally robust young cop who thrived on the cut 'n' thrust.

When I reflect on my time in the squad, it's incredible to think we didn't wear breathing masks or protective clothing when we seized heroin and other drugs. I've since learnt that the reason I'd go home from work with a wicked headache and feeling 'weird' was because heroin can enter the body through the skin's pores. I also saw some terrible sights. What hurt me the most was when kids were caught in the crossfire. Arresting couples who were involved in the drug trade was tough because we had to make arrangements for child welfare to take custody of the children. It was clear the kids were terrified. Most cried and screamed that they wanted their parents. Worse were the kids who showed no emotion. Their blank looks concerned me because I wondered what they'd seen. The kids always stirred deep emotions within me, the strongest of which was anger at unfairness of their plight. They didn't ask for parents like that – no kid does.

There are three areas within the drug squad: the parcel-post unit at the mail exchange; the drug response team, whose members could be sent to the airport when a mule is arrested, and long-term operations. Those officers require incredible patience because they could watch a target for over a year. I spent my time between the drug response team and the mail exchange, learning quickly that cartels could be as resourceful as they were ruthless. In one job we confiscated 2 kilos worth of cocaine in letters that were sent to an address in Sydney. It was drug supply by stealth – the cartel included 5 grams of coke in each envelope. They were well organised, with scouts locating 'dead drops': unoccupied houses where they sent their packages. The scouts also noted letterboxes that the residents of apartment blocks didn't lock, which they used to drop off their drugs.

The mail exchange was always a hive of activity. We uncovered cocaine, heroin and even MDA stored in machinery parts. Hang-gliders brought to Australia for a World Championship event and surfboards were also used to conceal stashes. It always felt like we'd scored a grand final try when we made a discovery that prevented drugs from hitting the streets. One memorable 'win' was when we extracted a tonne of hashish suspended in chickpeas, of all things! It took the better part of three days to extract it, and the stench was overpowering. I'm deadly serious when I say I couldn't eat hummus for many years without wanting to be sick.

However, I experienced worse sights, sounds and smells during my career in the drug squad.

In 1990 I was a detective constable assigned to the drug response team. One day we received a call from the New South Wales Ambulance Service saying they'd been called to treat a national from an Eastern European country at a doctor's surgery in Newtown. He had a stomach full of heroin, but when he and his girlfriend had attended the doctor's surgery earlier that day they'd refused to disclose what was wrong with him. The doctor advised there was little he could do if they wouldn't tell him what was wrong, and they left. A few hours later they returned, and while they were at the surgery the man collapsed and lapsed into unconsciousness. In her despair, the woman confessed he'd swallowed numerous pellets of heroin. An ambulance was called, and when they ferried him to the nearby Royal Prince Alfred Hospital, X-rays revealed he was holding around 70 pellets.

When a member of our forensic team and I arrived at the hospital we met with the two surgeons who were waiting to operate. Even though they wore surgical face masks, I could tell they were seething. They made it clear they were furious at being called back to the hospital after their shift had finished to save the life of someone who was feeding the drug epidemic. 'It's ironic,' said one of the surgeons, shaking his head in disgust as he glared at the man lying unconscious on the operating table. 'We're normally fighting to save the victims of drugs, and now we're saving *this*.'

The mule hadn't been to the toilet for days. Having blocked his bowels with intestinal obstruction medication, his stomach was bloated with gas, so when the scalpel was plunged into his abdomen his gut quickly deflated like a pierced soccer ball.

The stench released was pungent. The foul odour made me want to vomit, and even the two doctors recoiled. One of them broke the tension by saying, 'I'd say he's had a dodgy meal or two!' He then asked what my cricket skills were like and directed me to cradle my hands as though I was fielding at first slip.

My colleague, who was filming the surgery as part of the chain of evidence, and I watched in amazement as the surgeon removed the man's guts from his stomach cavity, plonked them on his chest and slit a fine line along the intestine. Once that was done, the surgeon glanced towards me and asked, 'Are you ready?'

He squeezed the intestine as if it were a sausage. The pellets of drugs – caked in undigested pieces of food – came flying out at speed. *Pop . . . pop . . . pop . . . pop.* I'd wait, watch, catch and drop the packages into a bucket full of Betadine disinfectant, and then repeat the procedure over and over again. Once the last of the drugs were removed, the surgeons, who'd earned my admiration for the incredible job they'd done to save this man's life, put his guts back into his stomach, and it struck me how they could just as easily have been stuffing a Christmas turkey. They then used catgut to stitch him up, and I thought how the man was going to have one hell of a scar to remind him of the lives he was prepared to destroy for a few dollars. It came as no surprise to any of us that, once the mule had recovered, he refused to be interviewed. His defence counsel insisted in court that he wasn't a willing party in the crime; he claimed his client acted under duress after being threatened with 'severe' ramifications if he didn't go ahead with the plan.

On another occasion, I was at a bedside bail hearing at
St George Hospital for another drug mule who also had a belly
full of contraband. He was refusing to cooperate with anyone –
us, the doctors or the nurses – and even though we had X-rays
that identified the position of the drugs in his stomach, all we
could do was wait for nature to take its slow course. We couldn't
force him to take anything that would help his bowels relax, so
it became a painful waiting game. Making an unpleasant job
even harder was the fact that he was an abusive, foul-mouthed
individual. I was happy to leave the bloke when my shift finished.
After doing the handover to the two relieving officers who'd
been assigned the night shift, I went home. I'd just started to
relax when one of them phoned me in a state of disbelief. The
officer, normally a reserved and calm character, was screaming
down the line. Once I deciphered what he was shouting my
guts churned.

What had transpired since I'd knocked off was extraordinary. The prisoner drove my colleagues mad with his abuse,
but what he did when his bowels erupted sickened them. In
his desperation to keep out of prison, he grabbed the capsules
as soon as they left his body and one by one *swallowed* them.
All I could think to say to my mate as he relayed the story was,
'That's bloody disgusting.' In the end the mule's actions were all
in vain – he was found guilty of trafficking and imprisoned for
six years.

The demand for mules is so high because drug barons have
realised Australia is a lucrative market. While our government
spends billions of taxpayer dollars annually on our war against
drugs – including our contribution to funding a paramilitary

force in Colombia that combats the cartels – our nation is renowned as the perfect dumping ground because of our unenviable reputation as world champion drug takers. That title was bestowed upon Aussies in the United Nations' 2014 World Drug Report, which confirmed we led the world in the use of the party drug ecstasy, and came third for methamphetamine use and fourth for cocaine consumption. It's equally well known to criminal gangs that Australians will pay through the nose for their next high. The Mexico-based Sinaloa cartel, for instance, will do whatever it takes to protect their Australian market; a kilo of good-quality cocaine that's worth US$2500 in Mexico will make US$180,000 profit when it reaches our shores. Australia's law enforcement agencies – the AFP, state police forces, Border Force and the nation's corrective services – are all doing their utmost to curb the influx of drugs. Indeed, the Australian Criminal Intelligence Commission noted in its 2016–17 report that these agencies established new records nationally for both the number of seizures of illicit drugs and the number of drug-related arrests. Among the haul they'd intercepted during that twelve-month period was 1109 kilograms of cocaine, double the amount seized in 2015–16. Make no mistake, despite the commitment and great work of those officers, Australia remains under attack from overseas drug cartels.

Most people have a stereotypical view of drug dealers. However, you can't pigeonhole them; they come from different walks of life and backgrounds. For every cheap gangster dressed in designer clothes and chunky gold chains, there's a sophisticated businessman or woman who has accrued property and a fine art collection. The would-be drug dealer who shocked me when he found his way onto my radar was a former sporting champion who many respected rugby league judges rank among the greatest players ever. He was one of the sporting heroes of my generation.

This shocked me to the core because I have vivid memories of seeing this bloke in the 1970s when I was a boy. He worked at Sydney's Darling Harbour when it was still an industrial area with workshops and rail yards. I'd take days off school to go there with Pa as he delivered goods for the state's freight trains, and even though Mum would be angry with him when she found out, it was always a great adventure. One day Pa pointed out the footy hero to me. As I watched him unloading crates from off the back of a table-top truck, it seemed as though he was doing an extra training session because he cut a fine figure as he cleared the cargo.

I lost count of the number of times I saw him at Darling Harbour, but his presence always generated a sense of excitement among the other labourers. It was as though he was a saint walking among the common folk. The workers, old Sydney hard nuts who were tough to impress, would nudge one another with their elbows and point their thumbs in the direction of their football hero. To them, he epitomised all that was good about Australian manhood because, while he was a champion sportsman, he was respected for not being big-headed. I admired him too because I'd watched him destroy rival teams on our black and white television, but I was far too shy to ask for what would've been a prized autograph in my school playground.

Fast forward twenty-odd years to 2001, when I'd only recently returned from working in Los Angeles. Due to my contemporary experiences in the United States I was assigned to the 'Cocaine Team' of the Transnational Criminal Intelligence Team, watching my fallen football hero with four men outside his inner-Sydney house. The conversation was becoming more animated by the minute. The ex-footballer was in our sights because the AFP had good intelligence that he'd planned to import a shipment of what was described broadly as 'a commodity' from South-East Asia. Our information suggested he wasn't too particular about what drug he and his cohorts smuggled into the country because essentially it was a cash-grab. However, we were certain it was heroin because they were arranging to obtain the shipment from the Golden Triangle, a place in South-East Asia where the borders of Thailand, Laos and Myanmar meet. Like most dealers, this bloke didn't take drugs – he was happy to profit off the depths of human misery.

This particular football great was well known to police. He'd been running close to the wind for a while on account of the people he was mixing with. I'd recently been promoted to the rank of sergeant and my team had run a substantial investigation into him and his activities, but we kept it close to our chests because we didn't want to risk details being leaked to the media. The longer our investigation continued, the clearer it became that he had signed on to drug trafficking, and I wanted to be there when he was convicted.

There's a long list of former Australian rugby league players who've been imprisoned because of their involvement in the drug trade. In what is perhaps the best-known case, the former Newtown Jets player Paul Hayward was caught by Thai police in a Bangkok hotel room in 1978 with 8.4 kilos of heroin in a suitcase. Hayward, who'd also fought as a professional boxer, maintained he only went to Bangkok to make a quick $20,000 by acting as a 'minder'. His job was to ensure the drug courier Warren Fellows didn't get 'burnt'. However, after being caught and photographed in chains with Fellows and their Bangkok connection, William Sinclair, he was tried and sentenced to twenty years in prison. Hayward received thirteen years less than the others because the Thai legal authorities believed he was 'used'. When he was released after serving ten and a half years, Hayward returned to Australia infected with HIV, the result of using a contaminated syringe in jail. He died in his Sydney home in 1992 after a heroin overdose. He was 38.

The only reason the former footballer we were targeting this time hadn't appeared on the list is because he had one trait that made him extremely hard to nail: acute paranoia. He took no chances, and his deep-rooted distrust of *everyone* in his circle suggested he had a good understanding of how things worked in the criminal world. He was also very patient; that I've learnt the good crims are the patient ones. However, eventually they need to stick their heads over the parapet to get things moving. My partner and I watched as he took his leap of faith. As the five men hatched their plan I felt confident *this* would be the day we nabbed him. He and his associates were engaged in heavy conversation, and I noticed that while the others appeared comfortable enough to talk, the old league legend remained hyper-vigilant, his eyes nervously darting everywhere as he scanned the streetscape.

I'd read the intelligence reports, which detailed his plan to ship heroin into the country, and it disappointed me to be watching a bloke who was once idolised by so many people. He must have known his plan involved profiting off the misery of others. There was so much at stake, but while the labourers at Darling Harbour in the 1970s extolled his virtue for being a tough bastard, I rued he was also a lucky one.

The group was on the verge of discussing their plan when out of the blue a university student walked towards them. The kid was carrying a backpack, and as he passed the men he suddenly bent down to tie one of his shoelaces. I reckon the blood must've drained from my face in an instant because I knew that would be enough to send the target's paranoia off the Richter scale. I heard myself yelling, 'No, no, no, no, no!' Fearing he'd somehow been set up, the footy legend threw his hands into the air and declared, 'It's off,' before storming inside his house and bunkering down. When we picked up on the group's chatter afterwards, they were ripping into one another, accusing different ones of 'gigging' to the cops, a tactic criminals sometimes use to either deflect blame or gauge who might be police informants.

Despite the setback we continued with the investigation, but his paranoia only intensified after the student's surprise appearance. I formed the opinion that he was trying to back out of the deal because he realised the ramifications of being caught. Ultimately, he either didn't have the finances needed to go ahead with the plan, or he was cutting ties with the suppliers. In the latter stages of our investigation there were also signs that the condition that plagued the final years of his life had started to manifest; he was often saying things that were garbled or didn't make sense. Reluctantly, we closed the file. While we had no doubt he'd intended to smuggle drugs into the country, for all intents and purposes he was getting out of the game.

There have been plenty of times since that day when I've cursed the fact that the unsuspecting kid suddenly needed to tie his shoelace. He'd never know that he'd unintentionally denied us an arrest that would have resonated widely. The media would have gone into a meltdown, and it would have stunned hundreds of thousands of people worldwide. Of even greater importance, his arrest would have highlighted the fact that you never know who is involved in the drug trade. For almost fifty years this man stood on a pedestal, but through either bad luck, ill fortune or pure greed, he was preparing to get involved in a trade that profits off heartache and despair. I haven't named the footballer because he's no longer alive to defend himself and his reputation, and I'm reluctant to upset his family. But the postscript to the story is that the former player didn't enjoy a comfortable old age. I have no pity for anyone who seeks to make money from drugs, but even so, it was sad as a one-time fan for me to witness such an inglorious end to a life once so widely celebrated.

19
A MORAL INJURY

*'Abuse manipulates and twists a child's natural sense of trust
and love. Her innocent feelings are belittled or mocked, and
she learns to ignore her feelings. She can't afford to feel the
full range of feelings in her body while she's being abused –
pain, outrage, hate, vengeance, confusion, arousal . . .'*
– Laura Davis, author, *Allies in Healing*

When Deputy Commissioner Phelan advised me in 2010 that
I was being transferred from the International Deployment
Group to high tech crime I was stunned because I only had a
basic understanding of computers. I was revelling in my role
as the Manager of Operations and Missions. We had hundreds
of people offshore in some exciting places, and I thrived on
the responsibility of looking after them. I thought my future
was there, but it'd been taken away from me in the space of a
five-minute phone call.

I turned up to my new post in Canberra feeling like a fish
out of water, although my mates and my partner, Kate, had
kindly bought me a cap with a propeller attached to it as a
joke so I could at least look the part when I turned up to work
alongside a group of cyber geeks (known as 'propeller heads' to

outsiders) who they imagined would be fluent in Klingon – the language from *Star Trek*. I soon felt quite foolish for holding such preconceived notions, because I'd soon consider myself blessed to work alongside some brilliant police officers and civilian staff.

One of our finest moments was in 2011 when a 25-year-old unemployed truck driver named David Noel Cecil, who gave himself the online alias of 'Evil', was jailed for attempting to hack into the system of Platform Networks, one of the thirteen service providers for the National Broadband Network (NBN). Cecil was a self-taught hacker who'd spend up to twenty hours a day on his computer. He came onto our radar when he hacked into a university website and made a racist comment on their home page about an employee. We obtained a warrant to monitor both his internet traffic and his voice communications, and we soon discovered he was attacking a number of companies. He bragged about his 'accomplishment' to hack into Platform Networks to members of the internet community. When he suspected the police were onto him, he directed his group members to follow him to an encrypted site, which he thought would guarantee him protection from prying eyes. However, one of my colleagues worked late into the night and broke into the secured site, and we were made aware of Evil's plans. It was because of such dedication that I removed the propeller cap from my office and took it home. I have kept it as a reminder about the foolishness of making ill-informed judgements about people before you get to know them. Those staff members were outstandingly capable people who were at the forefront of cutting-edge work, and the passion and commitment they showed in their objective to fight cybercrime, especially the heinous crime of child exploitation, earned my wholehearted respect. I will remember those colleagues as among the best of the best.

The role of the AFP's high tech crime unit is to protect Australia from malicious attacks on either our cyber institutions or places that are considered to be of national interest. An added responsibility was policing online child exploitation, as well as having the extraterritorial responsibility of dealing with Australians who travelled overseas and committed offences against children. This unit was formed in the early 2000s when I was working in surveillance, and it operated under the name of Operational Child Sexual Exploitation Team. Like those who went before me, and those who followed, I found it was a brutal gig. Indeed, everyone who worked on the team was left mentally scarred by the work.

From my time in what became known as the Transnational Sexual Exploitation and Trafficking Team, or TSETT (2002–2004), I will never be able to forget the image of a 6-month-old infant who was being used as a plaything by two paedophiles. It is evil. I'd like to write what these two lowlifes did – and said – in the vision they uploaded to the internet to properly illustrate the despicable nature that drives paedophiles. However, to do that would be to mentally transfer an image that is so awful and depraved that it would be very hard for most people to forget. It's harrowing to realise the incident is only one of thousands of violations against children that my team and I analyzed before passing them on for further investigation. The endless accumulation of such horrid images, and knowing innocent kids were . . . *are* . . . being treated so disgustingly by men, caused me and so many others to succumb to anguish. We'd never really be the same people again. When I saw what they put that poor baby through, I was enraged. As vile as that was, over the two years I was in the unit my team and I investigated far worse examples of child exploitation. I served alongside highly motivated people, all of whom were passionate about what they did because they realised the importance of their work, and we were all damaged by what we saw in some way. The graphic nature of much of the material exposed the depths of human depravity.

As the leader of the team, I worked hard to shield my staff from the worst of it, and psychologically speaking, it would eventually crush me. It reached a stage where I drank bourbon at the end of some shifts to try and unwind after the ugliness I'd been exposed to during the day at work, but I couldn't forget the horrid images. I didn't drink every night; it was only after the toughest of days. The 'moral injury' I suffered through my inability to rescue many of those children, combined with the women I would try to save in my work with human trafficking during a later appointment, would eventually metamorphose into gruesome nightmares about helplessness and innocence betrayed. And they would be the catalyst, later in my life, for what would be the development of catastrophic post-traumatic stress disorder. When that demon struck, not even the handfuls of painkillers and sedatives I took, or the gallons of alcohol I swallowed, could help me 'un-see' what I'd viewed. I would eventually devise another, more extreme escape plan.

Australians are among the highest viewers of child pornography in the world, which is a national disgrace. Some of the child sex offenders we've arrested haven't physically harmed a child, but they did view what's colloquially known as 'kiddie porn' – an offence that's punishable by a prison sentence. When we catch these (mostly) male perpetrators they cite 'curiosity' as the reason they were attracted to this material, even though they know it's immoral. And they know they're engaged in an immoral activity because their reaction to being caught is often to say, 'Thank God you got me, now it's over.' Once the serious-ness of what they've been charged with sinks in, they'll argue that they haven't physically harmed a child, but their hunger for the pornographic images they view has created a market built on exploitation and suffering. There is no such thing as victimless child porn.

In more extreme cases of paedophilia, there's a perverse pleasure in the pain and suffering imposed on vulnerable children. Such offenders are comparable to the Murphy brothers who participated in the brutal murder of Sydney nurse Anita Cobby in 1986. I've been asked on several occasions by jour-nalists to profile the 'typical' paedophile/child sex offender, but I'm afraid to say that the warnings we give our children about the grubby man in the trench coat who hides behind the bushes with a bag of lollies are a fallacy. There are, of course, occasions when a child is snatched off the street by a stranger, or when an adult exposes themselves to a child, but the odds suggest a child is in greater danger of being abused by someone closer to home – members of their family, family friends or acquain-tances who include school teachers, sports coaches, members of their church, a friend's father and the like. Although it is almost fifteen years old, the Australian Bureau of Statistics'

'Personal Safety Survey', which was conducted in 2005, found that 12 per cent of women and 4.5 per cent of men had been sexually abused by the age of 15 – and my father was one of them. The Bureau estimated that based on those findings there were 1,294,000 people living in Australia – 956,600 females and 337,400 males – who were victims of sexual abuse before they turned 15. Because the majority of perpetrators are known to the family, I tell people not to trust *anyone* with their children, because I've been cursed to see what paedophiles will do if given an opportunity.

The people who worked in the Child Exploitation Unit volunteered to be there. Because of the nature of the work, people were never transferred into the unit. Once they expressed their interest in joining us they had to go through a screening process that included a psych test. Indeed, we were solely guided by the psychologist's assessment on whether a candidate was accepted or not. If they had concerns about the candidate's ability to handle the nature of the work, their application was rejected. We quickly realised that the people who were drawn to the job were very passionate by nature, and without exception their motive for wanting to join was because they wanted to help kids. While there were many with the right intentions, we zeroed in on those who could view the most despicable images and then interview the alleged perpetrator in a controlled manner.

Resilience was an important characteristic. We worked long hours, and while our senses were bombarded with terrible sights and sounds, I found the biggest challenge was getting the crew to stop working, because they were so passionate about their job and wanted to get results. There was intense pressure. If we knew a child was at risk, it was all hands on deck. Before legis-lation in 2003 permitted the AFP to take criminal action against any vision we intercepted, my team and I spent two tough years examining every piece of material that was exchanged over the internet that had an element of child exploitation in it. We'd forward it to the Australian Communications and Media Authority, which had the authority to say whether the material was actionable. Once we received the green light we'd then refer it for investigation. Even now, half of the battle is that we're fighting twenty-first century crime with nineteenth-century laws, and while the AFP is trying to recruit more computer-savvy millennials to take on cybercrime, we need to ensure these officers will have at their disposal contemporary laws so they can fight highly skilled criminals without one hand tied behind their back.

The nature of the work was always going to take its toll on even my team's most resilient members. Our job was to con-stantly trawl the internet, and despite the grotesque nature of the material we came across, we didn't have access to psychologists. There was no official debrief procedure to help us unburden ourselves either, though I do stress the AFP has since addressed the issues we faced. These days there are annual assessments of staff, and the maximum time anyone will spend in the unit is three years. For us, it was all-consuming work. Sometimes it felt as though we were using teaspoons to bail water from a sinking ship, such was the sheer volume of material that swamped us from all corners of the world.

There have been, however, some memorable victories, including the AFP's involvement in 'Operation Rescue', a global policing effort that ran from 2007 to 2011 and ended up smashing the world's largest paedophile ring. I was in East Timor and then the International Deployment Group when this investigation was underway. The Australian commitment to the investigation was headed by Federal Agent Kel Mansfield, a good man. We worked together for a brief time in Sydney when he was a junior officer, and he was a very talented detective. When I was transferred to high tech crime in 2010, the investigation had been underway for three years. I realised the people working on it were at the top of their game, and I made it my priority to act as a buffer between the officers and the bureaucrats, and to ensure they continued to be well resourced.

Operation Rescue is a brilliant example of what can be achieved when law enforcement agencies band together to fight crime. The Dutch, Brits, Australia, the United States Immigration and Customs Enforcement Agency, Europol, and police from Canada and New Zealand combined their resources when a Netherlands-based server landed on the Dutch police force's radar after the AFP and British police independently found the website. It ran an international online child abuse forum which, at the height of its popularity, boasted 70,000 global members. It was run along the lines of a business, with an owner and directors, and in a brazen attempt to fly under the radar they called it a 'discussion only' forum, which allowed people to share their sexual interest in boys without committing any specific offences. However, it also allowed others, who among a variety of perversions discussed having sex with babies, to suss out like-minded people. They'd then move to secure channels to email child porn to one another. In effect, this online forum was a front for the trade in millions of child exploitation images and film, some of which were made to order.

The AFP also discovered that some members of the forum ran orphanages in Thailand, and tracked down – and charged – an 84-year-old Australian for physically abusing children. When the Dutch arrested the site's owner – 37-year-old Amir Ish-Hurwitz, a Netherlands resident – he signed over the rights to the server to them, and it proved to be a goldmine. After harvesting the IP addresses, officers assumed the identity of Ish-Hurwitz and some other alleged sexual perverts in order to make contact with suspects. That allowed for the thirty-one Australia-based members to be identified. Among their number were lifesavers, school teachers, scout masters and even farmhands, and their ages ranged from 19 to 84. In the UK, among the 121 people British police arrested were teachers, police officers, youth workers and even a woman. The woman surprised us because it's not the norm. We've found that when women get caught up in this scene, it's usually because they're in a relationship with a paedophile. These women are more often than not besotted with their partner and literally do whatever the male wants. They're often used as the 'hook' to groom victims because children are naturally inclined to trust females ahead of males. Some Australians were among the forum's senior members – they were 'directors' – and as well as arresting 184 suspected paedophiles globally, the AFP helped to rescue 230 at-risk children from around the world who were in danger of being abused. Four Australian boys under the age of 14 were among them. Some of the children were infants, who were being groomed for sex; others were forced to wear nappies as they were violated in the most degrading ways imaginable.

That operation took four years from beginning to end, and while it was relentless, the results were rewarding. However, elation swung quickly to anger when, after attending a press conference in the Hague alongside my Dutch and British counterparts to discuss the breakthrough, the Australia-based 'security advisor' for the network, Melbourne IT consultant Evgeny Potashnik, was sentenced to community service after pleading guilty to two counts of knowingly possessing child pornography. I was outraged. I thought he was culpable for more than that – after all, he'd employed his IT knowledge to protect thousands of paedophiles from being exposed. That feeling of disbelief that he'd escaped real punishment was perhaps best summed up by Hetty Johnston from Bravehearts, a group that fights for the interests of abused children, when she told *The Australian*, 'The police do all this work to catch these people and then they walk – it is pathetic.'

Despite the magnitude of what they're up against, there are committed police officers around the world who pore over online vision in the hope they'll find even the smallest clue that will lead to a conviction. And that was what happened the day when a Brit who'd recently visited Australia was on assignment with Interpol in Europe. He was in the office when they intercepted a video that had been uploaded by an organised child sex offender group in Czechoslovakia. It showed a terrified young girl, about 7 years old, in a cabin. She was being injected with a drug that would (mercifully) knock her out, but the Brit's interest was piqued by the noise a bird outside the house was making. He realised that the distinctive laughing sound belonged to the kookaburra, and when he studied the vision he noticed gum trees outside the window. He forwarded the material to us in Canberra, and one of our team displayed great initiative by taking some photographs of the trees to the Forestry Department at the Australian National University. She asked them to pinpoint where that specific species could be found. As it turned out, these particular gum trees grew in north-western Victoria and the highlands of NSW. It was a huge area to scour, but at least we had a starting point.

Something else we noticed from the video was that the perpetrator injected his victim in a professional manner. There was a theory that he was either a doctor or someone who was trained in medical procedures, which provided us with another line of investigation to follow. We'd arranged to do a nationally coordinated exposure campaign across all media in the hope of identifying the offender, but the NSW police took it upon themselves to release it on Channel Nine's *A Current Affair* without letting anyone else know. This decision to break ranks put a few noses out of joint from other agencies, but fortunately it worked. The mother of the child came forward, and we learnt that the offender was the girl's grandfather. He was also a former Tasmanian police officer, and his competence in administering the drug was because he'd served as a medic in the military. When the NSW police arrested him, they discovered he'd put his son and daughter – the little girl's mother – through the same hell when they were children. But the grandfather insisted he wasn't a sex offender – he was 'only' using the images of his granddaughter as merchandise to trade for the adult pornography he preferred. He was a piece of work, and he ended up committing suicide, but not before having a horrendous impact on the lives of his children and granddaughter. Other paedophiles have been caught by similar means – there were occasions when the radio station playing in the background was used to help identify them – but it pleases me to tell people that, of all things, a kookaburra helped us hunt down a child molester.

Few people will ever understand how hard it is to sit face-to-face with someone who has committed despicable acts on a child, and I'd be an extremely rich man if I was paid two bucks for every time a civilian has told me they'd 'shoot the bastards' or 'break their necks' if they were locked in an interrogation room with a 'rock spider'. While I've confronted paedophiles who are happy to be caught because they say 'it's all over', I've also crossed the unapologetic ones who'll try to goad you, saying things that are designed to provoke an unprofessional reaction. I remember one suspect who sneered at me during an interview, bragging about his physical endowments and what he did to his victims. What he said revolted me, but I focused on the end game, which was to have him charged and sent to prison where he would no longer be a threat to children. I continued to ask questions about his crime in a methodical, monotone voice, and when he realised I wasn't taking the bait, he had another crack, offering to show me the attribute he was so proud of.

Again, I ignored him, and continued with my line of questioning. In policing, you always need to remember that criminals are great manipulators; it's what they do for a living. This particular creep hated that I'd not reacted, so he took another tack and attempted to make it personal by talking about my wife. I didn't even blink. He didn't know her, and the more a suspect focuses his attention on trying to make you react to their taunts, the more likely it is they'll slip up and provide the information needed for the case. So I kept pressing, and he was eventually charged and put away. As a society I think we could do a better job of punishing paedophiles when they've been found guilty. While the charges laid against them can attract a maximum of life imprisonment, they often get as little as twelve months, with time off for good behaviour or, as in the aftermath of Operation Rescue, community service. And unfortunately a victim of child sex abuse can suffer first at the hands of their abuser, and then again when they learn of the kind of sentence that's been handed down to their attacker.

I'm a police officer of more than thirty years' service, and I'm still haunted by some of the terrible vision I watched in my role at the Transnational Sexual Exploitation and Trafficking Team. I have no idea how any victim of the sorts of degradation I saw could summon the courage to try to get on with their life, but the fact that they try says plenty for their spirit and heart. I've also heard the dismay in some prison officers' voices about child sex offenders being kept together in a security wing to keep them safe from the general prison population; this is a necessity because they would otherwise be killed for committing a crime that's deemed, even by murderers and rapists, to be the lowest of the low. However, for many paedophiles prison opens more doors because they're living among like-minded types and can openly talk about their perverted fantasies – or even 'conquests' – without the fear of judgement or violence. Consequently, most return to society better armed with the knowledge of how to avoid detection from the police, and they've also benefited from the mentor they'd managed to sniff out on the inside.

I remember reading some letters that had been intercepted and referred to us because they were written by a sex offender who had sent correspondence to his former cellmate, updating him on what life was like on the outside. It was particularly chilling to learn that he'd taken his cellmate's advice and sought out single mothers with children who hit his fantasy point. And he had the patience of a crocodile. Over an eighteen-month to two-year period he befriended some single mothers, and finally one of them felt comfortable enough to leave her child in his care so she could go out with friends. The monster gloated in his letters that he was successfully grooming the child because he was now regarded as 'uncle'. He was pleased that the family trusted him and was about to escalate his plan to have sex with the child, as the child was now comfortable enough to lie alongside him in bed as he read stories.

From Canberra we referred the matter to the relevant state police and they wasted no time in taking the appropriate action. However, there were many important messages to come from that correspondence: he was galvanised by his time in prison because he'd found a confidante; the confidante mentored him on how to access children; being sent to prison did not stop him from seeking out children to satisfy his sexual fantasies; he won the trust of a mother and committed himself to a two-year process of grooming a child for sex. And that is the hallmark of a paedophile – they never take their eyes off the prize.

These days police face the demands of a media that operates on a 24/7 news cycle, which can be a problem. Despite my upset with the old *Hinch* tabloid television program, overall my dealings with the media have been great, and I have a high regard for many journalists. Getting to know them I've realised that they do their job for the right reasons: to unearth the truth; to keep the bastards honest; and to inform the public about the machinations in the corridors of power. I believe a robust media is healthy for our society, even though that opinion was challenged during one case I worked on. We were set to arrest a school teacher from an exclusive private school for possessing child exploitation material. When arch rival media companies NewsCorp and Fairfax caught wind of the story, it became a huge yarn, and despite my pleas for both newspapers to do nothing until we'd affected the arrest, both seemed determined to run the story. Regardless of the consequences, they were hell bent on beating each other to the punch. While that might be great for sales or hits on their websites, it would've all but destroyed our chance of getting a conviction.

Ultimately, to ensure our case wasn't harmed, I met with the editors of both newspapers, and while they appreciated the seriousness of my dilemma, the general distrust between the organisations was reminiscent of what I would later witness between warring factions in Afghanistan. Finally, to get them to shake hands and agree to hold off on running the story, I arranged to make the arrest at a time that, apart from being exclusive for the papers, was also convenient for their respective deadlines. I felt caught between a rock and a hard place. If I didn't agree I risked having the case blown out of the water. These kinds of challenges in contemporary policing are not generally known or understood by either the courts or the public, and they make an already stressful job even more so.

If a police officer asks a member of the public for their personal details, there's every chance they'll cry 'civil liberties' and demand to know why Big Brother wants to watch them. What many people don't realise, however, is that the poor cop is asking for a valid reason, such as completing an incident report. Strangely, those same people don't think twice about sharing their details – and often much more – on social media or other internet platforms. The carelessness with which many people, especially children, use Facebook, Twitter, Instagram and the like is manna from heaven for a predator. I was shocked when a friend posted photos of his naked infant child splashing about in a blow-up plastic pool. The nature of the photographs was innocent, and when I asked him why they were on Facebook he explained it was so his parents in England could see their grandchild. He couldn't grasp why I suggested he delete them and use private messaging to share such shots in the future, so I had to tell him in the crudest manner that there are paedophiles who'll see those photographs and find them arousing. Anyone who posts a photo of a child on social media should keep that in mind. As I say, it was a blunt, crude way to make him understand, but my friend took the tip and deleted every photo he'd posted of his child.

As parents our job is to protect our kids, and the first step is to educate them about the dangers of the internet. When my eldest daughter, Emilee, turned 15, I did an exercise with her to highlight how much personal information she'd posted on social media. When I asked her how many people she thought had access to her personal information, like all kids she laughed it off, saying only her friends were interested in that stuff. We then pretended to be bad guys wanting to find out about her. After going through her social media accounts we had her full name and her date of birth. We knew the school she attended, the bus route she took, and the times she went to school and returned home. We also found out her address and through her posts we easily ascertained when Emilee's mother wasn't at home. At the end of it Emilee realised how easy she'd made life for a would-be stalker or identity thief. Her response of 'holy crap' said it all. It's imperative kids understand that if they upload explicit photographs of themselves, the digital footprint is there forever. By the same token, trusting a boyfriend or girlfriend with a compromising photograph is courting danger too; once they share the image, no one has control of where it might end up or what it might be used for. We all need to be smarter.

One way to become better informed about this growing problem is to visit the AFP-run website www.thinkuknow.org.au. ThinkUKnow is an evidence-based cyber safety program that provides information on the technologies young people use, the challenges they may face, and importantly, how these can be overcome. It has been around since 2009 and is based on the UK's highly acclaimed Child and Exploitation Centre. I've recommended this site to a lot of people because I believe it provides tools anyone can use to create a safer online environment for the young people in their care.

On a personal note, it concerns me that there are paedophiles who are adamant they are no different to homosexuals, and attempt to justify that man-to-boy or man-to-girl relationships fall under the category of 'love is love'. But it's an insult to gay people that child molesters think they are one and the same. Paedophilia is not love; it's exploitation. And it destroys lives.

The biggest issue I believe that needs to be examined by our lawmakers is how far they're prepared to go to protect children from someone who, while they mightn't have a criminal record for offending against children, displays all the characteristics of a child molester.

I raise this point because although police officers are expected to keep the community safe, they'd risk getting into serious trouble if, when asked to screen someone who'd applied to work with children, they warned the organisation to steer clear of that particular person even though they didn't appear on the Child Sex Offenders Register. Sometimes red flags are raised during such screenings, but under Australian law it doesn't matter if someone appears predisposed to being attracted to children; the only way they can be blocked from working with kids is if their name appears on the register.

That rule makes it very difficult for government bodies, such as the Department of Foreign Affairs and Trade (DFAT) – the nature of their work in developing countries means it can attract questionable people because it provides access to vulnerable children. In my experience, the majority of people who work for DFAT are great ambassadors for our country;

they do their job for the right reasons and they certainly make a difference. However, over the years the AFP has investigated some DFAT employees. One former employee who lived in a village in Thailand was being investigated after allegations were made that he'd groomed local children by providing funds to educate them. However, he'd paid off the villagers to protect him. It wasn't a lot of money, but it was enough to buy their silence when we started asking pertinent questions. In the end he denied us the opportunity of nabbing him by committing suicide.

The quandary for DFAT is that it may have intelligence that suggests a candidate's character is questionable, but warning bells often amount to nothing. DFAT won't stand a chance if they're taken to court and a candidate says they have shown bias in their decision. We've seen organisations accused of bias, and while I don't doubt they overlooked candidates because of concerns for the welfare of the children who'd be at risk, they were heavily scrutinised by the court, and sometimes even berated for acting 'unfairly'. I'm well aware I could be heavily sanctioned for advising a humanitarian organisation not to take on a particular candidate because of information I'd unearthed during the screening process. But this is problematic. Under the law, a person is either guilty of a crime or they're not – there's no in-between, and I'd welcome more debate in regard to the in-between, especially if there's the possibility of a child being harmed.

I mention humanitarian organisations because in the immediate aftermath of the 2004 Boxing Day tsunami in Indonesia and surrounding countries there was a rush of

Me, aged 19 months.

Mum, Dad, Jenelle, aged 22 months, and me, 3 years.

Nan and my beloved Pa.

Opening ceremony at the 1982 Seoul (Junior) International Open, where I won the bronze in shot-put.

Throwing the hammer at Interclub, E.S. Marks Athletics Field, Sydney, 1989.

Playing rugby for the Woy Woy Lions, late 1980s.

The Australian bobsleigh team at St Moritz, Switzerland, competing on the 1991–92 World Cup circuit. *L to R:* Justin McDonald, me, Ted Polglaze, Jason Giobbi, John Trutwin.

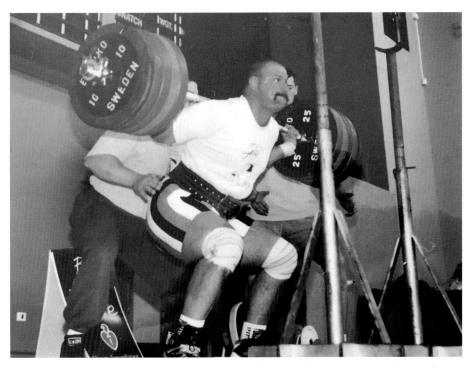

I took up powerlifting in 1994 as a stress reliever and in 1995 was pleasantly surprised to win the NSW title and place second at Nationals.

Above: World Series Strongman, 1997 at the Sydney Royal Easter Show. I'm in the centre, third from the right.

Right: World's Strongest Man, Malta, 1999, doing the loading event – 90kg sand bags.

Below: Lordy assisting as I pull a Boeing C-17 Globemaster III at the Dover Air Force Base, 2017. (© *Dudley Little/Alamy Stock Photo*)

Australian Federal Police class 5/85. Sadly, since 2016 I have been the only one left standing.

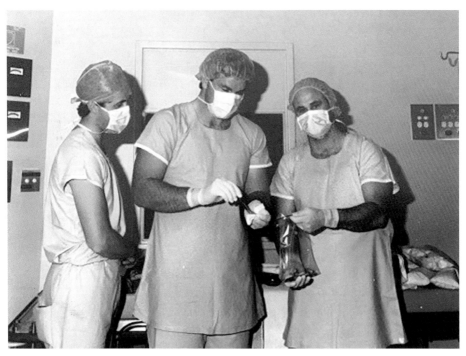

Overseeing surgery on a drug courier during my time in the drug squad.

With the Prime Minister of Timor-Leste, Xanana Gusmão, 2009, at his home celebrating the 10-year anniversary of liberation.

Children at the Timor orphanage we supported, 2008.

In Timor. *L to R:* Brigadier Bill Sowrey ADF – CO for the International Security Assistance Force, AFP Station Sergeant Melia Zelonko – attached to UN, UN Police Commissioner Luis Carrilho, me, Police Commissioner of the National Police Force of East Timor (PNTL) and former Prosecutor General Longuinhos Monteiro, Deputy PNTL Police Commissioner Afonso De Jesus, c. 2009.

Handing over specialist equipment in conjunction with the European Policing Mission to assist the Afghanistan National Police in investigating crimes against women, 2013.

My last photo in Afghanistan as I leave on completion of my mission, 2013.

With my wife, Lordy, in our beloved Green Bay Packers NFL football team jerseys.

Above: With my daughters, Emilee aged 22 and Jacinta 4 years, 2014.

Left: Emilee and Jacinta, 2018.

people volunteering to help. The majority were big-hearted and decent citizens. While organisations needed people on the ground urgently, one in particular contacted us because they'd heard 'Person X' and 'Citizen Z' weren't of good character. All we could do, however, was reply that neither of them appeared on the Child Sex Offenders Register. The charity asked again whether they needed to be careful, and again all we could do was play a straight bat and tell them we couldn't say yes or no. Believe me, that was very tough. An officer could take the risk and say *they* wouldn't allow so-and-so within a mile of the organisation, but it would be at a huge personal risk. If the applicant took the organisation in question to court (because volunteers have employment rights), the trouble could fall back on the police officer.

As I see it, this is wrong. Some days I really struggled with not being able to say anything, and I felt sorry for the group I was dealing with because I thought they deserved full disclosure, but our hands were – and still are – tied. It's a situation that needs to be scrutinised. In this age of litigation and accountability, I have no doubt the day will come when a volunteer commits a child sex crime after going through the screening process, and there'll be hell to pay if it's found that police could have saved a child from being molested by telling an organisation why they wouldn't personally endorse that particular applicant. Unfortunately, it sometimes takes a court action and bad publicity to introduce common sense.

20
THE STRONG MAN

*'What we face may look insurmountable. But I learned
something from all those years of training and competing.
I learned something from all those sets and reps when I
didn't think I could lift another ounce of weight. What
I learned is that we are always stronger than we know . . .'*
– Arnold Schwarzenegger, Seven-time Mr Olympia

I was almost seventeen when I started lifting weights during my school lunch hour with my PE teacher, Peter Hadfield. Apart from wanting to build up my muscles, I threw myself into strength training because it was a fantastic way to release the stresses from my home life. I actively looked for ways to escape the madness at our place. I thought drinking alcohol in the pub was a way out, but I realised that was a dead-end solution before too much damage was done. When I was in Year 11 I was fascinated by the traditional Chinese practice of tai chi after hearing someone on the radio extol its stress-busting benefits. This person said it was a natural way to reduce what I'd later learn were my bouts of anxiety and stress, so I bought a book on it. I devoured the pages covering meditation and breathing exercises, and they helped a bit. However, as a kid full of testosterone and teenage angst, nothing cleared my head quite like hitting the gym and heaving heavy metal. It was the same calmness I gained from throwing the shot-put.

I hurled myself into weight training and spent a fortune buying bodybuilding magazines imported from America, including *Muscle and Fitness* and *Iron Man*. I'd read articles about the techniques used behind the Iron Curtain to develop explosive power and strength. I also learnt about the emphasis Eastern Bloc nations were placing on psychology. They believed a strong mind was as important as a strong body, and that made sense to me. I became so interested in the mental side of sport that I even saw a sports psychologist when I was 18. I took a lot out of the session – it centred around the value of goal-setting and techniques to build self-belief, but the sessions were too expensive for me to continue.

My fascination with strength meant Channel Nine's *Wide World of Sports*, which aired during the late 1970s, was part of my television diet because it showed strongman contests from overseas. Mum and Jenelle knew not to disturb me as I'd stretch out on the lounge, transfixed by creatures of gargantuan proportions doing things that wouldn't have looked out of place in a superhero comic book. Big men with gigantic personalities, I watched in awe as they heaved – and even threw – what would be immovable objects for mere mortals. I was a huge fan of England's two-time Commonwealth Games shot-put champion Geoff Capes because of my passion for shot. A three-time Olympian, Capes actually became better known around the world for his strongman feats. He had incredible strength in his hands and arms, and he did things like tear a London telephone directory in half with the same ease as a child ripping a sheet of paper. I even tried doing it to a telephone book in one of the phone booths that stood near the East Hills train station to see how hard it was – but failed miserably. Capes won two World's Strongest Man titles, but his raw strength was mesmerising: bench pressing 300 kilos and squatting 380 kilos.

Other people were equally impressive, including the American world champion powerlifter Bill Kazmaier and Lou Ferrigno, who starred alongside the actor Bill Bixby in the 1970s television show *The Incredible Hulk*. Then, of course, there was the Icelandic warrior, Jón Páll Sigmarsson. Many aficionados consider Sigmarsson the world's greatest ever strongman, despite his dying at 32 after suffering cardiac arrest during a 1993 training session at his gym.

I'd watch our television and imagine how cool it would be to be strong enough to do such things as the 'Loading Race', where contestants ran 50 metres then packed several objects weighing between 100 and 163 kilos onto the back of a truck. In the 'Keg Toss', they attempted to hurl a beer keg or a kettle bell over a 4.42-metre bar. For the 'Vehicle Pull', anything from a tram, truck, bus or plane was dragged 30 metres. The jewel in the crown, the 'McGlashen Stones', featured five round stones weighing between 100 and 150 kilos (they're 200 kilos these days!) being lifted from the ground and put on top of a barrel. It was all incredible stuff, and the strongmen enjoyed a huge following around the world. However, there was one reality about my new heroes that I needed to wrestle with. Apart from being great entertainers and highlighting the power and explosiveness humans are capable of, some of them were chemically assisted.

When I retired from bobsleigh in 1994, I was transferred from Sydney to Canberra to work in internal investigation. The work, the weight I was putting on, the study I needed to do for the degree in anthropology that I'd started in 1993 at the University of Newcastle and my failing marriage meant I needed an outlet to release the stresses that were weighing me down. I couldn't take any time off work to recharge my batteries because I'd chewed up all of my leave attempting to qualify for the Olympics. Maree and I were paying off a mortgage, making it impossible for me to go without pay. I took up powerlifting in the hope that I'd enjoy the same benefits from weightlifting and throwing the shot-put as I had as a schoolboy. My biomechanics meant I was at a far greater disadvantage than shorter folk, because tall powerlifters have longer legs and arms. Any lifts we attempt require 'greater absolute strength' than a shorter person because we need to lift the weight further. With that in mind, in 1995 I was pleasantly surprised to win the New South Wales title before finishing second in the under-125 kilo division at the National Championships.

After relocating to Canberra, I was able to complete my degree at the Australian National University, and that gave me access to the campus gymnasium. Most cops study law and psychology, but I was interested in anthropology because it studies how societies evolve over time. I was shocked when some of my superiors questioned my decision, but I pointed out that we police society, so it would be advantageous to have someone who'd studied the norms and values of societies. They still scratched their heads, but my degree gave me an advantage over 200 candidates in 1996 when I applied to be posted in the AFP's bureau in Los Angeles.

While I was using the gym I met David Huxley, a hammer thrower who I'd competed against on quite a few occasions. As co-founder of the strongman group Tartan Warriors, David invited me to compete in an event at the Brigadoon Highland Games. I agreed to compete in the Bundanoon Stones, Australia's answer to Scotland's *Clach cuid fir* – or the 'Manhood Stones' – which for many centuries has been used to test an individual's strength. I had enough on my plate, but this was my chance to do what I'd dreamt of as a kid – try and emulate big Geoff Capes and the crew!

When I arrived at the 1995 Brigadoon Highland Gathering in the NSW Southern Highlands township of Bundanoon, it had been transformed into William Wallace's – aka Braveheart's – Scotland from the early 1300s. Despite the ominous grey clouds and chilly weather, there were 15,000 people celebrating all things Scottish, many of them dressed in kilts. Bagpipes blared, traditional dancers kicked up a storm and food stalls sold such Caledonian delicacies as haggis and shortbread. The odd drop of whisky was also consumed – but that was only the half of it!

As part of the Tartan Warriors, I found myself in a veritable Land of the Giants, competing against the likes of former World Strongest Man winners Jamie Reeves from England and Gary Taylor, the Welsh Dragon. It was an invitation-only event, and we cast a large shadow. Even though I weighed 119 kilos, I was the 'wee laddie' of the troupe. Taylor strained the scales at 139 kilos, and Reeves was 150 kilos of prime British beef. Other competitors included Andy Andersson from Scotland, Colin Cox from New Zealand and Wayne Price from South Africa, all of whom would have easily qualified for the 130-140-kilo weight category. I took in the sights and sounds, and probably laughed a little too loudly when I heard a proud Scotsman reply 'the future of Scotland' when a woman asked what was under his kilt. I was flying.

The Manhood Stones event had been part of the World's Strongest Man competitions in the 1980s, and I vividly remembered how the likes of Sigmarsson and Capes had manhandled the stones, which were named after the Scotsman, McGlashen, who carved the first set of lifting stones. The stones used at Bundanoon were carved from sandstone from a local quarry and placed in front of five evenly spaced old whisky barrels. The steel legs at the bottom and the truck tyres placed on top of each of the barrels meant we needed to lift the boulders to a height of 1.5 metres, and then run 5 metres to the next station to repeat the feat. The winner was whoever successfully completed the course in the least amount of time. At 110 kilos, the first stone was the lightest; the others went up in increments of 10 kilos, with the heaviest being 150 kilos.

I was still coming to grips with what was expected when Huxley said I'd be the first out of the blocks. Shocked, I protested. I'd never done anything like this event before and wanted to see how the more experienced blokes performed. But Huxley didn't seem too concerned and dismissed me with a wave of his hand, saying that seeing as I'd watched the event on television as a kid I ought to know what to do. Of course, it was harder than it looked, but as the first man up, waiting for the signal to start, I was keen to avoid embarrassing myself in front of a massive crowd and some of the strongest men on the planet.

I don't mind admitting that I was intimidated by the behemoths who were to follow me. My main goal was to not look out of place, so I decided to go as slow as I had to. I surprised myself by double-lifting (a two-movement lift) and loading the first two stones without too much trouble. When I lifted the 130-kilo boulder, however, I felt my hands, legs, core and everywhere in between strain. My back was screaming. When I picked up the 140-kilo rock it felt as though my internal organs were being crushed, but I managed to get it on top of the barrel. The fifth one defeated me though. Despite my best efforts and the urging of the crowd, I couldn't budge the 150-kilo monster and waved the white flag.

However, my sense of achievement at lifting and loading the first four stones turned into a triumph of sorts when Taylor, the 1993 World Strongman champion, was the only competitor to complete the entire set. It was exhilarating, and the euphoria I felt was intoxicating. When Huxley paid me $200 and asked whether I wanted another crack the following day at Sydney's Darling Harbour, I said yes. Of course, I hadn't taken into consideration how my body would react to the shock I'd just put it through. By the following morning I'd seized up and was walking like the Tin Man from *The Wizard of Oz*. I was so stiff and sore, it hurt just to move. However, there was no way I was going to back out; I'd given Huxley my word. When I saw the large mob that had gathered to watch us compete, I fed off their energy. To my amazement, I somehow repeated my feat of lifting four stones. But I also had to do the 'Farmer's Walk', which is carrying 100 kilos of weight in each hand, and that destroyed me.

Even though I wouldn't be able to walk properly for the better part of the next week, I loved 'the stones'. They were the iconic strongman event, and I worked hard to master them. As I drove home to Canberra I realised I'd discovered another sporting passion. And a new personal challenge was born: I wanted to become Australia's strongest man. To achieve that ambition I needed to be selfish, and that included eating so much that there were times I couldn't bear to look at food, let alone shovel yet another spoonful of tinned rice down my throat.

Huxley – who made the *Guinness Book of Records* for dragging a 38-tonne Concorde jet 12.19 metres across the tarmac at London's Heathrow Airport – was a great promoter. Through his efforts we were sponsored by Weet-Bix and ran a Strongman series during the Sydney Royal Easter Show. With the full support of my superiors I was a part of the Tartan Warriors from 1994–2000, giving up at 38 when my body said 'enough'.

We travelled around New South Wales for exhibitions and competitions at Westfield shopping centres. Channel Nine picked us up and we appeared on all of their top-rating programs, such as *The Footy Show*, fronted by former rugby league internationals Paul Vautin and Peter Sterling; *Kerri-Anne* with Kerri-Anne Kennerley; and *Hey Hey It's Saturday*. We were considered a 'freaky fun thing' by TV executives, and our many stunts included carrying Daryl Somers onto the set of *Hey Hey It's Saturday* as if he were a Roman Emperor.

We enjoyed an enormous amount of publicity in the mainstream media, and as a result of the Tartan Warriors' popularity, I had a regular stint on Canberra radio, updating the listeners about our latest feats and antics. We had some outstanding characters, one of the most colourful being the big, bold, jovial Englishman Jamie Reeves, who was always cracking jokes. Another brilliant character was my fellow Aussie Mike Sidonio, known as the world's strongest astronomer, who in more recent times discovered a galaxy! We were all competitive and wanted to win, but at the completion of the day's events we'd all enjoy a meal and a few beers, and laugh together.

Channel Nine broadcast our events of a weekend and assigned a genuine heavyweight to head the commentary team in the larger-than-life Darrell Eastlake, whose booming voice revolutionised how weightlifting was called. 'Big Darrell' was joined by a young bloke from Brisbane named Leigh Diffey, who now works in America as NBC's motor racing and Olympic track and field commentator. The *Wide World of Sports'* Kim Watkins – whose brother Mick was an AFP colleague of mine – was assigned to help bring the event to life with her interviews. Dad loved it, and he even became my unofficial publicity officer, calling local newspapers and pitching stories to the editors about his son, the strongman. It was great to see the *World's Strongest Man* program was as popular with viewers as when I was a kid – we achieved ratings that apparently made Kerry Packer, the TV station's billionaire owner, smile.

It was impossible, however, for me to not get caught up in the strongman lifestyle. I not only grew physically – I packed on 41 kilos of muscle – but I also developed a greater mental strength through my ability to focus. And then there was the incredible sense of self-belief that came with success. Finally I'd learnt to use my mind to overcome the adversity my University of Hawaii coach, Dick Tomey, spoke about, and it was powerful. If only I'd had that awareness when I was a teenager – I might have done better at not only rugby league but also American football.

21
DOIN' THE LOCOMOTION

'He got out there and lifted heavy things, pulled things
that people would normally sit on and buy a ticket
for – and he loved it . . .'
– Kate Lord, *Australian Story* (2018)

Throughout 1996, most of my weekends were spent competing in strongman events. I could be found straining and sweating, attempting anything from the Manhood Stones to holding traditional heavy Scottish axes with outstretched arms for as long as possible. I was gaining tremendous experience by competing against quality opposition, including the likes of Ver Magnússon and my former University of Hawaii football teammate, Joe Onosai – a tribal Samoan prince who weighed 190 kilos and stood 1.95 metres – in the main arena of the Royal Sydney Easter Show. I peaked at 160 kilos in 1998, and had to step on the scales that were used to measure freight at the post office because the bathroom scales could not handle the strain when I stood on them. News of our feats travelled around the world. The British television program *Record Breakers*, a BBC 1 institution, sent Cheryl Baker (most people of my vintage would remember Cheryl from the 1980s English band Bucks Fizz) and a production crew to Sydney. They were putting together their 25th anniversary program, and were hoping to capture some vision of new world records being created for feats of strength such as pulling the 386-tonne replica of William Bligh's *HMS Bounty* (built for the 1984 movie *Mutiny on The Bounty*, starring Mel Gibson) on Sydney Harbour, completing the Manhood Stones event or dragging a 201-tonne steam train – complete with the coal and water trucks – over 14 metres.

It was exciting, but by the time I was to pull the train I was in the mood to rip the thing apart and turn it into scrap metal. I was feeling frustrated. After setting a new world record the day before by dragging the *Bounty* across the 25-metre course in 2 minutes 16 seconds, I lost my place in the *Guinness Book of Records* when the last competitor bettered my time by less than a tenth of a second. So I descended upon Thirlmere, a quiet semirural town about 90 kilometres south-west of Sydney's CBD, with the intention of doing something special at the New South Wales Rail Museum. The event was held during the school holidays and my nephew Stephen, as well as my former sister-in-law Tracey's four kids, were among the army of school children *Record Breaker*'s producers had bussed into the township. I overheard the director prepping the kids on when to cheer: 'If anyone gets near the world record mark of 14 metres I really want you all to go berserk!'

When the time came, their cheering broke my heart. I'd arrived with intentions to destroy the museum's pride 'n' joy, but as I stood next to the mighty nineteenth-century wheel and piston locomotive, I couldn't help but wonder how anyone would be able to move it, let alone break the world record. As I was preparing to move his train, the engineer climbed down from the cabin with a concerned look on his face. He addressed all of the competitors and said he was terrified – if anyone slipped, he'd run them over because the nose of the train was so long he wouldn't be able to see us. 'Boys,' he gasped, 'mark my words, this baby will destroy you.'

I told him not to worry because we had guides walking on either side of us and they'd alert him if one of us slipped. But the engineer still looked nervous when he climbed back into the cabin.

I was first off the rank. After fitting into my five-point harness, looking like a parachutist and connected by a wire to 210 tonnes of heavy-duty steel, I positioned myself on the *Guinness Book of Records*-approved five-rung ladder, which had been laid flat on the ground to provide us with a staging point to kick off our challenges. When the starting whistle sounded, I remembered the advice Ver Magnússon had shared with me during the bus trip from Sydney. He'd suggested I 'caress' the train gently, as though it was my lover. Rather than being crude or forceful, I needed to treat it tenderly because the train would respond more favourably to a gentle touch. I knew it was left-field thinking, but because of Ver Magnússon's standing in the sport I was all ears. Besides, our chat confirmed everything I'd heard about his outstanding success being due at least in part to his intelligent, scientific approach to the sport.

I used the strength in my hips and legs and moved the train an inch. As I continued to strain and pull forward, it moved a couple more. Those inches slowly but surely turned into a foot. I built up momentum by utilising my height to grab each track of the ladder and pull the train with my arms, The foot became a metre. Once I'd clawed past the last rung of the ladder, I found that taking little steps was the best way to keep going. On one side of the track Ver Magnússon was ordering me to 'caress it'; on the other was Cheryl Baker, screaming wonderful encouragement with each step.

The organisers had clearly identified the world record mark, and while I occasionally looked up and saw it getting closer, I continued to be the tender lover, concentrating on every small step. I had another quick peek ahead. The record was now within my grasp. All I needed was to edge the front of the engine over and it was mine. Then the kids started to cheer. It felt awesome to see them raise their arms above their heads in celebration. Inspired, I felt as though I could pull the train to Couridjah, the next station on the disused Picton–Mittagong loop line . . . but then the train came to a sudden halt. *What the hell has happened?* I thought as I drove my leg forward again. But . . . nothing. *Come on, lover, I was so tender!*

I strained and I pulled, but it refused to budge. Perhaps there was a rock on the track stopping my progress. I strained again. *Nothing.* In my bones I felt I needed to prevent any of the other six from bettering my effort. I gritted my teeth and gave another mighty surge. *Nothing!* Then the producer yelled for me to stop pulling and explained that the driver had applied the brake. I was crushed. Through absolutely no fault of my own, my chance at a big world record was over – and it felt cruel.

My outrage eventually turned to understanding when the driver apologised. He explained that he'd stopped the train because, in 'rail speak', when someone raises both arms in the air it means there's an emergency. So when he saw a few hundred arms shoot into the air his instinct kicked in and he thought I'd fallen over. It was an honest mistake, and while I was bitterly disappointed I told the engineer it was okay. After all, he'd said before the competition started that our wellbeing was his only priority, not world records.

I watched as the other competitors took their turn, and I was happy to see them retire before reaching my mark. I decided to ask the organisers if I could have another crack, feeling I still had a bit left in my tank. I was annoyed when they told me that was dependent upon the other competitors giving their consent. It wasn't my fault that I had stopped. It says a lot about the character of the other competitors that they agreed to my request. So after the last of the contenders, Wayne Price, a powerful 150-kilo South African, dragged the train 28 metres to double the distance I'd established in my first attempt, I prepared for my second go. It was a massive effort as I once again summoned Ver Magnússon's advice to be the perfect lover. These days I smile when I wonder what on earth people must've thought as he yelled, 'Treat her tenderly, Grant.'

The second time around I was more comfortable with what I needed to do. I chanted to myself, 'I think I can . . . I think I can', from the children's story *The Little Engine That Could* – which helped me remain calm. In the end, the only reason I didn't continue was because the slag hadn't been cleared after 37 metres because they didn't think anyone would be able to go beyond that. Even so, I was exhausted and collapsed face-first into the dirt and stones, with Cheryl screaming into the television camera, 'I can't believe what I have just seen!' It had taken me 1 minute and 16 seconds to pull the train 36.8 metres, and I was thrilled that it was ratified by Guinness as a world record.

All up I spent four years as an amateur strongman, and while it is one part of my life that many people want to talk to me about, my body took a battering as I pushed the limits. During a competition at Darling Harbour in 1998 I dropped a 200-kilo block of sandstone on my ankle during the 'Carry and Drag' event. It was my own fault; I took too much of a run-up and lost my footing. When the block fell the pain was so intense I feared I'd shattered my ankle, which immediately blew up like a balloon. Thankfully it wasn't broken, but I'd damaged all of the ligaments and tendons. I had a six-week, around-the-clock battle to take my place in the Australia's Strongest Man competition – and I got there. Then in 1998, I attempted a second train pull in Canberra – a 220-tonne monster – but collapsed in agony when I felt something go in my lower leg. The ACT's chief minister Kate Carnell, who was also a pharmacist, was in attendance that day. After taking a quick look she correctly diagnosed that I'd suffered a lateral tear of my right Achilles' tendon.

I also lost a chunk from my right pectoral muscle when it tore as I bench pressed 200 kilos at training. I've torn my quadricep muscle, suffered multiple hamstring tears, and I've had to undergo ankle surgery and a number of knee operations. I also have three herniated discs in my back as a legacy of competing in strongman events. But despite the pain and the gruelling recoveries, I can't complain because the sport opened many doors for me.

Sport was important because I learnt great values, such as integrity, and even time management. Being a member of a team meant I had a role, and we were only as strong as the weakest link. Playing on rugby league, soccer and American football teams taught me not to be selfish, and to appreciate that my actions affected every other person on the side. I also learnt through team sport to celebrate other people's successes, even when they overshadowed mine.

Competing as an athlete and strongman was the opposite. I realised there were times when I needed to be selfish, because despite having wonderful coaches, I was on my own whenever I entered the thrower's circle or braced to pick up the Manhood Stones. I learnt the importance of self-discipline, training hard and giving my all because if I failed due to a poor effort there was no-one to blame but myself. Sport countered what was happening at home, where, through Mum's general poor taste in men and our home becoming a drop-in centre for drug addicts and criminals, I was exposed to what today's youth would describe as 'losers'.

I remember the pride I felt when I was presented with the very first Canberra tartan to wear when I competed in the World Highland Games Championships in Scotland. The highlight of my trip there in 1997 was winning the Scottish heavy throws contest at the Rosneath and Clynder Highland Games. Among other achievements, I successfully pulled a RAAF C130 Hercules, a 78-tonne mining truck, the steam engine in Thirlmere, a New Zealand tram and an 18-tonne semi-trailer, which I pulled by rope hand-over-hand. I also succeeded in pulling the majestic *HMS Bounty* for a second time.

In 1999 I was fortunate to be granted leave from my work yet again so I could compete at the World's Strongest Man competition in Malta, although by then I'd be based in Los Angeles in a completely different role. After collecting my athlete's ID, the event's medical staff asked me to provide them with a full and detailed list of the 'stuff' I was 'on'. I rattled off the *legal* nutrients and supplements that were part of my daily existence. One of the medicos must've thought I was worried about possible recriminations; after all, I weighed 140 kilos and looked BIG. When I repeated the list, he interrupted me: 'No, you don't understand. We only test for recreational drugs, but it's important we know what steroids you're on.'

The question threw me, and I'm sure I bristled. Even these days as a competitor in the over-50 age group in masters athletic events, I pride myself on being clean – always have. As both a police officer and an athlete, it's in my DNA to be anti-drugs, regardless of whether they're cocaine, methamphetamines, heroin or the performance-enhancing variety. My stance stretches back to my childhood. When I was 13, two no-hopers who used our place as a drop-in centre hid their marijuana in the lounge room. They intended to sell it later that day at the pub. I was lying on the couch, pretending to be asleep as they stashed it under the cushions on our other couch. I disposed of it when they left. Fortunately, neither was smart enough to realise I'd taken it, because I would've copped a terrible hiding. I did it for two reasons. I was always scared that if the police raided our house and found drugs, it would be Mum, and not the no-hopers, who'd be sent to prison. Secondly, I was angry that they treated our place the way they did. I thought our home was constantly disrespected by people who weren't respected. When I joined the police force I saw the damage drugs did to the community, and I wanted to get them off the streets. Drug barons aren't worried about the human cost of their trade. They don't care that users will suffer terrible health complaints – even death. They don't think about the anguish they cause the families who'll do whatever it takes to try and get a loved one off drugs. It doesn't bother them that drug users will stoop to such degradations as prostituting themselves to fund their next hit. While drug barons and dealers see dollar signs, emergency workers contend with the real price that's paid by people addicted to drugs.

In my opinion, doping has always been the domain of the cheat – people who steal the glory of winning by gaining an unfair advantage over athletes who are otherwise better than them. In my early days as a young constable in Sydney I'd worked in a covert capacity to root out supplies of steroids, but there wasn't the same desire to investigate them then as there is today, now that criminal networks are involved in the distribution. That said, as a strongman competitor I was never torn about competing against athletes who were pumped up on chemicals, because everyone knew it was tolerated. If anyone wanted to match it with the *really* big boys, they could swallow the same pills or inject the same gunk into their bloodstream.

However, while the blokes who took anabolic steroids did so to build lean muscle and body weight without increasing their fat mass, they did this at a great risk to their health. It's been well documented that athletes who rely on 'gym candy', 'pumpers' and steroids for their edge are vulnerable to an array of potentially fatal health issues, including liver trauma, tumours, cysts, kidney disease, shrinking testicles, heart disease, heart attack, stroke, male infertility, and menstrual irregularities and excess facial hair in women. While I can't understand why anyone would take such drugs, I was motivated by the goal of making the world's top 30 as a clean athlete. That would be a victory in itself! So that day in Malta, after the medico picked up his pad, having assured me everything was okay, I repeated the list of the World Anti-Drug Agency-approved nutrients and supplements I used. And I made sure he realised I was 100 per cent clean by stressing, 'I DON'T DO DRUGS.'

Some strongmen have paid the ultimate price for their choices, but surveys over recent years show there are still athletes who'll risk everything. A high proportion answer 'yes' when asked whether they'd take drugs if it guaranteed them the gold medal or a world title, even if it meant risking death ten years after the victory celebration. Their preparedness to take that risk reflects the mindset of some elite athletes who'll live – or die – for glory. From 1996–1999, when I reigned as Australia's Strongest Man, we were drug-tested under the terms of our sponsorship agreement with Sanitarium. While we set the standard, such testing was never going to happen globally because the 'freak' nature of the event drew sponsorship as well as media exposure overseas. My winning Australia's Strongest Man guaranteed my passage to the World's Strongest Man competition, which was an incredible experience and a chance to lock horns with some big names, including Sweden's defending champion Magnus Samuelsson, Finland's Jouko Ahola and Janne Virtanen, as well as the charismatic Norwegian, Svend Karlsen, who'd habitually scream 'Viking Power!' during the competition.

That year, I injured my right hamstring in the Lift and Load event, and when I faced off against Samuelsson in the 'crucifix hold', I struggled just to climb onto the platform, let alone hold the two stone pillars, each of which weighed 175 kilos, for as long as possible. While it was all deadly serious – you'd see guys psyching themselves up by yelling, beating their chests and using smelling salts – there were still opportunities for sportsmanship. Before we were to compete I heard that Samuelsson didn't have hand chalk, which absorbs the sweat, allowing you to get a better hold on the stirrup-shaped grips we used to keep the pillars upright. I shared mine with the Swede, despite knowing it could help him beat me.

I was the first competitor up, and as the television commentators spoke about how the pillars tested 'strength, stamina and character', I was determined to set a reasonable time. And even though I was injured, I didn't want to finish last. This turned out to be a source of great inspiration. My then 6-year-old daughter Emilee was in the crowd that day screaming her support, and I wanted to show her to never give up, even when things are against you. It was good to have Emilee there for moral support. Things weren't good on the home front; Maree and I were engaged in a Cold War. I didn't feel she was supporting me as I wanted to be supported, be it in the police force or as a strongman competitor – even though I was excelling in both fields. We'd stayed together in the belief it was the best thing for Emilee. I think the reason I hung in when the writing was on the wall stemmed back to my childhood. I thought I'd missed out on something by not living under the same roof as both of my parents, and I didn't want my daughter to experience that.

I managed to hold the pillars for 37.8 seconds, and I held my breath as the other four competitors tried to better my time. The Scotsman Jamie Barr let go after 34.53 seconds, and while Samuelsson growled like a demon summoning the hounds of hell, he let go after 36.49 seconds. I was awarded six competition points as the event winner.

However, Samuelsson, the defending champion, turned the tables when we were pitted against one another in the Log Lift, an event where you lift a 140-kilo log above your head and then repeat this until you reach ten lifts. He defeated me 10–2. There's no question he was a powerhouse, but my injured hamstring meant I didn't have the foundation needed to lift and heave something so heavy. Not finishing in the top ten meant I didn't qualify for the finals, but in terms of the World's Strongest Man competition, to this day I consider winning the crucifix hold my own personal gold medal.

During my time in the strongman world I was never offered steroids, but the inference from fellow competitors, as well as trainers and coaches on the circuit, was that I'd be a 'monster' or a 'beast' if I ever went down that path. Taking steroids had no appeal to me. I always found it amazing whenever I heard that a competitor in a strength sport had announced that the reason he used 'juice' was to get bigger for the cameras because he felt inferior when compared to the other competitors. I didn't have that ego problem, but I do remember how furious I felt in the late 1990s when I competed in the AFP's tug-of-war team. We defeated the team representing the ACT Brumbies Super 12 Rugby franchise and one of the footballers accused me of being a 'steroid-muncher'. We had some big and powerful men on our team, and I don't think anyone was more surprised than the Brumbies when we cops made short work of them.

The event was staged to raise funds at a well-known annual charity event held outside of Canberra at the Hall Showground. While I understood the Brumbies' pride was hurt, the foolish accusation angered me. At the time I did security (in my own time, and payment was a ticket to the footy) at the Brumbies' home games with my old boss, Superintendent Laurie Pyne – our job was to keep a quiet eye on the VIP area and ensure there weren't any problems. I supported the Brumbies. They played the game with a great spirit, despite the experts dismissing them as the 'reject' team because the squad consisted of players who weren't wanted by the NSW Waratahs or Queensland Reds. And I admired their first coach, Rod Macqueen. As well as guiding the Wallabies to the 1999 World Cup, Rod proved himself to be a great manager of men. However, the comment after the tug-of-war burnt me, and I told their chief executive at the time, Mark Sinderberry, that I thought some of their players needed to learn about being gracious in defeat. It felt good to get it off my chest, because I'm still a diehard Brumbies man and love what they've done for the game.

In 1994 when I competed in my first strongman contest I weighed 119 kilos. But after spending a fortune on food and following a regimen where I ate every 90 minutes, I ballooned to 160 kilos. For three years my life centred around my next meal, and I wasn't alone. I quickly learnt that my fellow competitors had equally monstrous appetites. After competing in a strongman event at Darling Harbour, the poor manager on duty at the Star City Casino bistro looked stricken when he announced that we'd eaten every crumb in the place! There are times when I feel physically ill just remembering how much I ate in those days. At my peak weight in 1997 I was eating eleven meals a day, adding up to 6000 calories – three times the daily recommended amount for a healthy adult male. I took four tins of creamed rice into work every day. It reached the point where I couldn't bear looking at the stuff, let alone shovelling yet another spoonful into my mouth. I learnt about the weight-gaining qualities of tinned creamed rice from an English trainer. His job was to help prepare us for the World Series Strongman event, and he shook his head when he saw that my diet was low in fat and high in carbohydrates. After explaining to him that I struggled to stomach the amount of food required to become as big as my rivals, he recommended that I eat four tins of creamed rice a day because it's extremely dense in calories. The fat contained in the cream was just as beneficial as the carbohydrates from the rice. It was also simple to eat – the only preparation was opening the tin. However, I haven't touched a grain of the stuff since I gave up competing as a strongman!

It should come as no surprise that I was also living proof of Arnold Schwarzenegger's theory that 'what goes in must come out'. While some of my colleagues took their regular smoko breaks, I would be taking one of my frequent toilet breaks.

My old meal diary from 1997 documents the carnage, but what I failed to note was the 20–25 Weet-Bix I snacked on every day. But this, in conjunction with training, is how I reached my peak weight of 160 kilos:

- **Meal 1:** A large bowl of oatmeal with banana, honey and blueberries plus a large milk coffee
- **Meal 2:** A large protein shake with milk and banana plus 4 slices of bread with peanut butter
- **Meal 3**: First large tin of creamed rice with fruit
- **Meal 4:** Two chicken breasts with pasta and vegetables
- **Meal 5:** Second large tin of creamed rice
- **Meal 6:** Large protein shake with milk; fruit; two slices of bread
- **Meal 7:** Third large tin of creamed rice
- **Meal 8:** A large steak, vegetables and bread
- **Meal 9:** A large bowl of muesli with yoghurt and fruit
- **Meal 10:** Fourth tin of creamed rice but with ice-cream and fruit
- **Meal 11:** Large protein shake with milk

As you can imagine, day-to-day life was tough. There were numerous problems with having a 40-inch waist, a 52-inch chest and 36-inch thighs. I couldn't fit into my usual clothes. Flying became a nightmare – I remember the look of horror on the face of one poor person when they realised I was about to sit next to them. I traded in our Mazda 323 for a sturdier Ford. While there were many signs I was too big for my own good, reality bit the day I went for a medical check-up and my doctor said I had a fatty liver – something that can occur in any age group but is normally found in people aged in their 40s and 50s. I was 36 at the time, and the GP pointed out that most people who had the condition are at risk of heart disease, obesity and type-2 diabetes. I immediately cut back to five meals a day and discovered I didn't need to be that heavy to perform well. In fact, after I lost the excess kilos I moved more freely and quickly.

What I love most about my time as a strongman is that I actually *made* it. When I reflect on my days as a shot-putter, my stint in American football, my shot at the Winter Olympics and even my time in the two rugby codes, I had opportunities to make it but didn't for any number of reasons. Strongman, however, allowed me to fulfil my potential. Even though I was a drug-free competitor in a sport where many competitors were full of juice, I didn't merely match them – I had my victories! My reign as Australia's Strongest Man from 1996 to 1999 was very emotional because there had been times in my life – including the night when I hid under the bed with Jenelle while Mum was bashed by a boyfriend – that I felt useless, weak and vulnerable. Time has taught me that I'm a late bloomer, and while my previous sporting endeavours had their disappointments, the lessons I gained allowed me to eventually make my mark as both an athlete and a cop.

22
LA CONFIDENTIAL

'Tip the world over on its side and everything loose will
land in Los Angeles ...'
– Frank Lloyd Wright, American architect

In 1998 I was one of 200 officers who applied for seven positions overseas. It was always my goal to work in London because it's my favourite city. I love that while the English capital is steeped in history, the city's people haven't stood still. It's vibrant and modern, and whenever I go there I feel recharged by its energy. Unfortunately, London wasn't available on this occasion, so I applied for Los Angeles. LA appealed to me because the successful candidate would be responsible for compiling intelligence on America's outlaw motorcycle gangs, and finding what influence they had (or could have) in Australia.

Normally a candidate for such a role had to be a sergeant, but I was still a constable after my fourteen years. My rank was not a reflection of a poor officer – the AFP had flattened its ranks after I joined, meaning the traditional line of progression from constable to constable first-class, to senior constable and then sergeant had changed. Under the new system my class and the ones that followed went from constable to sergeant in one leap. Eventually the brass realised it wasn't the best system and reinstated some aspects of the old one. When I was finally promoted to sergeant in 2002 I enjoyed a rapid rise through the ranks, becoming a superintendent in 2004 and then my current rank – commander – in 2006.

I was surprised by the interview process for the Los Angeles job. Normally the panel of three senior officers followed a formula where they would ask a series of questions. My interview was more like a fireside chat. I was invited to take my coat off, a superintendent then motioned for me to sit in a comfortable chair, and we talked about my interests, my sporting achievements and some of the jobs I'd worked on. It was very relaxed, and one of the panellists was interested to see I'd taken Aboriginal studies as part of my anthropology degree. He asked how I would explain to someone in the United States what the Mabo case (the landmark land rights claim made by the Meriam people of the Murray Islands, situated between Queensland and Papua New Guinea) meant for Aborigines. My response was to point out that Mabo was actually a Torres Strait Island claim, which technically meant it wasn't Aboriginal. I went on to explain the reason why the Torres Strait Islanders were able to challenge the seventeenth-century British notion that they could colonise Australia without a treaty or payment because the land belonged to no one. The Mabo case acknowledged that the Murray Islanders had continuously inhabited and exclusively possessed their lands; they'd lived in permanent and settled communities and had their own political and social organisation. The panel was impressed, saying they didn't know any of that.

I'd find out much later that the nature of the chat was to see how I'd conduct myself, because some of the people who'd been sent on overseas deployments had embarrassed the AFP. When the interview was nearing its end, I mentioned that I was surprised no one had asked me what I knew about outlaw motorcyclists because I was more than happy to discuss the Hells Angels and The Outlaws. They indulged me, but their priority was not to send a boofhead to LA.

I joined the AFP's Los Angeles office in Century City, next to Beverly Hills, as a liaison officer and quickly set about accumulating as much intelligence as I could on outlaw motorcycle gangs. I also received an unexpected crash course in undercover work. The Laughlin River Run in Nevada is the biggest gathering of bikes and bikers on the West Coast and attracts up to 70,000 people. The American law enforcement officers I was with asked me to help them obtain intelligence on a little-known gang that was there. They wanted me to pretend to be a goofy Aussie motorbike enthusiast and obtain whatever information I could. They were especially keen on names or nicknames so they could trawl through their database to identify the individuals. A female officer acted as my girlfriend, and the others waited around a corner, ready to swoop if things went pear shaped. I knew my bosses in Canberra would have had kittens if they knew what I'd agreed to do, but I did it as a show of good faith for my American colleagues.

I rocked up to the stall the gang had set up and said that I loved one of their Harley-Davidsons. The lead gang member was initially on guard, but when he realised my 'weird' accent was due to my being an Aussie, he offered me a beer.

When I cracked the can open and said 'cheers' I grinned. As we talked about our respective Harleys, women and the differences in beer, this guy had no idea he was drinking with a director of the International Outlaw Motorcycle Gang Investigators Association (IOMGIA), an honorary position that – due to my role for the AFP – allowed me to work and share information with other law enforcement agencies.

I continued to play dumb as he asked me if I knew Crocodile Hunter Steve Irwin and whether he always said 'Crikey!' The biker then introduced me to other gang members, who provided tidbits of information, including where they were based. I asked for a photograph and they obliged.

Ironically, I'd applied to join undercover operations when I was a young cop, but the hierarchy didn't believe I was cut out for it. The people who ran the department said I failed the psych test, but where and how I'd failed was never explained to me. I actually ended up running the department when a restructure meant surveillance and undercover came under intelligence collection. I was the manager for intelligence collection in 2006–07, and I'm a huge admirer of those officers selected to go undercover. It's not easy, but I found the best operators have similar traits to an actor. They throw themselves into character, and live and breathe the role as they befriend some not-so-nice folk. They're brave, but they're also human; on one occasion we needed to pull an officer out of their job because they'd become too close to the people they were watching. I understand how that can happen; people respond favourably to kindness. It's understandable that some people will feel torn about being treated well and trusted – even being invited to family events, including weddings and birthdays – by people on the wrong side of the law. However, they're police officers, and they can't lose sight of the fact that they are dealing with criminals.

While my experience in Nevada was nothing more than a twenty-minute beer and being a friendly Aussie, it added to my admiration for undercover officers. That beer effectively put the motorbike gang on the US law enforcement radar because it helped my US colleagues identify some gang members and form profiles of them. But going undercover was just one element of the work I did. During my time in Los Angeles I accumulated as much intelligence as possible on the bikers and fed it to the authorities back home. Even though there were only three inter-national outlaw motorcycle gangs in Australia at that time, it was believed American gangs were looking to branch out into South-East Asia. I also needed to keep my AFP colleagues updated about which gangs planned to do 'world runs' – and when – so the state forces could be prepared.

My posting to Los Angeles was a dream assignment, especially for someone who was only a constable. My beat was the entire West Coast, which extended to the Kansas–Missouri state line, four Canadian provinces, Hawaii, Alaska and Mexico. Besides investigating America's outlaw motorcycle gangs, I was also involved in counter-terrorism during the lead-up to the 2000 Sydney Olympics. I forged a meaningful relationship with Mexican law enforcement agencies and was the first AFP officer into Panama. There was never a dull moment. One day I could be dealing with an Australian pilot who had been caught over the limit after he was seen urinating in a bush an hour before he was meant to fly a jetliner full of people to Japan. Another day

I might be instructing a Qantas cabin crew about the dangers of wearing fake Rolexes and other bling as they walked around the dodgy area where their hotel was located. My job meant I had to do some travelling, and while my career was booming Maree hated Los Angeles. We lived in Brentwood, an affluent suburb where many movie stars reside, and Emilee seemed to love being among it. She was five and made lots of friends. We shared an 'LA moment' during one of her karate lessons. I watched as she picked up – and threw – a boy her age around the dojo as if he were a ragdoll. The boy's father was reading what looked like a script, and when he looked up to see what was happening, I said, 'That's my daughter training with your boy.' The father was the actor Dennis Quaid. He immediately picked up on my accent, and without missing a beat joked that now his boy could say he'd been 'picked up by an Aussie girl'. Lou Ferrigno's son attended Emilee's school, and while there was so much I wanted to ask about his strongman career, he seemed reluctant to engage in conversation because he was profoundly deaf. On the odd occasion we spoke he wished me well in the strongman contests, saying he hoped I enjoyed it as much as he did.

One of the most disturbing incidents I dealt with was when it was alleged that members of an AFL club had assaulted a woman while on an end-of-season trip overseas. The AFL were very supportive and provided me with everything I needed, but they were very particular about brand protection. In fact, the story didn't emerge until years later, and when it did, to me it sounded quite damning, even though no one ended up being charged.

We'd initially received a call from police after a Los Angeles woman claimed she'd been raped by a club member and some players at a hotel. I visited the woman in LA and she was clearly upset. For several reasons, the case didn't get off the ground, including the fact that there were no witnesses other than the club personnel and no corroborating information. Another issue was that the particular US police department would have had to request a mutual legal assistance treaty to obtain evidence, but once the case was deemed weak they dropped the investigation and no charges were laid.

The Sydney Olympics were less than two years away when, in 1998, I became a member of the Los Angeles Terrorism Early Warning Group because my boss, Shane Castles, said that while the motorcycle gang stuff was interesting, we were about to start looking away from it. He told me to think about what else interested me. I was busy working on drugs jobs, doing work for state forces and investigating Australian paedophiles in the US. Terrorism wasn't on Australia's radar then, but I realised the Olympics in laid-back Australia could be viewed as a soft target by terrorist groups. My intelligence work allowed me to join the Los Angeles Terrorism Early Warning Group, an invitation-only coalition of counter-terrorism specialists from law enforcement, academia and government institutions, such as the Monterey Institute of Non-nuclear Proliferation. So I wrote to its leader, John Sullivan, asking for permission to join. He put my request to the group and they allowed me to become the first foreigner to take a seat at their table. And it was there that I had my first exposure to videos smuggled out of Saddam Hussein's Iraq, which showed beheadings and the impact of chemical weapons. They made for hard viewing, seeing the terror on the faces of people about to be beheaded and the close-ups of children dying terrible deaths after being exposed to mustard gas. They're images I'll never forget. I fed the information back to Australia, but our international policing focus was on the heroin coming out of South-East Asia.

No one seemed overly concerned about the reports that suggested the greatest concern in the US in 1999 was biological attacks or water supplies being targeted. At that stage no one had considered an attack like 9/11, which would completely shake up the Western world's approach to terrorism. Even so, leading into the 2000 Olympics the US wanted an aircraft carrier anchored off the coast in case it needed to evacuate people in the unlikely event of an attack, and I was pleased to have people who I could seek information and help from if the situation arose.

It came as a personal disappointment that despite forming contacts and opening up lines of communication with people in America who had their fingers on the pulse – and the intelligence I'd attained – I was overlooked by my superiors when the AFP formed its counter-terrorism unit. Unfortunately, I speak on behalf of many members when I say the AFP doesn't do that kind of thing well. I was equally demoralised when the force led the intervention into the exploitation and sexual abuse of children in Indigenous communities. I'd put my hand up to be the first commander there, because I wanted to help. However, after presenting my credentials – including my anthropology degree, my Aboriginal studies and citing my police career – they brought in a former army commando. It happens all the time.

While in the US I formed many strong alliances and was keen to liaise with the Mexican police. The world had good reason to focus its attention on the Colombians, but there were burgeoning cartels in Mexico, and the intelligence reports suggested they were ruthless. My gut feeling was that they were going to become a problem for Australia, so I wanted to establish contacts. The Mexicans were generally disrespected by their US counterparts, but I befriended Jorge Ricardo Garcia-Villalobos Haddad from the Attorney General's department. Jorge was a big Lebanese–Mexican with the most magnificent lisp, and he was thrilled when I accepted his invitation to visit 'Me-hi-co'. I arranged to meet with Interpol while I was down there, and when I disembarked from the plane there were six policemen decked out in black vests and armed with machine guns. As they escorted Jorge and me through the airport they brushed aside the poor customs officers who wanted to check my passport. We were quickly ushered into two armour-plated Hummers, and when we arrived at a luxury hotel there was a battalion of guards. A whole floor had been cleared to accommodate us! My jaw dropped – I was still only a lowly constable but the fact that a member of the AFP had made the effort to visit was seen as a sign of great respect.

The Mexican police were gracious hosts. Jorge was a tremendous guy, and even though I was stuffed from our lunch he was insistent I *had* to try the beef at his favourite restaurant that night. The feed was amazing, but what I remember most was other patrons being pushed out of the place by police officers so we could have the restaurant to ourselves. It took a few seconds for me to realise what was happening, and when it registered

I was shocked. I couldn't help but wonder what the reaction would be if Australian police were so heavy handed. However, as with the customs officers who had been pushed aside at the airport, it seemed to be the way things were done there. Years later in 2015, as the AFP's Commander for the Americas, I was proud when Canberra agreed with my view that we needed an office in Mexico. I have no doubt the Mexican law enforcement agencies will continue to be great allies to Australia at a time when Mexican drug cartels and outlaw Australian motorbike gangs are forming relationships.

In LA I had a mud map that allowed me to note which law enforcement agencies didn't get on with each other. And there were a few, on account of intense inter-departmental rivalries. It was good intelligence, and accurate, because when I took the initiative to head to Panama to establish contacts, my boss in Washington insisted I go through the US Drug Enforcement Agency (DEA), even though I told him the Panamanians and the DEA weren't getting on. Back then Panama was considered one of the most corrupt nations, laundering money from Mexican and Colombian crime gangs. We needed contacts there because many of the vessels that berthed in Australia came via the Panama Canal, making it a key drug-trafficking route. I had a colleague in British customs, Andy Davenport, who was happy to set me up with the new guy in charge of Panama's operations. But I did what I was told by my boss and saw the DEA's chief Jay Bergman, who became a lifelong friend to me and a long line of other AFP officers. Jay said that while he was on hand to help in whatever ways he could, his advice was to not hang off his department because the locals hated them.

He suggested that I link up with 'The Brit'; he'd get me into places that would otherwise be hard to access and that would only offer lip service. And that's how I came to hook up with Andy, a Cockney. I couldn't help but laugh whenever he spoke Spanish – his accent was hilarious – but because the Panamanians loved him, he opened doors for me that would otherwise have been impossible to budge. Through him I had very meaningful dialogue with high-level officials, which proved beneficial for Australia. As a result of the relationships that were forged in the late 1990s, Australia received tremendous intelligence from people who have progressed through the ranks in American, Mexican and Panamanian law enforcement, helping us enjoy important victories in the war on drugs.

My time in America did wonders for my police career. However, had it not been for Canberra and its red tape, I might also have had a shot at Hollywood, thanks to none other than Chuck Norris.

Most people who live in Los Angeles have at least one brush with fame. And while I was lucky enough to meet actor John Goodman and Micky Dolenz from The Monkees at an LA party hosted by Jeff 'Skunk' Baxter, one of the original members of Steely Dan and the Doobie Brothers, my biggest Hollywood moment came when I was seated next to action star Chuck Norris – of *Walker, Texas Ranger* fame – at the retirement dinner for John Hensley, the special agent in charge of US Customs, who apart from being a brilliant bloke was also a respected martial artist.

In the US, law enforcement agents can work on the side, and while Hensley was the bodyguard for a number of celebrities, Norris was one of his best mates. When I walked into the farewell bash I was stunned to find who I was seated next to, but even more surprised when Norris, one of my favourite actors, started peppering me with questions about the World's Strongest Man competition, which I'd only recently returned from. It was an incredible experience, and my heart skipped a beat when Chuck called out to his producer, asking if they'd ever 'kicked the crap out of an Aussie' on their show. They hadn't, and when he asked if I wanted to be the first, I stammered with excitement! He laughed when I asked whether I'd be hurt – I don't know why I asked – but he assured me I'd get training in how to fall and take a shot. I said I'd love to do it, but I made the mistake of asking my bosses in the International Division based in Canberra for permission to play the role of an extra. They knocked it back with the simple message, 'Nope, not happening.' I think they were worried about how it would be viewed if news got out that an AFP officer on a government posting had appeared in a television show. I got that. I wasn't planning to supersede Bryan Brown as the best actor out of the East Hills-Panania area, but I was disappointed because it would've been one hell of an experience.

One celebrity I befriended was Skunk Baxter, who worked as a defence consultant and chaired a Congressional Advisory Board on missile defence. He was a fascinating, well-read bloke. From talking with him it was obvious that while he always loved music – he has eight platinum records – he realised there was a higher calling. In due course, he became one of the world's best known counter-terrorism experts. Skunk claims he fell into that area by accident in the 1980s when his interest in music technology inspired him to wonder about hardware and software that had been originally designed for the military. His neighbour, who'd worked on a missile program, bought him a subscription to an aviation magazine, which piqued his interest further. He wrote a paper on missile defence and, after handing it to California Republican congressman Dana Rohrabacher, he commenced a new career as a defence consultant. Skunk loved Australia and had travelled here a fair bit. Apart from appearing regularly on *Hey Hey It's Saturday*, he also mentored Nathan Cavaleri, a well-known young guitarist in the 1990s. Skunk was a fascinating bloke, and we'd speak at great length about such things as nuclear non-proliferation, terrorism methodologies, and mechanisms for deploying noxious and deadly gases. I remember one meeting when he spoke about the 'mechanism to deploy' a biological or chemical weapon. I'd always thought if someone wanted to contaminate a city's drinking water supply they'd just need to sprinkle bags of whatever it was into the water, but Skunk explained they'd actually need to deploy it, and its success would depend on the right trajectory, the wind factors and other variables. Listening to him scared the bejeezus out of me, because he made me appreciate how easy it would be for someone to wreak havoc. Our conversations weren't always as heavy, though. He liked to hear cop stories, and I loved hearing him talk about his life on the road as a musician.

While I missed my chance at stardom due to red tape, my daughter Emilee hit the big time ... well, kind of ... when she was signed up to do some voice-over work at Paramount Studios for Tom Cruise's *Mission Impossible II*, which was filmed in Australia in 2000. They'd had problems with the audio and needed an Aussie kid to re-voice 'Ring a Ring o' Roses', which appears at the beginning of the film. Maree had her listen to Blinky Bill cassettes to help her 'rediscover' her Aussie twang, because after two years living in the US and mixing with neighbourhood kids she'd started to sound more like an American.

While Emilee's name doesn't appear on the credits alongside the likes of Cruise, John Polson and Richard Roxburgh, she had to join the Screen Actors Guild, the labour union that represents 100,000 show business people. Interestingly, she also had to deposit a portion of her earnings into the Jackie Coogan Trust. Jackie played Uncle Fester in *The Addams Family*, and when he'd been a child actor his parents squandered most of his earnings. In the US today kids are somewhat better protected by law when it comes to such things, and they can't access the money they earn from acting until they turn eighteen. For the record, *Mission Impossible II* is one of my favourite films because, well, I happen to know one of the stars quite well.

23
A NOT SO LUCKY COUNTRY

'The traffickers are barbaric, I have seen women with scars around their wrist and scars and burns on their upper body and torso. The women can't get away. These people know who they are and where they live . . .'

– Natalie McCauley, End Child Prostitution and Trafficking

One of my most heartbreaking experiences as a policeman – and the father of two daughters – came in 2003, as a member of the Transnational Sexual Exploitation and Trafficking Team (TSETT). I interviewed a man who had sent his daughter from Thailand to Australia, telling her she was coming here to become a hairdresser. Naturally, the girl was excited as she dreamt of the new life that awaited her in a country that throughout South-East Asia is seen as 'paradise' because of the standard of living we enjoy. However, the reality was that she'd be forced to have sex with a seemingly never-ending number of clients because this poor woman had effectively been indentured to human traffickers. When I asked how he, *her father*, could have made such a decision, the man responded pragmatically, saying even though he knew the horrors that awaited his daughter, sacrificing her would provide enough income to feed the rest of his family for the next four years. His reasoning reinforced why it's so easy for criminal networks to prey on people who have nothing . . .

I didn't volunteer to join TSETT but was pitchforked into it not long after I returned to Australia from Los Angeles in 2001. I'd been investigating the cocaine trade for the Transnational Criminal Intelligence Team, but I was plucked out of that by Assistant Commissioner Shane Castles, and my superintendent in LA. He asked, 'You know stuff about these prostitutes, don't you, Edwards?' Most appointments in the AFP are more formal than this, but even though Shane's line of questioning was in keeping with his at-times gruff character, I still wondered whether it was a trick question. The reason for his rather blunt inquiry was because he, and other members of the force's hierarchy, were frustrated about a series of exposés two journalists from *The Australian* were writing about women being trafficked into Australia for sexual exploitation from countries such as Thailand, South Korea, Malaysia and Vietnam, as well as a small group from Europe. It turned into a political football because Australia had been put on notice by the United States that it was on the verge of being added to its annual *Trafficking In Persons Report* (or TIP), which shames nations that aren't doing enough to stop the trade. Personally, I think it's interesting that the only country that is exempt from being added to the report is the United States. My research suggests their backyard is a long way from being the tidiest in the neighbourhood.

Regardless, the Howard government was nervous about being condemned as a Tier Two nation because it meant Australia could be exposed to a range of trade sanctions and other embargoes. As is the way with organisations such as the AFP, when the government of the day is nervous, we sweat profusely. We were tasked with the job of stamping out a heinous (but lucrative) crime on a budget best described as 'meagre'. On top of the government's orders to fix a terrible situation, the AFP was copping unwelcome blowback in the media after two women who'd informed on their captors were refused visas to stay in Australia. It was a mess, and Shane's question was far more complex than me simply knowing anything about 'these prostitutes'.

When I finally ascertained that he was referring to human trafficking, I reminded Shane I'd been on working groups in Los Angeles with US Customs. While I attended them mainly for the latest information they had on drugs, they'd discuss the trafficking of human cargo from Mexico to the States. They'd talk about victims being smuggled across the border in the consoles of cars, in false-sided semi-trailers, and within the rear seats of motor vehicles. While I understood some of the methodologies, I was not an expert. His response was, 'Okay, that'll do' and he sent me to meet Dr Adam Graycar, a respected academic who ran the Australian Institute of Criminology in Canberra. As I walked away Shane yelled out my brief, which was to simply 'do something'.

I respected the brevity of his orders because Shane was a man of action. When he was the AFP's Commissioner of Solomon Islands he was effectively kicked out of that country because he took on the allegedly corrupt politicians there, who rushed to protect themselves when they heard him coming. After meeting Adam, I was advised I'd be accompanying him to a Trafficking and Persons conference in Washington DC, but as I saw it the AFP's two-man delegation lost its firepower when the day before we were scheduled to leave I discovered I'd be flying solo and had no idea what I'd be thrown into.

In the week leading up to the conference – and during the flight to America – I'd done plenty of research. Still, there was no way I could have claimed to be an authority. All I knew about the subject was the scraps of information I'd picked up during my stint in LA and what I'd crammed in the lead-up to my trip. However, that didn't seem to matter to the organisers. When I arrived in Washington they told me I'd been made moderator of one of the most important sessions, along with Bernadette McMenamin, then the CEO of Child Wise, an Australia-based service committed to the safety and wellbeing of all children. Apart from being able to lean on Bernadette's expertise, I was extremely fortunate that Alastair MacGibbon, who was the Deputy Director of Cyber Security in the Department of Home Affairs, was our liaison officer in Washington. He provided me with essential material to digest, and it was a huge help.

The conference was a massive event – there were five thousand people in attendance across the board, and in some ways it was similar to attending the United Nations. There were rooms full of interpreters for six different languages. When I took my seat the enormity of what I was doing hit me. Behind a table of invited VIPs hundreds of people filled the room – and every pair of eyes was fixed on me. After I delivered my pre-prepared welcome, I opened the floor to whoever wanted to get the ball rolling, and it started with a bang. The delegate from a Middle Eastern nation immediately stood up and, before saying a word, smashed his fist on the desk and proceeded to shout that they did not have the problem of prostitution in their country. He demanded to know why they were being listed on the US-compiled TIP report.

Before I could remind him the conference was about human trafficking and not prostitution, the entire room erupted into chaos. NGOs hurled abuse towards the by now even angrier delegate, who was yelling insults back at them in Arabic. I managed to quell the uprising with some basic diplomacy – I banged my fist on the table to get his attention and explained that the conference was not about apportioning blame. We had, instead, an opportunity to learn from each other and work out how to combat a terrible problem. However, the delegate still maintained that his country didn't have a problem, and when I requested he share with us what exactly his nation was doing so we could learn from it, he looked stunned and became mute. However, after a few seconds he rallied and shouted that he was angry because the *Americans* thought his country had a problem. After I spent a few more minutes explaining that we weren't there to argue about what the US thought, we got the meeting back on track to discuss more pertinent issues.

The role was mentally challenging, to say the least, and the three nights I spent in Washington for the conference were very tough. I burnt the midnight oil trying to learn as much as I could about this horrific subject so I could do my job properly. When the conference was over I thought that would be the end of my commitment and expected to return to my normal duties. However, journalists Natalie O'Brien and Elisabeth Wynhausen from *The Australian* were tenacious in their pursuit of the subject.

Their exposés had people from all spectrums of the government and bureaucracy jumping up and down and saying they wanted the problem fixed immediately. The AFP was copping criticism from all sides. I was told human trafficking was now my beat. After all, apart from anything else, I knew enough about the subject to be the moderator at a keynote conference in America.

So, that's how I was put in charge of creating the Transnational Sexual Exploitation and Trafficking Team, and the pressure was intense. It was coming from the top, too. During John Howard's prime ministership the AFP received greater funding, but with that we were having a variety of things tacked onto our daily business that we didn't have a lot of experience in, which included human trafficking. The bosses didn't want problems; they wanted people like me to find solutions. I embraced the challenge of being given a blank canvas, but it was a hard slog. During this stage of my career I learnt all facets of voluminous government reporting. I also learnt to prepare for the plethora of briefings that were part and parcel of the job, especially the process known as 'questions on notice' in Parliament. However, few people appreciate that police are hardly ever properly resourced because of tight budgets, and what our critics didn't realise was that my team was far from the army that was needed to combat the problem at hand. We only had four members: me, two unsworn women (that is, civilians) and an unsworn analyst. I was also advised that I needed to write proposals to obtain extra funding. I had no idea where to start. I'm thankful that I was supported in that process by Meegan Fitzharris, a brilliant policy writer who weaved her magic to produce proposals that allowed me to eventually build a team from scratch.

I did everything possible to give us a rock-solid foundation. Initially, I reached out to the Americans for support, and while they were extremely helpful, our legal systems have distinct differences that made many of their suggestions redundant. I turned to the British and formed alliances with people who were doing brilliant work for the Metropolitan Police. I also drew on Interpol's expertise. When the funding started to trickle through the clogged pipes better known as 'government bureaucracy' I recruited a group of people who were passionate about the mission. However, our progress before we reached that point was snail-slow because I was forever in meetings that centred around the media's reporting of the issue.

The agenda for my week's work was basically determined by what had appeared in the weekend's paper. It was a stressful time. My bosses wanted me to make the problem of trafficking go away, but because they wanted to focus on what they considered the 'real' issues, which included terrorism after the Bali bombings, I seemed to be forever chasing my tail and I achieved very little during my first few months in the job. My people were equally frustrated because as an 'intel' team they wanted to collect information and data that could be used to combat the criminal networks trafficking people. However, their time was consumed instead by the constant need to write briefs and prepare circulars for politicians and bureaucrats. It was early days and we really needed to blaze a trail, but because our superiors – and the politicians – either didn't understand what we were doing or were preoccupied with other matters it felt as though I was forever sinking in quicksand.

The journalists' work was two-pronged. They were blaming us for Department of Immigration issues, so I was annoyed that the AFP was being unfairly targeted. And by reacting to screaming headlines and unfavourable reports on radio news bulletins we weren't properly doing our job to help the trafficked women. This way of operating couldn't continue. Ultimately I decided to take a leap of faith. I met with someone from the newspaper and put everything on the table. I told them the AFP was being criticised for something it wasn't responsible for and explained that we didn't have the legislation to control visas; that was the Department of Immigration's domain. This was dangerous, I knew. If things backfired, my approach of seeking forgiveness rather than approval wouldn't hold water, and the repercussions for my career would most likely be severe. Thankfully, the person I met had the common sense I believed they had, and the newspaper's ensuing investigation zeroed in on what it needed to – immigration – and the AFP was finally left alone to do its work.

The hours and stress of my new role did nothing to help my marriage. We'd moved onto a 16-acre farm at Wamboin, a 35-minute drive from Canberra. It was quiet, and while it should have been a dream location, I didn't enjoy it as much as I should have. The demands at the office made everything that should have been appealing about living at such a place a chore. It became an inconvenience to have to fix the fences that were falling down, or to stop the grass from becoming a jungle, because I was so invested in my role. Mobile phones had become popular at that time, and I was forever fielding calls from a variety of people wanting to criticise us. I was the team leader, and I went above the call of duty because I thought it was my responsibility to take the pressure off the team.

I always felt punch-drunk. This was one time in my career when I'd take one step forward and two back. No one was interested in hearing my gripes. I didn't have enough people, we didn't have the legislation that was required to work with, and my budget was pathetic. I'd tell my superiors it felt like I was trying to put a massive bushfire out without water, but they weren't interested in analogies; they demanded results. I decided to play rugby union for Easts (Canberra) as a way to deal with the stress. Most of the players were cops, but due to the pressures of work I played in only three games, and only rarely attended training sessions.

In the course of this work I also gained some insights into the determination and spirit that allowed the women being trafficked to rise above their horrific circumstances. One of them told me the reason she serviced up to twelve men a day was because every client represented a cross, and every cross next to her name on the brothel owner's list was another step towards regaining her freedom. Many of these women had no previous experience as sex workers, and as part of their 'induction' were given 'desensitising' activities, which is essentially *rape*. For want of a better word, they also received 'motivational' talks. They were told by their captors that once their debt was paid off – and the average debt was $40,000 – if they continued working in the brothel they'd make more money in six months than they could in ten years in a regular job in Thailand. However, that was yet another lie. Once they'd 'earned' their freedom, the traffickers phoned Immigration and provided information about these 'illegal immigrants' they'd 'heard about'. As the women were deported to their country of origin, shells of who they had once been, a new batch of naive girls was being shipped to the brothels. It was, and remains, a vicious cycle.

I spoke to the father who sold his daughter into slavery to feed his family after a series of AFP raids on homes and a brothel in Sydney and Melbourne resulted in four people becoming the first to be charged with slavery under Australia's sexual servitude laws. Although Federal legislation had been amended in 1999, the government hadn't provided the AFP with any operating funds. This left us open to criticism in the media because there was a perception that we'd dragged our heels regarding human trafficking and thrown a lot of our resources into burgeoning terrorist threats. Eventually the purse strings were opened and TSETT received $40 million to create what were called 'virtual teams' across the country. The support was a huge breakthrough. Prior to this it had been difficult to do anything, and while the arrests were a watershed moment for TSETT in terms of our aims and objectives, the four individuals were imprisoned but did not suffer anywhere near the level of indignity or hardship that the women who worked in their brothels.

Following these raids, six Thai women were placed in protective care. When some of them finally spoke to us the picture they painted of their lives was harrowing. They lived in filth and squalor, were constantly threatened, were told their families would be killed if they escaped and were isolated from the rest of the community. One woman, who became a confidential informant, told me she worked through her menstrual cycle by using a sea sponge. Another revealed that once a month they were allowed to keep whatever money they made from working on a Sunday – a brothel's lowest patronage day. But many of these women sent that extra cash home to help their impoverished families. And another woman, who'd been a sex worker in Thailand, said that when she'd agreed to come to Australia no one had told her she'd need to spend the first four years working off her debt bondage.

This was all new territory for me. Up until joining the unit my work had basically been focused on faceless crimes, such as fraud and drug trafficking. I describe them as 'faceless' because we only followed paper and commodity trails and didn't meet the people who were affected. However, witnessing the putrid living quarters of a brothel and listening to the stories of women who'd been lied to, abused and, in some cases, betrayed by their loved ones, had a profound impact on me. There were occasions when, rather than shuffling papers, briefing politicians and deflecting the criticism of the media, I would have preferred to be in the thick of the action, kicking down doors and making arrests. However, my days as an operational cop were over. The path I was on after working in LA meant the only way I could have continued in that role was by transferring to ACT policing. I knew there was no way that transfer would have been rubber-stamped because my superiors wanted the intelligence I'd gathered in America to be 'reinvested' in the AFP. In any case, when you build a new department as I was, intelligence is king. It's what allows you to achieve results, and results are what bring credibility and respect.

One of the most terrifying moments I endured while working in TSETT was the day when my informant was kidnapped.

This woman was courageous because, even though her life was endangered by working with us, she was determined to save other women from suffering the same fate she had. She had a wealth of knowledge, and it was through her we learnt how the people smugglers kept their books, who did what in the business, their structures and the fronts they had created to legitimise the money they made. We learnt that they set up a number of false businesses, including language schools where young girls went to supposedly learn English.

We were meeting at McDonald's in the south-west Sydney suburb of Liverpool when I noticed she'd turned ashen. One of the traffickers – a man from the Balkans – was ordering food. My informant was an agitator; she drove her bosses mad with her questions and demands for rights, but she enjoyed some liberties. She'd paid most of her debt off and served a purpose for them because she was being used to recruit other women from Asian nations to become prostitutes (although, in the AFP we only ever used the term 'sex worker' as a sign of respect). In the few seconds we had before the trafficker came over to find out why she was meeting with two men, I gave her a cover story. I told her to say we were migration agents, discussing the possibility of her staying in Australia. But the trafficker smelt a rat and she was nabbed that night. My informant was imprisoned at a brothel in Wagga where a guard was kept on the door of her room. She sent messages via her mobile phone saying she feared for her life. We tracked her phone and discovered where she was being held. I was obviously concerned for her welfare, but without going into the details, she was eventually released unharmed.

One of my most immediate priorities as the head of TSETT was to shift the typical cop's mentality so that the women who'd been trafficked were no longer seen as 'just' prostitutes, but as people with families, women who were in turmoil because they'd been exploited. Most of these women had been deceived into thinking they'd work in Australia as waitresses, hairdressers or kitchen hands, but they were coerced into sex work the moment they arrived. Their passports were confiscated, and they had to work off their debt for the airfares, accommodation, food and medical expenses – and it destroyed them.

An amazing woman from Burma named Ma Khin Mar Mar Kyi – or Dr Mar – proved to be a great friend and ally to both me and the women in need of help. She'd buried thirty-eight trafficked girls who died on the Thai–Burma border, and when she arrived in Australia Dr Mar wrote articles and lectured on trafficking while she completed her PhD at the Australia National University. We met in Melbourne as members of a panel that addressed the issue of trafficking. I explained to Dr Mar that I needed women who could play the roles of girls who'd been trafficked to Australia in order to help me devise a training program for police involved in raids. The program would cover how to deal with traumatised victims and how to appreciate cultural differences in order to ensure victims were treated properly during recovery warrants. Dr Mar assembled a wonderful group of women, and their efforts helped us formulate a program which, over time, would be acknowledged by international observers as 'world class'. As a result of our achievements, I'd eventually become the co-chair of Interpol's expert group on the trafficking of women and children, along with my good friend, Detective Inspector Lori Lowe from the Royal Canadian Mounted Police. Our roles were to guide the international community's pursuit of human traffickers, particularly the exploitation of women and children. Dr Mar coached the women on how to react in simulated police raids on an empty ACT government house. It had been made to resemble the sort of place where trafficked women were housed, and their role-playing was so authentic it changed my colleagues' mindsets. Rather than thinking they were going to arrest hookers, the police involved now understood they were rescuing women who'd had their freedom taken from them by people smugglers. Still, it wasn't an easy job for any of us. Trafficked victims had an inherent distrust of law enforcement authorities, based on their experiences in their home countries. What we eventually did after we made a raid was to hand the women headsets with messages in their native language saying the Australian police would help them. Nevertheless, it was extremely difficult to convince them to give evidence against their captors. They were terrified of the consequences because the people who'd enslaved them knew where their families lived.

In tackling these problems I stepped outside of the box and sought the advice of people who didn't necessarily support the AFP, including Melbourne-based Kathleen Maltzahn, who at the time was our fiercest critic. Despite her many criticisms of us, the community is a far better place for having the likes of Kathleen. She was the founding director of Project Respect, an NGO that opposed the trafficking of people into the sex industry, and she petitioned long and hard for a greater response from the police. So I viewed her as someone whose heart was in the right place. She was fighting to save these women, and I admired her for that. I also respected that she knew her business, so I didn't hesitate to invite her to join panels that we chaired at conferences and meetings to further develop our capabilities. I wanted someone who'd challenge our direction and methods, and, to her credit, Kathleen helped me look at things from a different perspective – namely, the victim's view – because she taught me a lot about what needed to be done to help the women, and that included working in conjunction with NGOs through our embassy in Bangkok. We arranged for the women who returned to Thailand to learn trades that could give them employment, such as becoming make-up artists, hairdressers or anything else that would stop them from falling back into the sex industry.

I immersed myself in my work. One of the great things about being a member of the AFP is that the work is varied. If you open your mind there is always an opportunity to learn new things – although some insights don't show humanity in the best light. The more I researched, the uglier the picture became. In the 1990s it was suggested that the Australian trafficking industry netted approximately $1 million per week to the organisers of the trade. By 1995 an estimated 500 trafficked women were working illegally in Sydney at any given time. A Queensland study in 2002 found that illegal migrant women working under a 'contract' were forced to provide sexual services to between 500 and 700 clients to repay their debt before being free to either leave the brothel or continue working in it. A Sydney study found that 80 per cent of immigrant sex workers were from Thailand, and 90 per cent of them were working off their debt.

The social impact of trafficking for the sex trade was highlighted by Moldova back in the mid-2000s when the number of women taken out of the nation to service men in Macau meant there were no women aged between 13 and 24. While the country has recovered now, the disproportionate number of men to women at that time created a huge social fracture.

Human trafficking is a very broad domain. It extends to trafficking people into a country to provide cheap labour and includes organ trafficking. There are also some big discrepancies when it comes to interpretations of fair payment for work done. I learnt that there were some well-off migrants who brought their own chefs with them to Australia but didn't pay them.

However, no matter how much we investigated the other aspects of human trafficking, back in the early 2000s the focus always came back to sex work. The breadth of this was mindboggling, and we often hit brick walls. We investigated reports that Indigenous women were selling sexual services to long-haul truckies for as little as $10 to buy petrol or tins of paint so they could get high off the fumes. It was unacceptable, and I felt angry that such a situation could be occurring in modern-day Australia. As my career comes to an end, I'd like to think Australian policing will increase its efforts to address the obvious disparity between remote communities and the rest of the nation. We also received reports that some women were being ferried to offshore oil rigs to service the men who were stationed there for extended periods of time. I believed this was occurring, but we were unable to substantiate the facts.

Another investigation we conducted concerned Australian women being trafficked overseas. We were aware that Caucasian women were going to Japan to work as hostesses, and had reason to believe the Japanese crime syndicate, the Yakuza, was involved. We came extremely close to making an arrest, but as was the case with the Thais trafficked to Australia, we found that the women sent to Japan were terrified of the likely consequences if they took action. They too felt shame about what had happened to them.

24
EAST TIMOR

'My message to my people is please forgo violence and
hatred with weapons, machetes, with arson – we only
destroy each other and the country . . .'

– Jose Ramos-Horta, President of East Timor and Nobel laureate

In 2008, I was one of ten officers at the AFP's inaugural Senior
International Command Program that took place at the
Australian Institute of Management in Sydney. It was facilitated
by Warwick Jones, a former lieutenant colonel in the Australian
army, and someone whom I consider an extremely competent
operator. He was using the experiences he'd gained throughout
his military career to help prepare us to serve overseas at a time
when the AFP was represented in a number of regional trouble
spots, including the Solomon Islands and Timor-Leste, the place
most Australians know as East Timor.

While I was doing the course, Commander Mark Walters,
the AFP's Manager of Operations and Missions, tapped me on
the shoulder and signalled for me to follow him outside. He
said there was going to be a deployment to East Timor the
following month and he wanted to know whether I was interested
in going. Emilee, now 14 years old, was my only tie to home

because I was divorced by then. I eventually decided to go, not only because I viewed it as a great opportunity for me to broaden my career and horizons as the AFP's Mission Commander, but also because I thought I could provide Emilee with great life experiences by flying her there during some school holidays to observe a culture that is completely different to Australia's.

I landed in the former Portuguese colony's capital of Dili with the Timor-Leste Police Development Program, which was a bilateral arrangement between the governments of Australia and Timor-Leste to promote and maintain a safe, stable environment throughout Timor. The general consensus was that if that could be achieved it would contribute to social and economic development, and reduce poverty. The program also represented a $53 million dollar commitment by Australia to help train the Policia Nacional de Timor-Leste (PNTL).

However, despite the amount of money Australia was ploughing into our nearest neighbour, I arrived at a time when East Timor's relationship with Canberra was at a crossroads. While Australia was hailed as a liberator by the Timorese when our troops headed the multinational peacekeeping taskforce in 1999 that ended Indonesia's rule over them, that love had vanished long before I arrived in February 2008. Anti-Aussie sentiment runs even deeper in the nation's capital today because the Timorese believe our government exploited their vast gas and oil reserves. There's also ongoing resentment that we were seen to have abandoned them when the Indonesians invaded in 1975, heralding a brutal twenty-four-year occupation in which up to 180,000 local soldiers and civilians died through either starvation or conflict-related incidents. The Timorese believe the Whitlam government that was in power when Indonesian paratroopers landed in Dili – as well as subsequent governments – conveniently forgot that 60,000 Timorese had been executed by the Japanese for assisting the Australian commandoes who fought a guerrilla-style of warfare against them in the Second World War.

I'd been in East Timor for all of three weeks and was still getting my head around my duties when an attempt was made on the life of the nation's president, Jose Ramos-Horta. A group of 'mutineers' from the military, headed by Major Alfredo Reinado, opened fire and Ramos-Horta was hit in the stomach and chest as he returned to his official residence. Reinado was killed by the president's bodyguard during the shoot-out, and when Prime Minister Xanana Gusmão's convoy was attacked not long after the assassination attempt, the government announced there'd been a failed coup. I saw the ambulance responding to the assassination attempt as it hurtled along the streets to get Ramos-Horta to surgery, and I soon received a call from the Australian Defence Force to advise me they were considering going into lockdown. They couldn't be certain how catastrophic the fallout would be.

They had their reasons for being on guard. In 2006, at the behest of the East Timorese government, they took action when another crisis required intervention by forces from Australia, New Zealand, Malaysia and Portugal after 600 East Timorese soldiers were dismissed from the army. Their anger escalated into a coup attempt, which in turn sparked an outbreak of violence that left thirty-seven dead and forced 150,000 people to leave their homes. Now, while surgeons at the Portuguese base fought to save Ramos-Horta's life before he was airlifted to Darwin, Dili was alight with suggestions that factions within the East Timorese army would use the shooting as an excuse to go at one another. The place was a tinderbox, as I would find out in the aftermath when I needed to drive my car during a curfew.

When I stopped at a security checkpoint I was dragged from my vehicle by members of the East Timorese military, one of whom stuck the barrel of his weapon into my throat. There was a lot of shouting and nervous energy among the soldiers, and I had no idea what they were saying. It was obvious they were jumpy, and that scared me because in most situations where you have nervous people with firearms, there's a good chance it'll end in bloodshed. The soldier putting the gun to my throat demanded to know the nature of my business, and while I was seething inside about the way I was being treated – after all, I was in their country as a friend – I managed to speak in a clear, calm manner. I hoped that would help settle down the soldiers, who were becoming even more agitated with each passing minute. I explained that I worked for the Australian Federal Police and was also an advisor for his government. None of this seemed to matter because he just pushed the gun's barrel even deeper into my neck as he kept shouting. The only time something seemed to register with him was when I rattled off the names of the government ministers I'd sat alongside in a series of meetings that day. After a few heated words between him and his comrades, the soldier finally lowered his gun and told me to move on. It was a nerve-racking experience but that soldier provided me with an insight into the feeling on the streets.

Canberra reacted to news of the assassination attempt by contacting me to say they were despatching eighty members of the AFP's newly formed Special Response Group (SRG) to help maintain law and order. It was the last thing that was needed – as I said, we had more than enough people on the ground and sending more police from Australia would only unnecessarily ruffle the feathers of the UN and the Portuguese Guarda Nacional Republicana, a paramilitary police force that had proven to be highly effective in restoring stability to Timor-Leste. My concern was that the UN had the mandate to police Timor (and the Portuguese were a part of that), and by sending extra police Canberra was sending the message that they didn't believe the UN and the Timorese could handle the situation. However, Canberra overrode my advice, and the reason behind it was pure politics. The government had specifically funded the AFP to form the SRG, and it was an opportunity for the powers-that-be to justify the expense. I implored my superiors to at least consider stationing them in Darwin for seventy-two hours, and wait and see what happened, noting that if Dili erupted they'd be only an hour's flight away. However, they were committed to sending in the cavalry. This meant the Australian ambassador, Peter Heyward – a great man – and I needed to negotiate with Dili the 'status of forces', which formed the legal basis for the new batch of officers to be allowed into Timor.

Our negotiations were made even tougher because the lawyer the Australian government sent to discuss the terms of the SRG's deployment was recalled when he reached Darwin because a bureaucrat realised the Aussie army already had a lawyer in Timor. However, as I soon discovered, the army major in question specialised in Intellectual Property; by his own admission he would've been as useful to us as 'tits on a bull' in this instance. His concession meant Ambassador Heyward and I were left to sort it out, and Heyward had only been in East Timor a week longer than me. The Portuguese, who had colonised Timor from 1702 to 1975, did the negotiations on behalf of Ramos-Horta's government and, after a lengthy night of discussions, we basically agreed to their demands in order to ensure the AFP officers would be legally allowed into the country because by now we were in a race against the clock. The ambassador and I *had* to get the deal done; we risked an international incident if the SRG were forbidden from stepping foot in the country. It's fair to say the Australian government wasn't pleased with what we agreed to. However, when they realised their army lawyer specialised in IP, there was silence.

In the days that followed the ambush, members of the Australian army patrolled through the scrub, trying to track down the people who were involved in the assassination attempt. Indonesia's president, Susilo Bambang Yudhoyono, provided his private jet to his nation's police, and Jakarta flew in a group of specialists known as 'The Hunters'. Because they don't have the same rules imposed on them as Australian law enforcement officers in intercepting telephone calls, they arrived armed with the covert technology that allowed them to pinpoint where the members of the group were operating from. Each of the twenty-four rebels was eventually captured, and they were imprisoned until Ramos-Horta pardoned them. The president's decision to commute the sentences (after he'd recovered from his wounds) was met with anger and dismay from the United Nations and rights groups. They believed his decision undermined the rule of law and was yet another example of 'crime without punishment'.

I flew to Darwin with the nation's Prosecutor-General, Longuinhos Monteiro, when Ramos-Horta woke from his coma. He demanded information on an Australian woman he alleged was behind the ambush. We had many robust conversations about his theory while he was in Darwin because our investigations had ruled her out as a suspect. It was typical of my first few months in Timor – my life was consumed by politically charged issues. I also needed to address the AFP's concerns about issues arising from the actions of other UN police. Apart from their abuse of alcohol, some were overtly disrespectful towards the locals, and this was a source of friction among our officers, who couldn't tolerate seeing the people we were sent to help being belittled by the UN's cops. We didn't tolerate it because my officers and I had thrown ourselves into getting to know the locals, helping them wherever possible. We did that because, apart from being a rewarding experience, it allowed us to feel as though we had some ties to the Timorese.

We supported an orphanage that was run by the locals. The children they cared for were either disabled or had lost their parents during the 'conflict' – which is how the Timorese refer to the Indonesian occupation. We became aware of the orphanage because there were some women from the UN who'd visit it during their days off. The kids were beautiful, and they appreciated the attention and support. We did all number of things to try and lift their spirits. For instance, before the 2008 Beijing Games we ran an Olympics for the kids. We had an opening ceremony, athletic events and a party – it was a brilliant day.

I channelled the generosity of my teacher from Padstow Park Public School, Miss Hurley, and made sure these children always had more than enough pens and paper for their school lessons. I was pleased that most of my officers got it when I said we were being paid very good money to serve in an impoverished nation. I pointed out that it was fine to eat in the best restaurants all the time, but I also said it wouldn't hurt for us to throw a few bucks in to show some goodwill to the people. The officers' acceptance of that allowed for us to make regular donations to help the people who ran an orphanage pay for the things they needed, including a playground. We, of course, weren't the only ones who were helping; a Rotary group from Australia often visited the orphans and they built wheelchairs for the kids. An Aussie company also kindly donated the rubber-based shock-absorbing material that was laid on the floor of the playground to prevent any of the kids from hurting themselves if they slipped from the equipment.

It was very tough to know that many of the people who worked alongside us in our office lived in abject poverty. Our cleaner was a lovely lady, a very hard worker who was paid thirty American dollars for her week's work. She was a single mother with three kids, and I guess there was something about her situation that reminded me of my own mother. Her husband had abandoned the family and with that came the social stigma that she was 'barren' (if I correctly interpreted what I was told). That meant she would struggle to attract a new husband. I realised how tough life must have been for the woman and her children, so I paid her extra money out of my wallet each week to allow her to buy some more food and other items for her family.

There was a terrible monsoon that swept through Dili, and I was devastated to learn from her friend that she'd lost all of her furniture in the deluge. I found out she and her kids were eating and sleeping on the floor of their hut, and that broke my heart. This woman had never asked for anything – like my mother, she was far too proud for that – so I went out and bought new furniture for her. When I left Timor I paid for her to receive English lessons, because I knew that was one way to help her get ahead.

We were also able to help some other East Timorese colleagues. Another young woman, a local police officer attached to our office, had teeth that were so badly mangled the only way the disfigurement could be rectified would be if she underwent facial reconstruction surgery. I could only imagine her despair when she looked into a mirror every day and realised it was highly unlikely that any man would marry her because of her teeth. It wasn't fair. A dentist mate of mine from the ACT, Dr Rob Waites, regularly travelled to East Timor with his wife, Nancy, to provide free, basic dental care for villagers. He'd do things like extract decayed molars, fill cavities and clean their teeth. It was impossible for him to do any surgical work on our colleague in Timor because at that stage the Guido Valadares National Hospital in Dili was not up to the required standard. When Rob said he could help our colleague if she travelled to Australia for the operation, my officers and I chipped in the money to get her to Canberra. He did a wonderful job and his work changed the woman's life. I don't think there was a dry eye in our office the day she returned, and after beaming the most beautiful smile you could ever hope to see, she told us she was confident that one day she would marry and have children. I understand that day did come.

There were, however, many work pressures. The UN set up the Timorese police force in 2002 before sovereignty was handed to the state, but the handling of the police was hindered because of competing lines of command and cooperation between successive UN nations, Portugal and also Australia. I had my own concerns that the East Timorese police force were being instructed by member nations that had poor human rights records, and I was concerned about the methods they may have been teaching the local law enforcement officers, including excessive use of force.

What normally happens in situations such as Timor is that the highest contributing nations are *developing* countries because they're paid a lot of money from the UN for their support. However, I'd heard whispers that set off alarm bells. I was told the selection process used to pick the instructors from some of those nations was corrupt, with allegations that some of the people who'd been employed to train the locals weren't even qualified cops – they were just handed a uniform and the promise of a good pay day because they knew people. The other issue that concerned me was that training was usually delivered along national lines, so while Australian policing methods were being taught by Australian officers, the other thirty-four nations represented in the UN were teaching local police their style. It doesn't make for a homogenous force, and I pointed that out. I managed to cope with such stresses by simply accepting that I was involved in a challenging position and that I'd been selected to deal with it on behalf of the AFP, and my government. I did my best to make my two years in East Timor count.

My father and Emilee visited me in Timor on a couple of occasions, and it was a great experience for both of them. Dad spent a lot of time at the Castaway Café, which had a beautiful view across the water. The Castaway served gourmet pizzas, hamburgers and other Aussie staples, but Dad liked going there for his coffee. However, I never worked out whether he enjoyed drinking it or just telling the barista how bad a job he'd done of making it! Believe me, my dad was a *MasterChef* judge long before the popular television show started. It was good for both of us to have that time together because we spoke a lot and it allowed us to understand one another better.

Emilee came up twice, when she was 15 and 16. I wanted her to see that the way most of the world lived wasn't as fortunate as Australia. I also hoped she'd learn that there was more to life than the materialism that drives most Western countries. During her time there she saw kids make their own fun by getting old tyres and using a stick to roll them along the road, and fashioning toys and ornaments out of old soft drink cans. She witnessed kids, who had a life span of twenty to thirty years less than what she could expect, making the most of what they had. She was a keen photographer and a few of the women who worked in the office were very good amateur shutterbugs themselves, and they helped her capture some great photos. Over a decade later, Emilee still has vivid memories of Timor, and the one that has endured best is the hospitality of the people. She met folk who, despite being dirt poor, would have given Emilee their last bit of food if she told them she was hungry.

After the assassination attempt, Prosecutor General Longuinhos Monteiro said he needed the AFP's help because he lacked both the capability and the people within the East Timorese ranks to build a strong police force. When he requested the secondment of some of my officers, I explained that the AFP cops were invited guests to his nation and there were international protocols that needed to be observed if we were to help him. His response was to smile and say he'd do whatever was necessary to make it happen – and he did. Within days I received an official letter from Xanana Gusmão, requesting help with the investigation.

I took my position as an advisor for the East Timorese government seriously, and that frustrated the fifty AFP officers and other contributing nations who were assigned to the UN because my role meant I had access to information they needed for their investigation into the attempted assassination of the president, but me and the other officers who'd been seconded couldn't tell them anything. There was a lot of friction, and it reached the stage where the UN police commissioner, a representative from El Salvador, said I was obliged to share whatever information I had. I explained that if I was working for the AFP I'd share everything, but I was assigned to the East Timorese. Besides, it was a matter of personal integrity for me to abide by international law. I couldn't afford to breach the trust we had with the Timorese – if that was broken, everything would be ruined.

One question I constantly asked myself in East Timor was who would become the scapegoat once the UN withdrew and things didn't go the Timorese way? The answer was obvious: Australia would be blamed for every misgiving. This concerned me because every day I saw the valuable work the ADF, AFP and numerous aid agencies were doing. Australia was pouring money into Timor and *everything* was aimed towards helping these people, who live in what remains the most impoverished nation in our region. I discussed the matter of Australia becoming the whipping boy with a very sharp academic who was working for me, an Oxford-educated Irishman named Dr Gordon Peake. He was a brilliant ally, tapping into global issues and breaking them down so they were relevant to our mission. During one of our many discussions he noted that Portugal held sway over the Council of the European Union, which he suggested could be helpful because the Timorese valued their link to their former colonial rulers. He was right. The ties that bound Dili to Lisbon were reflected in such things as Ramos-Horta (who fled to Portugal after the Indonesians invaded in 1975) arranging for the Portuguese to negotiate matters on his government's behalf. And at a street level, the Portuguese police who arrived after the bloodshed and violence of 2006 received a returning hero's welcome.

After my discussion with Gordon, I attended a meeting with Timor's Secretary of State Dr Francisco Gutierrez. We discussed the possibility of travelling to Portugal and the EU headquarters in Brussels to float the idea of keeping a small component of EU representatives in East Timor after the UN withdrew. At the time there was concern in Dili's corridors of power about the direction their military and the police might take when the other nations withdrew, and the suggestion struck the secretary as a worthwhile venture. We arranged the trip through the Australian embassy because East Timor didn't have a foreign ministry, but just as everything was about to be rubber stamped his travel approval was withdrawn by Prime Minister Gusmão due to pressing government issues. Nevertheless, Gutierrez gave me his blessing to go as his representative.

When Gordon and I went to the EU we found they were receptive to our suggestion. They realised all it would require was forty Guarda Nacional Republicana to stay after the UN pulled out. However, even though the Portuguese didn't warm to the proposal like the EU had, I was pleased they'd at least received the idea. I also met with their police, which were facilitated by then UN Police Commissioner Luis Carrilho, a very intelligent, extremely competent and well-liked individual who was formerly the chief of the Portuguese president's security detail and was well connected in all areas of Portuguese politics. I was confident our idea would get across the line but the AFP blocked it, saying what I was attempting to do wasn't Australia's business. I responded that I was an advisor to the Secretary of State (at Canberra's will) and they were now preventing East Timor from taking my advice. It was a crushing blow.

When I advised Peake about Canberra's reaction he had a brainwave. He suggested we see his mate Lord Jeremy 'Paddy'

Ashdown, a former Royal Marine and politician, best known for his efforts in Bosnia and Herzegovina as the international community's high representative when that country was still recovering from the 1992–95 war, which left half the population displaced and the country's infrastructure non-existent. As the person who oversaw the reconstruction of the Balkans, Gordon said Lord Ashdown held a lot of political sway; he could go to Timor and advise the Council of Ministers on how to coordinate their reconstruction. It was a brilliant idea and we workshopped it over a few pints in Portugal, writing up a detailed proposal.

We had to return to Dili via London and during our stopover we met with Lord Ashdown's chief of staff in a park by the River Thames. Paddy was quite excited, we were told, and open to visiting East Timor twice a year to act as an overarching mentor for the nation's leaders. For Timor, this was akin to winning the lottery and I sent a briefing paper to Australia detailing why this was a coup. All Lord Ashdown was asking for was $30,000 per trip – nothing. As part of the arrangement he was also prepared to travel to Australia and meet with AFP and senior government officials to discuss the reconstruction of developing nations. Such an offer was unheard of, but sadly it didn't strike a chord with my superiors.

Despite all of the good Lord Ashdown could do for East Timor, I didn't get a response from Canberra. When I phoned a bureaucrat, he said they'd consider it. He then asked, 'Who is this bloke, anyway?', which hurt. Even though he'd been in possession of the document for a few days his question made it obvious he wasn't interested. However, I remained upbeat and told him about all the great work Lord Ashdown had done.

The only thing the pen-pusher heard, however, was that he was a Brit because he replied, 'What good is that to us?'

While Canberra dilly-dallied, I was being pressured by Paddy's office. He'd left his diary open but was being approached to work for other parties. I phoned Canberra for an answer and received a crushing two-line response the following morning along the lines of: 'The problem of doing this is it would take us down a pathway we can't control. Not approved.' Frustrated by the message's ambiguity, I phoned someone else to clarify what it meant, and these days I use his answer in my leadership talks as an example of one of the worst conversations I'd ever had. When I asked what pathway he thought this might take us down, he replied, 'I don't know, but it might not be where we want to go.'

Talk about an opportunity lost. However, that sort of attitude was indicative of the old AFP and a time when there was a reluctance to take any risk. We have a different culture now, and that change is for the better. I also acknowledge that hindsight proves Lord Ashdown (who sadly passed away while I was writing this book) wasn't needed in Timor. However, I make no apologies for the lengths I went to in preparing for the UN withdrawal. I was reacting to the information I had at the time, and it didn't bode well for Australia.

I was vigilant about my health and hygiene while I was in Dili. We had all number of health problems up there, and diarrhoea was one of them. It was concerning to see water trucks fill their tanks up with a normal hose after dumping excrement at the back of the beach at Dili, and we were careful to only drink bottled water. I secured a very nice place for us to work from when I was given the lease to a terracotta-coloured house, and one of the attractions was that it had a water purification system, which we'd use for washing our faces and hands and cleaning our crockery and utensils. It concerned me that many of my officers would become terribly ill during Timor's rainy season. I had some experts come in to check our water and they found it was a breeding ground for all sorts of bacteria. Further investigations unearthed that we had a septic system set up near our reservoir, so when it rained heavily the septic tank would overflow and contaminate our water. Maintaining good health was a never-ending battle.

The mosquitos were just as dangerous and I'd have my residence fumigated every day to kill mozzies that carried any number of diseases. When my replacement, Commander Charmaine Quade, arrived in Dili, I did the courteous thing and moved to a local hotel. It was an open building, and not surprisingly I was attacked by a swarm of mosquitos each of the three nights I was there. I was also bitten a few times as I loaded luggage into the back of my car before I drove to the airport. I arrived in Canberra and met Emilee at the gym to train together. When we started our workout I felt terrible, and after a while I was tripping over equipment and feeling out of it. Emilee was horrified because everyone was looking at me; she even asked if I'd been drinking. When we went home to our new house I felt lousy and decided to lie down for a minute. It was 6 pm when my head touched the pillow, and when I woke up three hours later I was sweating profusely. I also had a terrible headache – it felt as though someone had stuck a knife into my eye. Emilee confirmed that I looked as terrible as I felt. When I put both feet down on the ground to get up, I thought they were going to crumble. Every bone in my body felt as if it had been hit by a baseball bat. I was so sick I told Emilee – who was on her learner's permit at the time – to get the car keys because she was going to drive me to the hospital.

The doctor looked at me and initially said I had malaria, but when the blood tests came back he advised that I had dengue fever – and not the good strain. He wanted to admit me to the Dangerous Disease Centre, insisting that I needed special care, but I didn't go because I feared I'd never get out. I asked him what I needed to do to take care of myself. I was advised to keep hydrated and eat soup. The doctor prescribed the strongest possible painkillers for me, but nothing worked. For three months I'd fall asleep at lunchtime and wake at eight that evening. He did more tests and found I had chikungunya, a mosquito-borne virus. Surprisingly, he said I'd had it before. It laid me low for quite a while, and I have no doubt its effects meant I was far from my best when I was sent to work in my next major posting: high tech crime. It was a stressful time, and having to watch the most horrendous vision of exploited children, uploaded online by paedophiles, took a further toll on my health.

25
LORDY, LORDY

*'I was attracted to Grant's genuine nature and I loved
his strength ... not his physical strength, but his
strength of character.'*
– Kate 'Lordy' Lord

Composer Franz Schubert's 'Ave Maria' is popular at weddings, but I relate more to something he said in the 1800s: 'Happy is the man who finds a true friend, and far happier is he who finds that true friend in his wife.' It's true! Even though ours was not a conventional courtship, I found my soulmate – and best friend – when Kate Lord, otherwise known as 'Lordy', asked some friends at the Canberra gym we trained at in 2010 to find out whether I liked her.

Of course I'd noticed Lordy. Who wouldn't? She's a beautiful person who always makes her presence known. But I'd just come out of a nightmare relationship and had sworn off women, as many blokes do after a rough voyage. Police work had a negative impact on my relationships, although I hasten to add there are two sides to every story. It's also a fact that life in the force can leave officers feeling jaded, and that can affect their personalities. A lot of us don't communicate as well as we ought to, but I never talked about what I witnessed because I wanted to protect my partners from being traumatised. I adopted the same approach as most cops by downplaying the images and memories that kept me awake at night. When I'd return home from a shift I'd sum up my day by saying, 'It was a rough day at the office . . . What do you want to do for dinner?' While I thought I was protecting my partners from the harsh realities of policing, they became frustrated and accused me of being distant or not in the moment. Many officers become distrustful as a result of police work, and consequently tend to be more comfortable hanging out with like-minded people.

I was so lucky to meet Lordy. She'd also recently come out of a relationship and had no intention of being hurt again. We met at a gym called Elite Physique not long after I returned to Canberra from serving in East Timor. I was the Commander of Operations and Missions for the International Deployment Group. My job was to oversee the more than 500 officers who were serving in such countries as the Solomon Islands, Cyprus, Timor-Leste and Somalia. I also had to help prepare those officers who'd been selected for an overseas posting. The job consumed my thoughts, and I had no idea Lordy was interested in me. I had never been very good at picking up on signals. Despite growing up surrounded by females – my mother, my sister and their friends – women remain a mystery to me.

My cluelessness led to an embarrassing episode in Hawaii when a local girl I'd befriended named Dana saw me days before I left for Australia. She told me about a 'friend' of hers who liked a guy who was about to leave Honolulu. However, she didn't know if the guy liked her. Well, I offered all sorts of suggestions for her friend and returned home. It took six months before it dawned on me that Dana was actually talking about us!

So as a slow learner I'm grateful Lordy didn't hold it against me when I dawdled out of the blocks, because she thought I might be someone worth knowing. Lordy and I had noticed one another, and it may sound like school playground stuff, but one night my monster of a mate, Stevie Sugars, asked me whether I liked Lordy and if I'd go out with her. Sugars is a beast. He stands 6 foot 1 and is 150 kilos of brute strength. When Maree and I divorced he helped me collect my gear, even carrying my fridge out of the house – on his broad back. I once saw him walk into the gym straight from work wearing his overalls and boots, and he lifted 300 kilos off the ground without even warming up. He was a loyal friend, but when I said I wouldn't mind going out with Kate his next sentence was to the point: 'If you hurt her, I'll fucking kill you. She's like family to me!' I said 'No worries' and left the change room to lift weights.

As I walked past the office, Billy Giampaolo, the gym's owner, asked if I had a few minutes for a chat. He delivered the same spiel as Stevie, also adding that if I hurt her he'd kill me because she was 'like family' to him too.

'Steady on, Billy,' I said, wondering what I might be walking into. 'I haven't even taken her out for dinner yet.'

Despite the threat of being murdered if I put a foot wrong, Lordy and I went out to a little restaurant in Woden. I liked that she had old-school values. She placed family first, and I could see she was a caring, nurturing person. She was also an elite athlete, and her story about beating Cathy Freeman – the hero of the Sydney Olympics – in a running race when they were kids caught my attention. However, she was now a rower and had come painfully close to qualifying for the Australian team. I could sense that not fulfilling her dream was a hurt she carried, something I could relate to because I was still scarred by the way my bobsleigh team had been treated by the AOC. The mental strength and discipline Lordy had developed as a rower wasn't wasted though. Along with her loyalty, love and patience, those traits would prove invaluable only a few years later, and would hold our family together.

However, that was a long way down the track from dinner that night. As we swapped stories about our lives I was struck by the company I was in. Kate had a natural warmth and it was very easy to relax with her; we saw a lot of each other over the next five weeks. Whenever my mates saw us together they'd ask Lordy where her seeing eye dog was because they thought I was punching above my weight. And maybe I was – I'd never met anyone like her before. She was so confident in her own skin. Indeed, she was confident enough to drop a bombshell one afternoon when we walked up Mount Taylor, which offers majestic views over Canberra. It's a special place because the air at the top is so clean, although on this particular day I don't know if it was the altitude or Lordy's words that made my head spin, albeit in the best possible way. Lordy put her cards on the table and told me she was falling in love with me. I listened as she continued: 'I'm of an age where I know who I want to be with; you're of an age where you know whether or not it will work. But I'm not missing out on having a child, so I'm giving you an out if you want one.'

The great thing with me and Lordy was that neither of us hid anything from the other. Our lives were open books. She knew that I was useless with girls. My marriage with Maree had been good for a few years, but we'd drifted apart. We were blessed to have our beautiful Emilee, a kind, caring kid who values those close to her with a fierce loyalty. I had a few relationships after the divorce but they headed south.

Lordy and I clicked because we share so much in common. We're both homebodies; we share a love of country music, American football and cricket. The two of us believe in family and commitment. That trait came to the fore when I was working in Afghanistan and my father and his partner, Terry, were suffering from Alzheimer's disease. Kate was very strong through their illness, arranging for them to go into care and visiting them almost every day. She helped clean their house and settled their dogs into new homes. As they said, she was 'an angel'. She was also a huge comfort to me when my father passed away, helping me to accept things for what they were.

Dad's death was a huge blow. I picked up that things weren't quite right with him in 2008 when I flew him to Dili so we could spend time together. He'd become forgetful, and some of the things he said didn't make sense. He was in his early seventies, so I simply put it down to his getting older. Four years later it was obvious Dad was in the grip of Alzheimer's, and that was hard. He'd tell me he had just had a blazing row with Mum, who'd been dead since 1987. After Terry passed away, Dad would say he'd seen him earlier in the day.

Compounding Dad's health problems was that he'd broken his leg while staying at Nambucca Heads on the NSW north coast. He'd had a few glasses of wine and tripped over a small brick wall in the dark. He lay in agony for four long hours, his leg shattered, before his hosts returned home and rescued him. The impact on his health was dreadful. He was sedentary and developed lung problems. All this conspired to make his final three years a struggle.

Lordy shouldered the responsibility for Dad when I was deployed to Afghanistan. She was his rock. After Dad broke his leg, she and our daughter, Jacinta, drove from our place on the Gold Coast to Tweed Heads four times a week. Lordy wanted to ensure he wasn't alone. Dad's decline was rapid, though. When he caught pneumonia towards the end of 2014 he lapsed into unconsciousness not long after doctors put him on a ventilator. I knew Dad didn't have long to live when I sat with him on what was to be his final night. We'd made our peace long ago, and as I looked at him I remembered how Terry told me Dad had always longed for a hug from his son. On this occasion I farewelled Dad with a kiss on his forehead. 'You know I always loved you, Dad,' I whispered. 'I'll see you on the other side. Just be good to yourself – don't take any crap from Mum.' I'd like to think that made him happy. He died a few hours later, and while it was sad, I was happy my father had finally found peace.

At this stage of my life the demands and pressures of my job were causing me to unravel. That invisible backpack of pebbles I'd accumulated in thirty long, tough years as a cop was overflowing. Even the simple things in life were a battle.

Although it was not Dad's doing, his illness added to problems that were becoming insurmountable in my mind, and I didn't know why I felt that way. Thankfully, when Dad died I wasn't gripped by the same anger that had raged within me when Mum passed away. Unlike Mum, who neglected her health, Dad had lived a good life. It hurt me and Jenelle deeply to know that had Mum hung on for just a few months she would have become a grandmother, and I have no doubt that would have turned her life around.

Lordy has said she was drawn to my strength of character. She thought I was genuine, but that was exactly what I saw in her, along with her unbridled confidence. She is a school teacher and a personal trainer, but at 36 (there's a thirteen-year age gap between us), she wanted her own child. When she made that clear to me after we'd been going out for five weeks, I was blown away by the fact that she knew what she wanted. I was immensely grateful that a mere eight weeks after Lordy and I started going out, and just three weeks after she was brave enough to tell me what she wanted out of life, she fell pregnant with Jacinta.

Our daughter is the mirror image of her mother – genuine, caring and sensitive. Ever since she's been able to walk, Jacinta has skipped and danced her way through life. She has a good spirit. When she turned eight she asked that instead of receiving a bag full of presents, we head to Australia Zoo on the Sunshine Coast to see the animals. When she said that, I felt the same surge of the love and wonderment that overcame me when I laid eyes on her for the first time. It was exactly how I'd felt when I first saw Emilee twenty-six years earlier.

As I said, the start to my relationship with Lordy, was different to most others, and while we've had our challenges, it's withstood all tests. I know that over the years I wasn't easy to live with, and there was a huge challenge looming on the horizon that would be very hard on Kate and Jacinta. However, even during the worst of it, my love for them kept me strong. As Franz Schubert said, a man is lucky to have his best friend as his wife. I might struggle to express my emotions, but when I tell Lordy I love her they're the most honest, heartfelt words I've ever said.

26
MISSION AFGHANISTAN

'The Federal Government is considering expanding the
AFP's role in Afghanistan – currently restricted to just
four officers – as part of its plan to widen Australia's
effort in the war-torn country . . .'
– *The Age*, 24 February 2008

In October 2012, I replaced Wayne Buchhorn as the commander of the thirty AFP officers based throughout Afghanistan in Kabul, Kandahar and Tarin Kowt. When the Royal Australian Air Force Hercules I was on landed at the Hamid Karzai International Airport in Kabul, I commenced an assignment that was the most challenging I'd ever undertaken. Our mission in Afghanistan was the first time a civilian police force from Australia had been deployed to an active war zone, and I had a number of briefs, responsibilities and orders from my superiors in Canberra. However, my overarching concern was to do everything within my power to ensure each of my officers returned home in one piece.

Going to Afghanistan was the crowning moment of my career. Besides my duties for the AFP, I was also the Deputy Commander of the International Police Coordination Board

(IPCB-A). I inherited that position because of Wayne's foresight. The board was responsible for the police officers representing the member nations – Australia, Canada, Denmark, France, Germany, Italy, Japan, the Netherlands, Norway, the United Kingdom and the United States – and Wayne (who these days is an assistant commissioner) realised the AFP could have an even greater strategic role if it became a part of the command.

My superiors realised I was interested in going to Afghanistan in 2011 when I requested leave without pay to travel there as a member of the Australian Civilian Corps (ACC). The Corps recruits civilian specialists to provide their expertise in order to assist developing nations in times of conflict or natural disaster. It was formed in 2009 and has deployed people to such places as South Sudan, Afghanistan and Haiti. In 2012, a former AFP officer and a great personal friend of mine, David Savage, had the misfortune of becoming Australia's first civilian casualty in Afghanistan when he was badly wounded by a suicide bomber while serving in the corps. It shocked the world because a 12-year-old boy was identified as the person who had targeted David and a group of Westerners outside a bazaar in Uruzgan. Adding salt to David's wounds was the fact that, not long after arriving in Afghanistan, he'd befriended the child who attempted to kill him. News of his injuries hit the AFP especially hard because David had served with distinction in a number of hot spots, including East Timor. Ultimately, I decided not to go to Afghanistan with the ACC because I'd only recently returned from Timor-Leste and realised I still had a lot to do for the AFP.

My running joke about the year I spent in Afghanistan is that it seemed like 'death by meetings'. The reality, though, is that it was the toughest job I'd ever undertaken. Apart from the obvious risks that came with spending a lot of time 'outside of the wire' (a military term for not being in the safety of a barricaded and highly secure base), I found myself in some dangerous situations. I know there were people caught in much deeper stuff during their service over there than I ever was, but I had some tough experiences. The Taliban attempted to overrun the Green Village, the place in Kabul where I and four other colleagues were accommodated. Moments after I disembarked an RAAF Hercules at Kandahar, was targeted by insurgents with a guided missile. I was also in Tarin Kowt during a rocket attack. I even drew my Glock pistol when a meeting I was at with local Afghan police generals seemed as though it was about to erupt into a bloodbath.

Despite the dangers, the reason why I nominate Afghanistan as my career's greatest challenge was because everyone I dealt with, be it the military or local police chiefs, all wanted their agendas rammed to the top of an exhaustive list. It was as much a juggling act as it was a test of my diplomacy. One day I could be dealing with the problems our AFP officers were working through as they trained illiterate Afghan police recruits, the next might be spent managing the expectations of three-star generals from the International Security Assistance Force (ISAF) with 250,000 troops serving under them. Then there was a battalion of ambassadors, diplomats, government officials, United Nations delegates, the European Union Police Mission (EUPOL), politicians, and senior Afghan police who I was constantly briefing about the work and end goals of the IPCB-A.

On top of that I also had my responsibilities to the AFP in Canberra, and that meant I oversaw budgets, finances and human resources, and filed a series of detailed reports about the work our people were doing around the country. There were clear and ever-present dangers. Anyone who drove in a vehicle outside of the Green Zone risked being picked off by a sniper or hit by a vehicle-borne Improvised Explosive Device (IED). The Green Zone is an area in Kabul where embassies, international news media organisations and a number of military headquarters are fortified by grey, blast-proof concrete walls. It's heavily guarded by Afghan and coalition forces, and among the safeguards are a number of protocols, including truck drivers who enter the place after being verified by biometric scanners. There were reports that diplomats based within the walls ensured they enjoyed the creature comforts of home by doing such things as flying in cheesecake from New York or cases of wine from Europe. Like many other people, I thought it was bizarre to be told that in a place of such suffering and misery, pet peacocks strolled the grounds of the United Nations compound.

That said, it didn't matter where you were in Afghanistan, you couldn't afford to drop your guard – *ever*. Even the few places that should have been safe havens, such as the police building in Kabul, weren't immune from bloodshed. One morning I was rushed out of a high-level meeting by my security detail when a female Afghan police sergeant drew her sidearm and shot an American civilian law enforcement contractor who was simply admiring some medals in a glass display case. Like so many others killed in Afghanistan, he didn't see death coming. It was sometimes hard to identify near misses. I'll never forget the time I disembarked a RAAF Hercules in Kandahar and thought nothing of the 'puff' overhead. Sirens suddenly started wailing and I followed the military guys who dived onto the ground. It was a rocket attack, and the plane I'd travelled on was the Taliban's target. While I was shaken, I couldn't help but smile when I heard a digger crack a joke that we'd be in serious trouble if the insurgents ever learnt how to use their stuff!

I was working in intelligence when John Howard's government sent our first four officers to Afghanistan in 2006, and one of my roles was to provide support to our people in East Timor and Afghanistan. The British Foreign Secretary had requested that Australia assist the newly created Counter-Narcotics Police of Afghanistan by providing some officers who could help mentor the Afghans. Two officers were attached to the British Embassy Drug Team in the opium heartland of Jalalabad, where they gathered intelligence on opium smuggling; the other two were assigned to the US-led Combined Security Transition Command (CSTC-A) in Kabul, providing senior Afghanistan National Police (ANP) personnel with mentoring and policy development.

The AFP's financial contribution to Afghanistan from 2007 to 2008 was noted in the Budget Statement as being $2.595 million, but our financial and personnel commitment grew substantially from there. In 2008, Australia's then Defence Minister Joel Fitzgibbon advised parliament that the nation needed to broaden its police commitments to Afghanistan to 'hold our military gains and enforce the rule of law'. As a result, we committed even more people and cash, and our officers mentored Afghans in Tarin Kowt, where most of Australia's defence personnel were based. By November 2010 our personnel numbers had grown to 28, and our financial commitment to help establish law and order in Afghanistan increased substantially. When people ask me why the AFP risked the lives of officers in a war zone, I often quote the findings of surveys conducted between 2006 and 2013 by the Washington DC-based Brookings Institute. These researchers found that Afghans nominated 'insecurity' as their nation's major concern – ahead of unemployment, the economy, corruption, education, poverty, suicide attacks and even the Taliban. When you realise the horrors that regime inflicted upon the population until they were overthrown by the US-led invasion in 2001, that says a lot!

When the Taliban era ended there were very few Western-style democratic institutions – including police – remaining in Afghanistan. The few police officers there were mostly untrained, ill-equipped and illiterate, and their reputation didn't encourage the population to trust them. Apart from their corruption, it was well known that their allegiance was to warlords and local commanders. The impact of Afghanistan's continued thirty-year state of conflict resulted in five million citizens – including members of the professional and educated class – leaving their homeland to seek refuge in more peaceful nations. The 30 million who remained were 'educated' under the Taliban's narrow and antiquated curriculum, and despite the return of some expats after the coalition's intervention, levels of illiteracy remained unacceptably high. There was also a noticeable dearth of competent professionals, officials and leaders. It was against this background that Germany took the lead of the coalition law enforcement partners to help provide a stable rule of law in Afghanistan. However, at the beginning of the mission there was a fixation on quantity rather than quality, and in the early stages of the restructure there was also an emphasis on counter-insurgency capability instead of addressing the need for a traditional community-based police force. This view was all but confirmed by Catherine Royle, the former British diplomat who was the director of the IPCB-A when I arrived. When Royle completed her term, she admitted, 'We built a security force, not a police force.'

The impact of this was reflected in statistics that suggested the counter-insurgency death toll for the Afghan police was double that of their army counterparts. Cops were being used to combat the Taliban because then President Hamid Karzai deemed the insurgents an organised crime entity, which made them the responsibility of the police. It was politics gone mad. While international forces had assembled in his country to fight the Taliban, Karzai didn't want to give his nation's former regime any semblance of credibility by declaring war on them. However, as local police took on more of a military role, the nation's insecurity ploughed the ground for Afghanistan to re-emerge as one of the world's main poppy producers. Despite the best efforts of international police in curtailing the trade, in 2012, the year I arrived there, Afghanistan was responsible for 90 per cent of the world's opiates. Many feared the money was being funnelled into the pockets of the Taliban and a number of corrupt politicians, and the financial windfall provided the Taliban with funds for even more operations by insurgents: suicide bombings, murders and kidnappings, which further destabilised the nation's security. It was a vicious cycle, and it hurt to read in a 2018 United Nations Office on Drugs and Crime (ONDC) report that the 2017 harvest yielded an unprecedented record number of poppies, with experts estimating there were enough to produce 900 tonnes of 'export quality' heroin.

The best way I can explain how my mind was in Afghanistan is to say it was engulfed by the static you see on a television set when it has poor reception. I rarely relaxed because I had so many thoughts running through my mind. One thought I couldn't shake was knowing how much I'd disappointed Kate. I'd accepted the posting despite Lordy being vehemently opposed to me going. When we started dating, Kate not only flew in the face of her mother's advice to never go out with a cop, she also made it clear she didn't want me to ever serve in Afghanistan. Her fear intensified a month before I left for Kabul when a friend of hers was one of three Australian soldiers killed in Kandahar when an Afghan, who'd earned their trust after serving alongside them for a year, opened fire on the troops. The assassin was fatally shot by the diggers who were on guard duty, but Kate's friend's senseless death only solidified her view that Australia was 'stupid' to continue sending troops and other personnel to a country she figured didn't want to be saved by *us*.

While I knew how Kate felt, when I was offered the opportunity to head the AFP's commitment to provide the newly formed Afghanistan National Police with world's best law enforcement practices, I didn't hesitate to step forward. Apart from the honour, I believed I could make a difference. Of course, this was of cold comfort to Kate, who was in the laundry when I phoned to say that in just two minutes' time I'd be in a meeting to advise my superiors whether or not I'd serve in Afghanistan.

It cut her to the bone that I'd all but agreed to assume the posting without first seeking her input. That troubled me while I was in Afghanistan, but over and again I buried that thought – along with many other feelings that surfaced during my time there – by focusing on my job.

I also obsessed about how I could ensure the officers serving under my command would return home safe and sound. I didn't realise it at the time but I was intuitively employing what are known as 'psychological distractions'. This meant I was always finding something to distract me because an idle mind is a magnet for destructive thoughts. I found Friday was always the hardest day of the week. It was our down day because that's the holy day for Muslims, and I'd keep to myself. As the weeks turned into months I'd sit outside and watch the C-130 Hercules flying troops home, and as I watched them soar above us I wished I was going home to Kate and Jacinta. I kept busy. I trained religiously, going to the gym at least once, if not twice a day, every day. I had terrible days, weighed down by terrible thoughts, but I couldn't escape through drinking alcohol because ours was a dry mission. Even though I was the leader I refused to sneak grog into my quarters, because I would have had to discipline an officer under my command if they breached the rules. However, before I left Australia I purchased a small pharmacy's worth of painkillers and sedatives to numb the feelings and thoughts that had begun to torment me: Mum. Dad and Terry. Knowing I'd hurt Kate. Leaving Jacinta. Learning about kids who were killed or wounded in Afghanistan. Always wondering what I'd do if our base was attacked. Whether my people in Tarin Kowt were safe. Why on earth didn't the AOC send our bobsleigh team to the Winter Olympics? What could I have done to be a better player for the East Hills Bulldogs all those years ago? Why didn't Canberra seem interested in what we were doing in Afghanistan?

They were just some of the thoughts that continuously swirled around inside my head. The only respite was the sleep provided by the painkillers. Sleep was my friend because I needed it to function. My mind was in a constant state of turmoil, and there was never any respite when I wasn't busy. It didn't help that I refused to talk to anyone about the thoughts that kept me awake at night. I know I could've spoken to Lordy, but I resisted making that phone call. The load she was carrying while I was thousands of kilometres away weighed heavily on my mind. I knew she was doing it tough. Besides not wanting me to go to Afghanistan, she was holding our home life together. Apart from caring for Jacinta, she was travelling four times a week to Tweed Heads to look after Dad and Terry. I've since realised I willingly entered a state of hyper-vigilance while I was in Kabul because it was the only way I could get through my many professional – and mental – challenges.

While most of the AFP's contingent in Kabul were accommodated at either the US military barracks or Camp Anjuman, a place that was operated by a private security firm, I was based at the Green Village in eastern Kabul along with four AFP officers. It was quite the oasis in this strict Islamic nation. Apart from the 1800 rooms that accommodated private security operators, contractors, non-government organisations, police officers from all over the world and other workers, it also provided wi-fi, a business centre, a fully equipped gymnasium and the Dough Re Mi patisserie, which I was pleasantly surprised to discover sold Baskin-Robbins ice-cream. There were plenty of restaurants, a juice bar, a day spa (which offered everything from a beard trim to a pedicure), outdoor garden areas, a games room, and even a shop that sold cologne and perfume. We were protected by Gurkha veterans, who were all battle-hardened warriors from Nepal, but it wasn't a military base. Some people described its atmosphere as being similar to that of a US college; certainly, it was the only place in Afghanistan where women could wear skirts, shorts or even bikinis without the risk of offending the locals.

My life quickly fell into a routine. I'd meet with the operation's lead, initially Catherine Royle, who was dedicated to her duty. She is highly intelligent, extremely confident and doesn't tolerate fools gladly. I liked that she valued a strong work ethic and had the rare ability to slice through military red tape and bureaucratic BS quickly – it's a gift. During my term she was replaced by a retired Brigadier General from the German police force named Gerald Stoeter. He was calm, considered and liked to deliberate while he thought through issues. He'd previously served in Afghanistan as a police officer and was dedicated the IPCB cause. It said a lot for his abilities that he was able to bring together many disparate elements to harmonise the IPCB approach.

I met with these commanders in a variety of places, including the IPCB office in Green Village or at Camp Eggers (during Royle's term). We also met twice a week in the Ministry of Interior (MOI) building, which was anywhere between a 45-minute and an hour's drive from the village. It seems ironic, but I viewed the MOI building as perhaps the most dangerous place in Kabul, despite it being one of the most heavily guarded. It always concerned me that as the Afghan military guards went over our cars with a fine-toothed comb, they'd nonchalantly be waving to locals in trucks straight out of *The Beverly Hillbillies*. I'd watch nervously as they'd share a carefree laugh and a chat with the driver and passengers as they drove slowly by. My protection detail couldn't contain their frustration every time they watched this scene play out, calling it a joke. There was always the fear that lives would be the price for such nonchalance. I raised my concerns to those in charge, but nothing ever changed. The reaction was always, 'Oh well, that's Afghanistan.' It struck me that the local guards were sending a passive-aggressive message, reminding us we were intruders.

The meetings I attended were an opportunity to discuss timelines and progress with the ANP. We'd worked with them to develop a two-year plan and a ten-year underpinning operations blueprint. We spent a lot of our time working on ways to have the ANP work as a unified force. Barriers were constantly being put up for us to climb over, with some Afghan generals wanting to defend their patch. I did a lot of strategic work but the number of meetings was at times overwhelming. Once a month we had two meetings with the IPCB Board of Directors, all of whom were ambassadors, senior military, EUPOL and UN officials. I'd then chair the meeting of the IPCB Committee with the deputy ambassadors and First Secretaries of embassies, senior police and UN officials. I had a weekly catch-up with Australia's ambassador, Jon Philp, and I also chaired the Senior Police Advisory Group (SPAG), a meeting of all the Senior Police Contributing Commanders who were supporting the development of the ANP and also harmonising our individual commitments to the ANP.

Each of these meetings was political and required a lot of preparation. There were numerous projects centred around policing reform, ranging from the salaries officers were paid through to the establishing of procedures for officers to gain promotions. We were forever building the basic structures Western police forces take for granted, because it was crucial to provide the Afghans with a solid foundation they could work from. Our desire was to implement a ten-year plan but the Afghans resisted, saying that was 'too long' in their lifetime. They were willing to accept a two-year strategic plan that included a series of projects they could work on over the next decade.

Many of my colleagues couldn't understand the Afghans' logic, but I chose to follow the advice of Lord Paddy Ashdown, who wrote about this kind of situation in his book *Swords and Ploughshares: Bringing Peace to the 21st Century*: 'Our task therefore is not to seek perfection, but to achieve the most acceptable form of imperfection possible . . . then let them complete the process of building the "police force" they want, rather than the one we dreamt for them'. That summed up the situation in Afghanistan brilliantly. In an environment where there are vast cultural differences, you need to aim for a 51 per cent success rate – not the 100 per cent that the Western mentality demands. An improvement of any sort is an improvement, and you can then build on it. We spent a lot of time engaging with the Afghans and putting in place the locals who appeared the best qualified to run the programs, having quickly realised many of their generals didn't necessarily have either the intelligence or the capacity required to see things through. Most of them had attained their positions of power through their family lineage, and I found that ancient system of inherited influence was retarding Afghanistan's development because good people were often overlooked. That included a major I regularly dealt with. He spoke perfect English, was educated overseas and had uncommon common sense. However, this man knew he'd never be promoted to a higher rank because he had neither the connections nor the money to bribe his way to the top. The tragedy was that this bloke really could have made a difference to a nation that badly needed it.

The international police community put the Afghan recruits through an eight-week basic patrol officers' course. They were taught their country's constitution and penal code as well as the need to respect gender and human rights – and there were massive shifts in mindsets. The AFP drilled 'blue-issue basic policing' into them, which included learning to read and write, community policing skills and soft policing diplomacy, open-handed combat techniques, baton use, controlling a riot and handcuffing. We also taught them how to manage a crime scene and investigate a sexual assault – which presented difficulties due to the Islamic culture. Progress in the various provinces depended upon which foreign nations were representing the IPCB-A, but by 2012 there were some slight improvements in the ANP's approach towards policing. This was a welcome change from such incidents as 'The Bridge' in 2010, when a group of Afghan police were ordered to guard an Australian-built bridge in Tarin Kowt. When the temperature dropped they decided it was ridiculous that they should be standing outside and freezing when there was a house right next to the bridge. So, they turfed the owner out onto the street and used his house as a sentry post. The evicted owner took his revenge by joining the Taliban insurgency and planting roadside bombs, which could indiscriminately kill or wound anyone from children to foreign soldiers to local police.

The behaviour of those police only reinforced the local view that the ANP members were corrupt, uneducated and lazy. When I first arrived in Afghanistan I met some recruits who clearly had only signed up because of the uniform and pay cheque; I could see it was not a calling for them. I also realised that an individual's motive for joining seemed to depend on what region in the country they hailed from and whether they saw it as an opportunity for corruption. As I soon found out, the salaries of the lower ranks were being siphoned off by their superiors, which meant many new police weren't getting paid. Those officers decided if their bosses weren't going to pay them, the people who they protected could.

However, during my stint in Afghanistan, I witnessed great enthusiasm in the ranks of the recruits the AFP trained. They realised there were people who believed in them, and for once they weren't being treated like poorer cousins to the military. Unfortunately, just as the AFP was working in collaboration with other nations to raise the policing standards, the Federal Government recalled us to Australia. To my mind, that was the AFP's most humiliating episode.

One bright spot I enjoyed in Afghanistan came about by taking a leaf out of my experiences in Timor-Leste. We enjoyed a lot of personal satisfaction from helping an orphanage in Dili, and I decided we ought to do the same in Kabul. We officers were on good money, and I figured it was one tangible way to show some goodwill to members of the population who'd welcome it. I felt deeply sorry for those kids. They were alone in the world after their lives had been turned upside down by a war they didn't ask for. The tragedy of Afghanistan is that, whether it was at the hands of the Russians in the 1980s, or due to the war involving the 'Coalition of the Willing' nations in the 2000s, there are many tales that detail the suffering of innocent children. My colleagues were enthusiastic in supporting the orphanage, and we'd often make visits. Some of the children had been disfigured and scarred by acts of war, and even though it would have been easy to shed tears over the injustice of their lot, we donned smiles and did such things as play sport with them. For all of the wishing I did to be back home with my family when I saw those C-130s leave the airport, the Afghans couldn't escape. I'll never forget the despair I saw etched in the face of a local who worked with us when he told us his nephews and nieces had been injured in a bombing the previous night. It was dreadful. I should have realised I was blessed by comparison, but my mind wasn't capable of registering such things.

27
THE BUNKER

'A previous attack on Green Village, in May 2012, left eight
people dead. The compound sits along a road brimming with
foreign facilities, including a United Nations compound as well
as numerous military and civilian bases. This summer, attackers
detonated a bomb and tried to storm a civilian base along the
same road, killing at least nine people in the assault . . .'
– The New York Times, 18 October 2013

My Glock 22 service pistol was trained on the door of the reinforced concrete bunker where my colleague, Superintendent John 'Ben' Cartwright and I were holed up. Should our worst fears be realised, we could have been trading gunfire with some of the heavily armed Taliban insurgents who had attacked our compound. Two suicide bombers signalled the moment the war came right to our doorstep by blowing themselves up and blasting holes in the perimeter fence that protected the Green Village. Their misguided sacrifice provided other fanatics with a staging point to storm into our base and attempt to slaughter the foreign police officers, contractors and workers who were accommodated in the maze of buildings. Ironically, the only reason any of us were there was to help the Afghan people.

As Ben and I listened to the gunfire being exchanged between the insurgents and our security detail of Gurkha veterans, we braced ourselves for the possibility that we'd have to fight for our lives. We were the only people in our bunker, one of many scattered throughout the compound. We'd almost taken refuge in another one not long after the gun battle started, but thanks to what I'd learnt in my training, I realised at the last minute that we needed to make another choice – and fast. The bunker was already crammed with people, and I feared if the Taliban succeeded in overrunning the compound it'd be tantamount to a turkey shoot because there were so many targets. I also noticed that a lot of people inside the crammed bunker were armed. In such a highly stressed environment, so-called 'friendly fire' could pose a far greater threat to an individual's safety than the insurgents. But while I was happy to at least feel safe in the new digs, we'd found perhaps the filthiest bunker in Afghanistan – we were blanketed in the thick cobwebs that hung from the roof, and a large colony of spiders were scrambling about, angry to have had their home disturbed by two intruders. And the incessant rustling from the back of our sanctuary suggested it was infested with rats.

However, as we attuned our ears to ascertain whether the gunfire was headed in our direction, neither Ben nor I were prepared to risk being caught in the crossfire to find another hiding spot – although the idea did cross my mind when I thought I spotted the outlines of giant rats. It was snowing outside but the heat trapped inside the bunker was oven-like. Perspiration flowed beneath my military-issue ballistic helmet and personal body armour. Ironically, I told myself for the hundredth time that the reason I was sweating and my hands were shaking was due to the heat and not white-knuckled terror.

As my Glock remained aimed at the door I worried about my four officers and the locally engaged staff of Afghan civilians. I'd checked on them in the immediate aftermath of the explosions and had been relieved to discover that everyone on duty had escaped the initial stage of the attack unscathed. But we'd been separated during the confusion that engulfed the village when I ran the 50 metres to my room to kit up and arm myself. People were running madly in all directions amid the shouting, screaming and unrelenting wailing of the siren that alerted everyone to take cover.

I was worried by the image of gun-toting insurgents kicking down the bunker door. But not knowing where my colleagues were, or the condition they were in, was torture. During our time in Afghanistan I'd done everything within my power – even fought pitched battles with powerful bureaucrats – to put my officers' safety ahead of the 'desired outcomes' a number of international bodies pursued. I was intent on fulfilling my promise to get each officer back to their loved ones in one piece. It was frustrating that at this moment I couldn't phone any of them. Neither Ben nor I had our mobiles with us, although the reality was that, even if we did, the powers-that-be would've already killed all communications in the village as a security protocol. Invariably my mind drifted to home. I was worried about how Lordy would react if the news had already reached Australia that the Green Village was under attack. I knew she'd try to phone me over and over again to ensure I was okay, and would become increasingly frustrated and worried about not being able to get through.

I had almost completed my latest report on our efforts to mould the ANP into a modern, functioning force when the Green Village was targeted. I remember taking a brief break to enjoy the sight of snow falling outside my window only seconds before the shockwaves that followed the explosions rocked our barracks and shattered all of the windows. In the split-second that followed the detonations, the unrelenting chatter of machine guns started as the Gurkhas stood their ground and tried to repel the attack. In places such as Afghanistan you always know something terrible could happen, but it still comes as a shock when situations like this one erupt. Luckily my training – and a healthy surge of adrenaline – kicked in. My immediate reaction was to rush down and check on my people, and my priority was to check on Ben, who I knew was training in the gym.

I was pleased to see that Ben wasn't buried under a pile of dumbbells, and he sprinted towards me at Usain Bolt speed. We then checked our other officers, and the Afghan civilians who worked for us either as translators or administration staff. They were all unharmed, although I discovered a few of the Afghans had been knocked off their seats by the shockwaves. While they were dazed, fortunately everyone was physically okay and able to make their way to the safety of the bunkers unassisted. After seeing them off, I rushed back to my room for my protective armour and pistol, knowing the Glock would be as useful as a bowl of spaghetti if the Taliban fighters succeeded in breaching our defences. The Canadians, French and American police carried long-arms – or machine guns – in Afghanistan, but our government only sanctioned for us to use pistols. I cursed whoever it was that had made that decision as I hurriedly kitted myself out in my protective gear.

Not long after I'd arrived in Kabul I started to play the 'what if' game. Every day a series of scenarios and questions would run through my head: *What if* we're attacked? *What if* the Taliban overrun our base? *What if* I have to get my people out of here? I had a whirlpool of questions that required solutions. Ultimately, I knew not only that lives were at stake, but that *I* was responsible for them. That responsibility weighed heavily on me. It dictated a lot of my actions and responses to situations. I spoke from the heart whenever I told the officers under my command that regardless of the reasons they'd been sent to Afghanistan, it was my sole intention to ensure each of them returned home to their loved ones intact. When I look back now, however, I realise what I had in mind was an image of them walking through the door of their homes with four limbs in place and their head still on their shoulders. Unfortunately, as I discovered through my own experience, I could do nothing to prevent someone's mental wellbeing from being scarred. I couldn't even do that for myself.

Nevertheless, I had an overriding sense of duty to do everything within my power – and then some – to guarantee their wellbeing in one of the deadliest places on earth. My determination to be their shield was akin to my attitude during my time in the cybercrime unit and TSETT when I wanted to protect everyone else from the vile vision being posted on the internet. This role I assumed as protector compelled me on several occasions to cancel some mission activity either because of a gut feeling or due to the intelligence we'd received. On some days it was a combination of both. There were many times when I was called out by senior bureaucrats for my call to abandon a particular job (for instance, a British official once mocked me by saying she never knew Aussies were such 'pussycats') but I could live with this. It was easier to cop a bagging than have to tell a grieving family they'd lost their loved one because I'd given in to the pressure to please someone else.

My definition of leadership is doing what is right with the information you have at your disposal. If your course of action means you put noses out of joint, well, that's the price you pay. True leadership is not tickling the belly of someone who rolls over on their back and demands satisfaction.

I tell people that one of the toughest responsibilities they can assume in life is leadership, because by becoming a figurehead there is always the risk they'll become the focus for every failure, every poor decision, every mistake and disappointment that befalls their organisation. However, there are those who embrace leadership as an opportunity to initiate change, take control, inspire and empower. I've often believed time and circumstance play just as much a part in determining how leaders are remembered as their personality and style. One figure from history who I admire is John Curtin, Australia's fourteenth prime minister. He was in office when the Japanese threatened to invade Australia in 1942. Curtin was an intriguing figure; suffering from stress-related ailments, including depression, he was known to be a heavy drinker. He was also self-conscious of a lazy eye that didn't allow for both of his eyes to align, and his natural inclination was to be shy. However, he was renowned for his virtues of tolerance, patience and integrity. His political rival, Sir Robert Menzies, said in tribute that despite suffering many wounds at Curtin's hands, none was ever in the back.

Curtin vehemently opposed the Australian government's attempt to introduce conscription during the First World War, but when the Japanese threatened to invade he went against his beliefs for the good of the nation and its people and forced many men into uniform. Some of them were among the first troops to fight on the Kokoda Track. He went against the British prime minister Winston Churchill when he recalled all Australian forces from the Middle East, and then made an impassioned speech in which he turned to the US for support. He was heavily criticised by Churchill and the American president, Franklin D. Roosevelt, for spreading panic. However, his words finally forced the Allies to acknowledge that Australia was vulnerable to an invasion, and they diverted much-needed weaponry and manpower Down Under. I admire Curtin because he was a man of conviction.

I tried to follow his principles in Afghanistan. As I've said, I was often belittled in meetings because I would not agree to a plan if I thought it unnecessarily endangered the life of a police officer – Australian or otherwise. I've seen some great police leaders – people such as the AFP's current commissioner, AJ Colvin; the former commissioner of the New York City Police Bill Bratton; James Comey, the seventh Director of the FBI; and James McDonnell, the Sherriff of the County of Los Angeles. Every one of them made their people count. All I wanted the people who served under me in Afghanistan (or in my other postings) to realise was that they counted.

My anxiety about sending someone into a potential hot spot stemmed from the fact that neither the IPCB-A or AFP had its own intelligence stream. We could only rely on information provided to us by other agencies, including the Americans,

Brits or the Australian Defence Force. The Australian military was tremendous, and happy to share their intelligence with us, but because we didn't have secure communications we couldn't receive any high-level intelligence or security briefings. Despite our best efforts to obtain the necessary secure lines, they never eventuated, which made what should have been a relatively simple job a highly complicated and dangerous one. Getting that information whenever we could sometimes entailed great personal risk because people needed to travel outside of the Green Village to learn what was what. There was always some potential danger in that process, but my quest to ensure the safety of my officers quickly developed into an obsession. Every day I'd play out in my head – often to the point of it being mental torture – the various explosive scenarios I might need to deal with. I'd keep myself awake at night, looking for more scenarios to worry about.

The job was always going to take its toll on me, and looking back I realise I should have taken the advice I gave to the others: take time during the day to zone out from work by reading, going to the gym, listening to music or doing whatever else allows you to relax. But instead of following my own tip, I was forever formulating a series of emergency plans and escape routes in case we ever needed to evacuate from the compound to the Hamid Karzai International Airport. The airport was only five kilometres away from Kabul's city centre, but if hell was ever unleashed, I knew every inch of that trip would be a battle. There'd already been two occasions when I'd had everyone get ready to head to the airport at speed, and both related to significant intelligence that there'd be multiple 'high-value, complex' attacks within the capital. When I received that information, I decided to get on the front foot. Rather than trying to assemble my personnel during a potentially chaotic event, I wanted to beat ISAF's 'black call', the code that meant no one could use the roads. Camp Anjuman, the place where the main body of the AFP was based, was attacked in November 2018, and it cost four Britons their lives. Our protection team were aware of my concerns, and they'd been proactive in devising a covert escape route to the airport in the event of an evacuation. However, when the Taliban finally came banging at our front door, all I could do was hope the Gurkhas on the parapet ensured we survived the onslaught.

I don't know how long we were in the bunker; time stood still. I believe it could have been an hour. When the all-clear siren finally sounded it took hours for me to check that everyone was all right. I went back to my office as the Gurkhas and Afghan police completed their mopping-up operation – collecting the dead, treating the wounded and securing the location. I didn't go out to inspect the killing field – I'd seen the aftermath of these battles before and it was gruesome. Streaks of blood, guts strewn over the ground, limbs torn from torsos and lifeless bodies is not something you want to look at if you don't have to.

As was the way in Afghanistan, life went on as normal. And that frustrated me. I was annoyed that it felt as though nothing had happened – the people who were in charge of the village did very little to upgrade our security. At best, their attitude seemed blasé, and that didn't rest well with me. The Green Village had a history of being targeted, yet its management still maintained the status quo and forbade us from carrying our weapons inside the complex. While the AFP observed that rule, I made it a standing order that my officers needed at all times to have their weapons, as well as their personal protection gear, close by wherever we were working.

Eventually, we found out that the suicide bombers who'd blown holes in the fence were no more than kids.

The odds of the two suicide bombers who attacked the Green Village not going through with the Taliban's plan were significantly further reduced because their overlords used a remote device to detonate their bomb vests. The only blessing that mad morning was that the bombing happened during the school holidays, which meant that innocent kids were saved from becoming casualties. Had the bombers, in their confused state, gone to the school on a normal day before launching their attack, the fatalities would likely have been horrific. Unbeknown to them, the ever-vigilant Gurkhas observed their every move. Upon realising they were in the wrong place, the bombers panicked. And, I can only imagine, once they realised there was no hope of surviving, they charged towards the compound fence as someone a few hundred metres away flicked the switch that made them martyrs.

It has been six years since that attack on the Green Village, and I'll forever be grateful none of my police or civilian staff were harmed. However, despite all I've read and all the documentaries I've watched about Afghanistan since I returned home, I still can't grasp the depth of the hatred that fuelled those insurgents who threw their lives away when they attacked us that day.

28
MARCHED OUT

I'd been in Afghanistan for the better part of a year when I received a phone call one Saturday afternoon in 2013. The nature of the call from Ambassador Jon Philp shocked me, and I needed to sit down. He told me he'd received news that the Afghan Council of Ministers in Kabul – Afghanistan's equivalent of the cabinet in Canberra – had decided not to renew the AFP Memorandum of Understanding (MoU). I was advised that all AFP personnel would be sent home within a fortnight when the MoU expired. Neither the ambassador nor I had seen this coming, and I felt as though I'd been blindsided, having spent weeks bunkered down in the Afghan Ministry of the Interior's office working on the two-year Afghan police plans.

The MoU is the binding, legal document that's required when a foreign government sends staff to a sovereign nation – which is what Australia had done in despatching the AFP to Afghanistan. (The ADF operated under a Status of Forces agreement.) The Australian government agreed upon a convergence of wills, as well as giving an indication of the line of action that underpinned the reason for us being there. In the case of the AFP, this was to help the ANP develop skills that would allow them to police their nation. Upon hearing about the non-renewal, I contacted the AFP in Canberra. After some high-level discussions, Assistant Commissioner Mandy Newton advised me we weren't going to push back and I was to start the withdrawal as soon as possible. When I spoke to the head of the IPCB, Catherine Royle, she was livid and tapped into her former ambassadorial skills in an attempt to have the decision overturned. She was adamant that if the AFP left Afghanistan the IPCB would collapse. It's fair to say that as she drummed up support from her political allies to pressure Canberra to change its decision, the communication lines between her office and the Afghan Ministry of the Interior went into meltdown.

My head spun as I tried to think of ways to convince my superiors that this decision would tarnish the reputation of the AFP among our allies. I also feared we'd be seen by our Afghan colleagues as no better than everyone else who'd abandoned them. That thought stuck in my craw because after working so hard to gain their trust through inclusiveness we'd seen some great results. In Tarin Kowt and Kandahar the AFP officers had done some outstanding work to train the local police recruits. In Kabul we'd made great progress in providing the structure and governance that was needed to build a police force, and just as I was told I was headed home, the Afghans were signing off on our plans for the twelve arms of their police force. That was a huge breakthrough, and one that had required months of hard work. I made it clear I wasn't happy with the order, but I received a call from a superior in Canberra advising me to pull my head in and to leave quietly. Still, I pleaded with that person, asking them to appreciate the ramifications of this decision in terms of our standing with our allies and the Afghans. I was advised that the order to get out came from the commissioner's office. The exact words were: 'We've got one foot in the door and do not let it out.' In other words, I was to hightail it out of Afghanistan.

Even though I was again told to immediately start getting our people home, I countered by saying I hadn't yet broken the news to the four-star General John Allen. But the voice on the other end of the line said they didn't care, which only added to my disappointment about the attitude that seemed to prevail in Australia about us being in Afghanistan. Apart from having people ask how the 'junket' was going, the impression seemed to be we were sitting in our offices living the good life, drinking coffee and eating pastries. Even though it was obvious the AFP had no intention of relenting, I still tried to reason with the department. I argued, *pleaded*, that they needed to understand that their order would have severe repercussions on many fronts in Afghanistan, particularly with the US and our other allies. There was no budging. The ambassador was soon on the phone, demanding to be told who'd given the order to pack up and pull out. When I told him it was my commissioner, he told me he'd do all he could to fight it. He worked the lines from the Australian embassy, letting Defence Minister Stephen Smith know what the withdrawal of the AFP meant when it came to Australia's overall commitment to Afghanistan. But he was simply told the decision to bring the AFP home was the commissioner's call. As the drama headed up the chain of command towards

Prime Minister Julia Gillard's office, I felt as though I was the meat in an unpalatable sandwich.

The decision caused a furore. Some people in Afghanistan and the Coalition feared this was the beginning of the unravelling of the world's commitment to their country. General Allen demanded a minimum of one month's notice before we pulled out. I was hammered left, right and centre by invested parties, including the United Nations, who wanted to know what the Aussies were doing – and why. There was plenty of blowback in Canberra, and when the Coalition made the Afghan Council of Ministers realise what they'd done, they recanted their initial decision, saying they'd be happy to recommence discussions with the AFP about extending the MoU. But the problem for them – indeed for all of us – was that ship had sailed, the Aussies were leaving. Everyone wanted an answer, and while I wasn't privy to why the Gillard government had decided to take the course of action it did, it seemed to me that, geopolitically, it was a dangerous way to pull out. The lesson from places such as Iraq and Timor taught us that when you withdraw prematurely you end up having to return, and often to a worse situation than what you'd left. Moreover, the way the AFP went about it was so rushed that it was difficult for me to meet the gaze of some of the people with whom I'd worked very closely. After I gave the order that we'd be leaving Afghanistan, superintendents in Kabul, Kandahar and Tarin Kowt started to shut down barracks, pull out electronics and pack up gear. I had to visit our people at those locations because they were so angry. One officer even locked himself in his room and could be heard shouting, 'I have to be here!'

People volunteer for postings such as Timor or Afghanistan for various reasons. While most officers are there to do good, some have issues at home they are wanting to escape. That said, people were furious because they'd invested so much of their time working with the Afghans. Ultimately, the AFP agreed to keep seven officers in Kabul, which was important because it at least ensured the programs we'd established didn't just fall over. While that itself was a small victory, I still felt like a rat. And I found myself in an unusual position: while I personally didn't agree with the decision, I still had to protect my government from criticism because I'd sworn to do that. Two people understood the difficult position I was in: General Allen and his deputy, now four-star General Mark Milley, Chief of Staff for the US Army. Both their fathers were members of the Boston Police Department. However, neither man pretended to understand the nuances of what drove the Australian government's decision. We'd done great work in Afghanistan, but when we finally left I felt like a thief sneaking out under the cover of darkness.

I returned to Australia seething. On one hand I'd considered it a case of mission accomplished. All the people I was responsible for got in and got out safely, and the work we did for the Police Coordination Board was unheard of. But while I was proud of our achievements, they now felt hollow. When Commissioner Tony Negus asked me to describe my experiences in Afghanistan, he seemed visibly shocked when I said it was the hardest job I'd ever undertaken. I explained to him we'd been in an active war zone, and despite the rhetoric the AFP and the government extolled, we weren't always working behind the safety of the Green Zone. In fact, we were outside of the wire on a daily basis – a point others back home were never made aware of. When I explained I was up to my neck in dealing with the highest end of politics, the upper echelons of the military and the highest level of Afghan society, he shook his head in disbelief. I also explained that part of my job was to brief three-star Generals with 250,000 people serving under them.

I've often wondered whether what we did was respected in Australia. In some ways it felt as though Afghanistan was the AFP's Vietnam. When it was mooted in 2004, Negus, who was then a deputy commissioner, told the government that the AFP didn't want any part of the mission to Afghanistan. However, the response was 'bad luck, you're going' and our achievements were never promoted while we were over there. While I was in Kabul I received only one call from a more senior officer, and we didn't receive a visit from either the commissioner or his deputy, or any welfare or support staff during the mission. I'd bristle when I'd look at the AFP's intraweb and notice that welfare and support staff were regularly rolling in and out of the Solomon Islands and Timor-Leste. I don't dispute it was a worthwhile endeavour, or deny that the officers serving over there had their stresses. However, we were in a war zone and seemingly left to fend for ourselves. It wasn't right. There were other aggravations. For instance, I put vision on the AFP's website of the ceremonial removal of the AFP nameplate in Tarin Kowt from the wall, which was done in the presence of the Ambassador. Our nameplate had sat alongside those of the other serving nations, and it was respectfully pulled down to signify we were leaving. However, no one wanted the public to know we were leaving and the vision was deleted. While the people on the ground gave their all, it hurt to think their efforts went unnoticed by our leaders, let alone by the nation. And when I tried to rectify that it only added to my anger.

My bitterness ran so deep that I refused to attend the National Recognition Day for Afghanistan, as did other officers who served over there. It had nothing to do with disrespecting the people who had died serving Australia. While I've always respected Australia's military, I have never been as proud as I was of the way they served in Afghanistan; they were honourable and professional. My decision to keep away was a protest against the way we were treated. It didn't feel as though the efforts of the 150 AFP officers who'd served in Afghanistan – their devotion to duty and their courage – as the first Australian police to serve in an active war zone, were sufficiently recognised. We ended up with a lot of damaged people as a result of their service, but a proposal that a superintendent and I forwarded to the AFP that they strike an operational medal for Afghanistan was knocked back on the grounds that the deployment was simply 'the work we do'. In the end, the officers were presented with the Commissioner's Group Citation for Hazardous Overseas Service, but it still didn't seem right to me; our people had been in constant danger as a result of their duties, and their families suffered too because they were rarely contacted by our organisation, and nor were they recognised.

We'd been sent into a war zone by the government. We had people do extremely brave things, including those officers who were caught in a rocket attack in Tarin Kowt but assisted a person who was severely wounded by shrapnel. When I was offered the Commissioner's Group Citation for Hazardous Overseas Service, I respectfully declined.

Serving in Afghanistan was a unique experience. Ultimately, what I value most of all is that the officers who served under me knew I had their backs. As I told them before we left Afghanistan, they ought to feel extremely proud of what they achieved; each of them has represented the AFP, our country and its people in a war zone, and in doing so they maintained the highest standards.

I was proud of them, and still am.

As I'd prepared to leave Afghanistan in September 2013 my security detail insisted I *had* to visit one of Kabul's most famous landmarks – Swimming Pool Hill – as part of the farewell tour they'd planned for me. They said the 152-metre high mountain was the perfect place to take a panoramic photograph of the city. But if the guys learnt one thing about me during our time together it was that I'm a stickler for rules and protocols, especially when it comes to personal safety. I was also conscious of not wanting those who served under me to think I was one of those officers who had one rule for them and another for myself. As former members of the British Special Forces, my detail respected that trait, but on this occasion the crew refused to accept that I was confined to the compound and promised a visit to the hill would make for a great memory.

The pool's bloody history reinforced my belief that despite the many risks and frustrations that pockmarked our time over there, we'd done the right thing by attempting to provide the Afghan people with a police force they deserved. To reach the hill we drove through Kabul's most exclusive suburb, Wazir Akbar Khan. Perhaps best described as the city's equivalent of Toorak or Vaucluse, it's home to a number of foreign embassies and grand mansions. I'd visited this part of Kabul once a week to attend meetings with the Australian ambassador at the embassy, and there'd been a number of attacks on the building because it was high on the list of the Taliban's prized targets. We then drove along narrow tracks, past the rusting skeletons of Soviet tanks stranded in unfriendly soil thirty years after their army's inglorious withdrawal. These once-mighty weapons weren't the only reminder of the decade-long Soviet–Afghan war that caused up to a million civilian deaths and forced millions more to flee to Pakistan and Iran as refugees.

The Olympic-sized concrete pool the Soviets constructed to provide troops stationed on the hill with some relief from the heat is an embarrassing monument to the Communist regime's folly, although it's just as likely the coalition forces will eventually leave similar icons when they withdraw. After levelling the top of the hill and building the pool, complete with a high-dive platform, it wasn't until the job was finished that someone realised it was impossible to fill. The angle of the incline was too steep for the water to travel uphill.

While never used for its intended purpose, the Taliban utilised the pool throughout the mid-1990s as the place to execute 7000 blindfolded and bound criminals, intellectuals and homosexuals. It struck me that had my dad been born in Afghanistan he would have endured a horrid life. Well away from prying eyes, they forced the condemned to climb to the edge of the highest diving board and after zealots read a passage from the Koran, the prisoner was shoved off. In the dry season these poor souls crashed the 40 feet or so to the pool's floor; in the wet season they drowned in the murky water that had gathered there. If by some miracle an offender survived they were deemed innocent and cleared of all charges. It's also been reported that during that dark period in Afghanistan's history, groups of people were lined up against the pool's blue walls and exterminated by machine-gun fire. Such was the fanaticism that drove the Taliban at that time – men were arrested for not having the required beard length (the size of a clenched fist) while women who didn't properly conceal themselves with a burqa were publicly stoned to death at the city's main sporting stadium.

When I climbed out of our car I remember thinking how silent it was – not even the sound of birds could be heard – and as we stood on the mountain it felt as though dust was just hanging in the dry air. The dust had nothing to do with me choking up though. As I stared at the place where so many people had been murdered in cold blood, I couldn't help but channel the fear and suffering they must've felt as death closed in on them. Most would have surely wondered why they deserved such an inhumane end to their life, and as a cop it cut me deeply to think there was no one to save them. Before I arrived in Kabul I'd read that above all else the people of Afghanistan craved peace, safety and stability, and the history of this pool was part of the reason they felt that way.

It didn't take long before we were 'greeted' by a dozen or so rascal kids dressed in a mixture of Western-style clothes and traditional Afghan garb. They were quite aggressive as they demanded 'baksheesh' – money – from me and the boys. The team had warned me during the drive that these kids would be up to no good and to swat them away when they got too close. I was quickly surrounded by them, and when one of the lads reached for my Glock, which was carried low in a leg holster because I was wearing a 40-kilo armour-plated vest that prevented me from wearing it on my hip, I instinctively grabbed his hand and pushed him away. To my surprise the others followed his lead by retreating. But it wasn't a victory. When we returned to the safety of our compound a few hours later I realised that as I'd secured my gun another kid must have pinched my mobile phone. I was astounded by how easily they'd robbed me, and was also mightily pissed off. I rang the phone a few times and unleashed some choice language at the kid who answered it, but he just laughed each time as I shouted down the line. It was embarrassing to report to my superiors that I'd lost my phone, and that was compounded by the amount of explaining I needed to do when I was grilled about the wisdom of visiting Swimming Pool Hill for nothing more than a photo (one that was taken by a member of my security detail and which appears on the cover of this book).

What I didn't tell my bosses was that the few minutes we spent on the hill allowed me to take a good look at the city of five million people I'd spent the better part of the past twelve months living in. While the pool was a monument to the terror the Taliban inflicted, the chaos of people getting to work or school and moving on with their lives told a powerful story about the resilience of the Afghans. It struck me that in just a few days

I'd be home with Lordy, Jacinta and Emilee, and as I stood there looking upon the capital of the nation that several great empires have failed to conquer, all I could do was hope the bloodshed in their country would cease. It surprised (and disappointed) me when I hitched a ride from Tarin Kowt to Kabul in an RAAF Hercules and heard some diggers talk about the future of that area. The soldiers had already taken bets on which faction would take control over the province after the Australians withdrew. And that is Afghanistan's problem. No matter how many of us wish peace upon the Afghans, their troubles seem never-ending. Despite the so-called American-led 'liberation' in 2001, there is still bloodshed occurring throughout the country. It's regrettable that despite the average person's prayers and desires, peace still appears a long way away. However, even though I was overwhelmed to be welcomed home by Lordy and Jacinta after almost a year apart, it would be a long time before I found peace.

29
LOSING IT

*'I put my heart and soul into my work, and
I have lost my mind in the process . . .'*
– Vincent van Gogh, Dutch artist

After returning from Afghanistan I returned as the Commander of Aviation (Queensland), but I was also assigned a number of jobs outside of that portfolio by my superiors at AFP headquarters, which kept me busy. I reviewed the effectiveness of the branch that was responsible for looking after the proceeds of crime, and I also compiled a detailed report on the state of the properties being used by the AFP throughout Australia to stockpile the drugs we'd confiscated over a number of years. The amount we'd seized had become a serious problem because we had too much of it – four tonnes to be exact – and it had become a serious health and safety concern. Besides the drugs, we'd also seized the precursor chemicals that are used to produce them, and long-term exposure to them can result in serious illness. We needed to destroy them.

While I was named Queensland's Commander for Aviation, I wasn't in great shape after returning from Afghanistan. I was struck down by a series of physical health problems, including the debilitating effects of schistosomiasis. It's a disease that is as terrible as it sounds and is spread by parasitic flatworms that are released by snails into fresh water. It's lethal for people in developing countries who come into contact with it because they unfortunately don't have access to treatment. The symptoms are dreadful and include abdominal pain, diarrhoea, bloody stools or blood in the urine. While it is known as a water-borne disease, I have no doubt I contracted it through the food I ate while I was in Afghanistan.

My health problems affected me to the stage where I was unable to even hold a coffee cup or open a door because the inflammation in my body was too severe. The pain was so excruciating, and it refused to go away. Even though work approved the compensation claims I lodged, I never considered that my problems were anything more sinister than an unwelcome legacy from my year in Afghanistan. I had no doubt my health problems were interrelated, but I didn't realise the cause of my biggest problem was my state of mind. I didn't worry anywhere near as much about the brain fog and the forgetfulness I was now experiencing as I did about my physical ailments.

One of my biggest problems was that I couldn't sleep unless I self-medicated with sedatives or over-the-counter painkillers. Indeed, drifting off to sleep without the assistance of the drugs was to consign myself to suffering waking nightmares before the nightmares that plagued my slumber. If I didn't have the sedatives to knock me out, I would lie awake for hours, troubled by the incessant stream of images from my time investigating human trafficking and the exploitation of children. My quality of life deteriorated. I had no desire to be around people, and I'm ashamed to admit that included my own family. Physically, I was at home with them, but my mind was always elsewhere. I was always stewing on something from my past, especially perceived injustices. I was angry all the time, no more so than during my daily drive to and from work on the M1 highway linking Brisbane and the Gold Coast. I was so frustrated by other drivers' behaviour, the trip was an hour-long exercise in road rage. My office was my sanctuary. It was the one place where I felt as though I was still in control, although the truth is I wasn't achieving much. I was battling 'presenteeism' – where people with a chronic illness hang in at work but their energy is spent on figuring out how to carry on despite their ailments, rather than on being productive.

Upon returning home to Lordy and Jacinta, I just wanted to collapse into the lounge because I felt so drained of energy. However, I managed to push myself to the gym. After all, I was 'the strong man': I had the mettle to overcome whatever was bothering me. I attempted to do that by following my tried and proven dose of hard training. However, when I couldn't hold a coffee cup, let alone lift heavy weights, I followed my Uncle Graham's example and took up running. He developed full-blown PTSD as a result of his forensics work in the NSW police, photographing fatalities. I started jogging, and like my uncle I'd run late into the night because apart from the painkillers, sedatives and bourbon I was swallowing, it was jogging that provided me with a respite from the war that was raging inside my skull.

It only took two weeks after I'd returned from Afghanistan for me to realise I had a problem. On this particular weekend I went to a nearby high school to practise throwing the shot-put when I heard bursts of rapid gunfire. I followed my training and hit the deck; I was sweating profusely. I remember thinking, *I'm in Australia, not Afghanistan,* but I could definitely hear repeated gunfire. I was wearing a Fitbit health-monitoring device and it noted my heart rate had spiked to 170 beats per minute. After a few minutes, I carefully made my way in the direction of what I thought was a battle, only to see paintballers having fun at a neighbouring complex. I was rattled, but when I spoke to the AFP's psychologists about that experience they dismissed it as nothing to be concerned about. They said it was 'just' hyper-vigilance and would eventually disappear. They said there was no need to give me any medication, and their nonchalant reaction to a situation that had scared the tripe out of me made me think that perhaps a part of my struggle was being soft.

As the Commander of Aviation, I was based at Brisbane Airport, but my beat also included the Gold Coast and Cairns airports. The greatest challenge of this role was trying to stop bureaucrats from involving themselves in it. Because of that, I needed to learn the legislation and obscure statutes that had to be raised in arguments with pen-pushers who mistakenly thought I was answerable to them. Under the legislation I had the power to shut down the airport in the event of a 'critical situation' – in other words, an incident that endangered the general public. In the aviation industry, the amount of time that an aeroplane is out of the air is lost money to the carrier, and there was pressure on police to rush things such as their forensic investigation if a passenger had passed away during a flight. I ensured the job was done thoroughly, though. In a bizarre way, I welcomed these petty arguments – apart from setting the record straight, they allowed my mind to focus on things other than the images in my mind that were driving me to despair. I ended more than one meeting by making it clear to someone who'd stuck their nose in police business that if there ever was a threat to my people – or the public – I wouldn't hesitate to make the call to shut the airport down.

Another part of my role was to ensure each airport was appropriately staffed with enough officers at any one time to either deal with community crime or act as first respondents to a terrorist attack. I also spent a lot of time dealing with the respective airport authorities, including the Australian Border Force. The nature of my job meant I fostered a close relationship with Queensland Police, seeing as though 99 per cent of our jobs were handed over to them because they fell under state juris- diction. I quickly gained a healthy respect for our Queensland counterparts; they were a very professional organisation, and we even seconded some of their officers to the AFP.

I embraced the challenge of my role, channelling my energies into getting on top of my brief. I also had good reason to be excited about the appointment because Brisbane was named the host city for the 2014 G20 summit. That mean I'd play a part in an event that involved the world's most powerful leaders. Among them was US President Barack Obama, his Russian counter- part Vladimir Putin, the United Kingdom's Prime Minister David Cameron, Germany's Chancellor Angela Merkel, China's President Xi Jinping and Indonesia's President Joko Widodo. There was a lot at stake for Australia's reputation as a 'can do' nation, and I *somehow* needed to be at my very best.

However, the constant battles being waged in my mind made my time in aviation unbearable. Even though I realised I wasn't well, I put my mental state down to getting grumpy like my father did as he grew older. In any case, I limped through my tasks at work by employing the same tactic I used in Kabul. I kept my mind occupied. I also returned to athletics and competed in the shot-put at a number of masters competitions for older athletes. Throwing was something that helped get me through the tough times of my life. The hours I spent in the throwing cage at training was the time when I could truly relax. As a teenager I realised I could throw the negativity out of my system, but it wasn't until years later that I found out the reason I felt elated at the end of a session was because of the endorphins, the chemicals your body releases when you exercise. By interacting with receptors in your brain they can reduce your perception of pain as well as triggering a positive feeling; scientists have compared that feeling to the effect of the painkiller morphine. I did everything I could to get a rush of endorphins because they made me feel better, but I'd eventually realise all I was really doing was the equivalent of putting a bandaid on a wound that required a hundred stitches.

The preparation for the G20 Summit was thrown into turmoil on 17 July 2014 when Malaysian Airlines Flight 17 was shot down while flying over eastern Ukraine. All 298 people on the flight were killed, twenty-seven of whom were Australians. Watching the vision from Ground Zero was gut-wrenching for a number of reasons. One of the most tragic for me was the sight of once-loved toys that had belonged to some of the eighty children who perished that day, strewn amid the wreckage and debris in a paddock. I think that vision struck a nerve because it took me back to that night in the 1980s when I was a volunteer in the Rural Bush Fire Brigade on the NSW Central Coast and attended a fatal car crash. Seeing the children's wrapped Christmas presents lying on the back seat triggered great sadness for me that night because of the innocence that had been lost, and for an extended family for whom life would never be the same. I felt the same pangs when I watched the reports from Ukraine.

There was a lot of anger around the world, and Russia was the focus of it. American intelligence said the Russians had armed rebel forces fighting the Ukrainian government with the Buk missile that had brought the airliner down. Both the Australian and Dutch governments (the Netherlands lost 193 citizens) held Russia accountable for the deployment of the missile. Despite concerns for their safety, a large contingent of AFP agents headed by former RAAF Air Marshall Angus Houston joined their Dutch and Malaysian counterparts in another active war zone. With armed separatists watching them, these officers from forensics, investigations and other specialised areas scoured the crash site to identify and repatriate any remains. They were also there to assist with an independent international investigation.

The only other world leader to publicly point the finger of blame at Russia, besides Ukrainian Prime Minister Arseniy Yatsenyuk was Australia's Tony Abbott. Mr Abbott was asked by reporters how he'd respond to Putin when he arrived in Brisbane. He gave an emotionally charged reply: *'I'm going to shirtfront Mr Putin . . . you bet I am. I'm going to be saying to Mr Putin that Australians were murdered by Russian-backed rebels using Russian-supplied equipment . . .'*

'Shirtfronting' is a little-used term that describes a shoulder tackle in AFL. It was viewed by many as an inflammatory statement, and it divided public opinion in Australia. Speaking as a citizen rather than an AFP officer, I was stunned by the Australian public's response. In fact, some openly supported Putin in the event of a theoretical punch-up. I'm not a journalist, or a political analyst, but my interpretation of Mr Abbott's use of the word 'shirtfront' was that he simply meant to engage in robust conversation with his contemporary and let him know that Australia, let alone the world, wouldn't tolerate an atrocity in which 298 innocent people were killed. Others, however, either took the word literally or chose to cause trouble by suggesting that Mr Abbott – who had won some amateur boxing bouts when he attended Oxford University as a young man – intended to physically assault Putin, a former KGB agent who has cultivated a macho image by riding horses bare-chested and performing martial arts exercises in public.

I was stunned by the response in the media. At the time my AFP colleagues and Dutch officers were still searching a crash site littered with bodies, which included women and children, but some Australians didn't support their leader's decision to make a stand on behalf of all the victims – even if the language he chose was clumsy. The Russians, however, did take the matter seriously. While Prime Minister Dmitry Medvedev warned that his boss was adept at sport, implying that he and Mr Abbott could have 'forceful' debates if necessary, at the time Russia also had warships in international waters off the Queensland coast. When members of the huge Russian delegation arrived for the advance meeting they were rattled and came very close to pulling out because they feared an international incident. We placed an officer who spoke their language fluently to sit near them. When I asked what they were talking about she said it was basically, 'If their prime minister is planning to "shirtfront" the president, he won't be coming.'

The Russians wanted – and received – their own area at Brisbane airport so they could run their control system and protect their aircraft. The Americans meanwhile utilised the RAAF base at Amberley on the other side of the city, which saved some headaches. The actual G20 summit only ran for two days but it was the biggest peacetime operation in Australia, with 6000 police officers and 1500 security specialists involved. Public transport was restricted in the CBD, a wing of a hospital was reserved for the exclusive use of the world's leaders, and the government hired sixteen bomb-proof vehicles at a cost of almost $2 million. It was a huge operation, and while I should have been firing on all cylinders, I was unravelling mentally. My sleep was constantly tormented by nightmares, and throughout the day I was often weighed down by a sense of guilt – I hadn't done enough to save the kids who suffered at the hands of paedophiles, or the women who were trafficked to Australia as sex workers. It drove me crazy – literally.

I didn't have flashbacks, but whenever my mind strayed it summoned intense memories of the terrible things I'd viewed. However, I had many dreams that would manifest into nightmares, and they always saw me failing to rescue someone who was trapped in a life-or-death situation. Without fail the dreams ended with the person I was trying to help experiencing the most horrific of deaths. While I was tormented by these dreams for years, I can only remember one of them. In it I was half-hanging out of the window of an aeroplane that was flying above the clouds, and holding onto someone who was outside of the plane. This person was screaming for me to save them. It was so vivid I could actually feel myself strain to hold onto them, fighting against the g-forces pulling them from my grasp. Worse still, I sensed the desperation of the person looking to me to save them – my determination to rescue them also seemed just as real. Throughout this dream I kept telling myself I had to be strong enough to ensure this person didn't die. But I wasn't . . . I let go. While I didn't see the person hit the ground, I could hear their screams as they cartwheeled towards the earth. I always woke from this kind of dream with my heart pounding wildly in my chest and feeling as though I'd failed. I didn't talk to a doctor about them, only because I still hadn't realised there was something wrong with me. These days I can only imagine that the reason I had the nightmares was because my subconscious had tapped into the guilt I'd buried about not being able to save some of the people who'd been subjected to the most awful of horrors on my watch.

That guilt was one of the many issues that were crushing me during the G20. Most of the time I was lost in the fog inside my head. I'd sit at McDonald's at the airport having a coffee and trying desperately to gather my thoughts. I consumed sporting supplements known as 'pre-trainers' which contain caffeine, guarana or creatine for an energy boost. But like the bourbon I was now regularly swilling of a night and the over-the-counter painkillers I was taking, it didn't help. I was becoming increasingly distant from everything, and everyone. It was a battle to get out of bed each morning to face the world. Fortunately, I was working with two great people, Superintendent Sharon Cowden (now Commander of South-East Asia) and Con Coutsolitis (now retired). They both realised something was wrong with me. It was tough when I realised Sharon had sensed I wasn't well. It floored me, actually. I thought I'd done a great job of pulling the wool over everyone's eyes. However, one day when I was at a very low ebb, Sharon suggested it would probably be best if I 'kept my powder dry' and only come out when an authoritative figure was needed, which usually was when someone without a security background tried to make a dumb decision.

I continued my routine of battling through each day. I went to work, jogged, watched documentaries on Afghanistan, took my sedatives and painkillers and tried to sleep. At home I was distant from Lordy and Jacinta. I'd stare blankly at the television screen for hours at a time because it filled my mind with something other than negative thoughts. This was at the expense of my time with Jacinta. Because I didn't want her to see the graphic images of death and destruction, or hear the obscene language of troops on the frontline, I'd tell her to leave the room. But all she needed was time with me to talk and play. I was more of a zombie than a father.

It didn't help that I didn't see my current job in Queensland as all that exciting. After all the responsibility I'd had in Afghanistan, I was now basically just watching planes take off and land. On the few occasions that I spoke to Lordy, it was to complain that being handed the control of the airports meant my career had been side-tracked. It hadn't, but that line of thinking was where my head was at. Nonetheless, I took my role seriously.

Apart from Sharon, and to a degree Con, no one else knew how tough I was doing it – except, of course, Lordy. I was constantly self-medicating with booze and pills. I don't have any idea how she managed to fight against the waves of anger and tides of exhaustion she must have been feeling, because while I loved her and Jacinta deeply, I really wasn't there for them, even though I'd be sitting in our lounge room watching yet another documentary on Afghanistan. I couldn't see how tough Lordy was doing it. She was fighting hard to be the glue that held us together, but I was too lost in my brain's fog to realise. Thinking back on this time of my life much more clearly now, it saddens me to realise that what must have seemed like my selfishness would have been slowly strangling her. While I was function-ing to an almost competent degree with my police family, competing in sports, training, attending medical appointments and getting massages, her wings were clipped. As she fought to shield Jacinta from the problems that accompanied me home, she'd essentially become housebound – and this was not Lordy, a former elite athlete, a PE teacher, a business owner, a personal trainer and a cycling instructor.

It's shameful to admit this, but at my very worst, when I saw her 'moping' about the house, I'd go on the attack and demand to know what was wrong with her. Why wasn't she motivated to do things anymore? Why was she always at home and not playing water polo, or riding her bike, or training? It's a sad joke that I told her to hit the gym because she'd feel better about herself. I realise now that as Lordy did what she could to help me, she was also losing her own identity. What's more, she couldn't trust me with our 3-year-old daughter because

I was shovelling sleeping tablets and whiskey down my throat at an alarming rate. Lordy was anxious that I wouldn't hear Jacinta if she cried out for my help in the swimming pool. Sometimes she would return home from shopping and find Jacinta playing too close to the road, or she'd get a call from a neighbour asking if Jacinta was meant to be at their house. I'd dismiss her anger by telling her she was being neurotic. When I think of the hurt she must have been going through as I battled my demons, it wounds me deeply.

A major tipping point was Christmas, which, sadly, held no 'joy to the world' for me that year. We'd planned to drive around the streets to look at the Christmas lights in our neighbourhood and get in the festive spirit, but just before we left I popped a night-time Mersyndol, which, while it relieves pain and fever, was enough for me to tell Lordy I wasn't feeling well and wasn't going. She and Jacinta went instead with a neighbour while I swilled bourbon and watched the newest television shows from the war zone. When they returned home, Kate came charging into the house to tell me Jacinta had vomited in the car. Apparently my eyes didn't even leave the screen as I shouted at her to make sure she not only cleaned up the mess but also got rid of the smell. It was official – I'd become the Grinch who stole Christmas, and every other day of the year.

And by now there was a destructive voice inside my head, telling me there was only one way to find peace.

I spent hours each week driving the round trip from the Gold Coast to Brisbane. The problem with that was it gave me too much time to think about things from my past that had hurt me. I was halfway between the Gold Coast and Brisbane when I decided it would be my last day on earth. I didn't have the intention to commit suicide when I left home, but somewhere during my one hour and twenty minute car trip it seemed the best solution to my many problems. I decided I couldn't go on, failing everyone I loved. I'd tried my best to wear a brave face at home, but the face that was exposed whenever the mask slipped disgusted me. What I saw was a husband and father who was lost, a policeman who was struggling to be decisive. Nothing in my life seemed to make sense anymore.

As I drove north along that highway my mind went into overdrive, dumping piles of bitterness and bile. Each negative thought stung my brain, as if it were a giant wasp. *The fucking doctors aren't listening to me. God, I'm pissed off about the way we were treated in Afghanistan – no one fucking well cares about what we did.* Then it swamped me: Dad, Pa, Mum, the lost opportunities, including Hawaii, the Winter Olympics, the dickheads at school who derided me as the 'poof's son', the parents at the East Hills Bulldogs who said I played football like a cat. *Fuck them. Fuck everything.* It was as if every ounce of bitterness had rushed from the crevices of my mind and I was drowning in it. I estimate the episode went for ten minutes, but it felt like I had been bombarded for hours. Finally, I thought, *fuck this*, and with tears welling in my eyes I felt my hands grip the steering wheel as tightly as they'd gripped my Glock that day in the Green Village bunker as I waited for the Taliban insurgents. But a battle to save my life was not what

I was seeking now. My eyes zeroed in on a tree a few hundred metres up the highway. I unbuckled my seatbelt and pushed my seat back as far as it would go to maximise the impact when my head crashed into the windscreen. My death was playing out in front of my eyes, but I didn't care. As I pressed the accelerator towards the floor the voice in my head urged me on: *Do it . . . it's easy.* The countryside sped past me, my heart rate rose rapidly, and I even felt beads of sweat break out on my forehead. I was so in tune with myself. My jaw clenched tightly. There were no prayers as I watched the tree getting closer by the second. The speedometer had hit 130 kilometres per hour – *surely forensics would say I'd just taken the curve too fast.* The voice in my head was cheering wildly as I hurtled towards death at my own hands. *DO IT! DO IT! JUST FUCKING WELL DO IT!* I had one foot in the grave, but at the very last instant my trance was broken. Of all things, I saw Pa.

Pa had been my protector when I was a little boy, and I have no doubt he was again on this day. As I focused on the tree his image came to my mind. My first reaction was to feel love, but in a nanosecond my emotions turned to anger because of the way he'd left me. Fucking suicide. *Why, Pa?* That was the circuit-breaker. It suddenly dawned on me: all I would be doing was heaping the same feelings of misery and abandonment that I'd experienced on Lordy, Jacinta and Emilee, the same as Pa had done to me when I was a 10-year-old boy, when he tied the bedsheets around his neck and jumped out of the window. I came out of the twilight zone and back to reality. *What the fuck am I doing? I'm about to do to my family exactly what my grandfather did to me. How the fuck can you put Lordy through*

the trauma of identifying you at the morgue? You weak bastard.
I realised I couldn't do it, dropped my speed, pulled off the
highway and parked outside a coffee shop. My heart was still
racing, I was shaking. I had no idea what to do next.

I finally climbed out of the car and walked hopelessly around
in circles. I felt so lost. The three cups of coffee I drank actually
helped calm me down. Finally, I breathed. When I forced myself
to think about what I'd just come so close to doing, it struck
me that I'd just watched a movie that had a different ending to
the one the audience expected. I can't explain why I had that
moment of clarity amid such turmoil and madness. I'm not a
believer in divine intervention, but sometimes I have to wonder.
In the years that have followed since that day, I've theorised that
there was a reason I saw the photographs taken of Pa after he
killed himself. Maybe they embedded themselves in my mind
should the day ever come when I needed something to help me
see sense. I somehow drove to work after that, but I wasn't very
productive. I explained to my colleagues that I was late because
I'd been on a long call to Canberra. Then I went into my office,
shut the door and spent most of the day staring out the window
in a trance. I didn't know what to do. It was – ironically – one of
the longest days of my life.

I went home that night and, apart from being my usual
uncommunicative self, swallowed my pills and drank more
bourbon. When I switched on the documentary series *The
Bomb Squad* that night, it was to help me forget what I had
tried to do. While I should've felt grateful that I hadn't gone
through with the plan that inner voice had for me, I was dogged
by feelings that I was a failure. It'd been forty-odd years since

I played for the East Hills Bulldogs, but it seemed as though my lack of guts to do what seemed necessary confirmed the opinion of those parents who accused me of being a 'dog' or not having the 'bottle' needed to be the big, tough footballer they thought I should have been. I was in a perpetual state of depression. Those thoughts soon passed, and I'm forever grateful that I did 'fail' that day.

I did, however, set out to fight my way back to being the man I once was. I again went to the gym and pushed myself; I constantly trawled internet sites, researching why I felt the way I did. Whenever I met a doctor or a specialist – and it didn't matter where – I'd corner them and tell them about my many ailments in the hope they might be the one who had a magic cure. None did. One day when I went to my local GP for even more sleeping tablets, he rocked me by saying that for some time he'd thought I was suffering from PTSD. Perhaps I should have been relieved because he'd provided an answer, but the instant he said those four letters he lost me and my mind filled with dread. What he'd diagnosed was a career-killer. If anyone at the AFP knew I was suffering from *that* I'd be dismissed as fragile and weak. They'd take my weapon and revoke my security clearance. I'd be drummed out of the organisation I'd devoted my adult life to. When I came to, I heard the doctor saying that the anti-depressants he was prescribing wouldn't cure me, but they'd give me the space I needed to be cured.

I went home, my head buzzing. Kate seemed pleased that a doctor had finally categorised what was wrong with me. She said it was the first step to returning to life as we once knew it. I should've felt some relief, but I was terrified that someone might find out. The same sort of fear had gripped me as a child at Padstow Park Primary School, knowing that once my father's 'shameful' secret got out I'd be teased and ostracised. There was no watching *Bomb Squad* that night. I was on edge, pacing around the house like a caged lion. I don't know how many times I angrily told Kate I'd be returning to the surgery the next day to demand the doctor remove his notes from my records. I was there first thing in the morning, panicked.

Somehow, life resumed as well as it could without the medical help I'd rejected, but my continued decline was impacting on Kate because my seemingly careless actions made her paranoid. She'd regularly get up at 1.30 am to make sure I'd locked the pool gate because she was tormented by the thought of Jacinta sneaking in and drowning. She'd programmed herself to wake at all hours to check the doors and windows. I'd often go outside in the early hours of the morning to think in the quiet, but because I'd left the door wide open on a few occasions when I returned to bed, Kate feared Jacinta would wake up and wander off into the night, never to be seen again. She also started to vacuum the floor three times a day. I was popping so many antihistamines, anti-inflammatories and sleeping tablets, I'd become blasé and had stopped picking up the pills I dropped as I threw them down my throat. Kate was worried Jacinta might swallow one, thinking it was a lolly. She was also forever looking to see where I'd stowed my gym bag or bum bag because there were usually boxes of pills in them and they were easy for Jacinta to access.

I still don't know why – or when – I stopped thinking like a father, but I hadn't enjoyed sleep for a long time, and now I was denying that to Kate. My nightmares had reached a stage where I'd flail my arms about desperately; other times Kate would wake in fright, straining her eyes against the dark to see whether I was still breathing.

I soldiered on at work, doing everything by the book and hiding the pain behind a smile, a laugh and some jokes. And while I was so tired – I was giving every ounce of my energy to getting through the day – Lordy was exhausted from trying to be the best mother she could possibly be by protecting Jacinta from what I'd become: a husband who would spend his family time either competing in athletics carnivals or watching television. Despite my coldness and inability to speak about anything except my job at the airports, I'm so grateful she had the strength to stick by me, even when I appeared to be nothing better than a selfish, insensitive creature. We didn't fight, I just had nothing to contribute to any conversation, and it still hurts me immensely to know that Kate took all this in her stride. She thought that by trying to be the perfect partner, and being attentive and caring, she might finally guide me out of the fog and back home.

If you are thinking about suicide or experiencing a personal crisis, help is available. I urge you to PLEASE call Lifeline Australia for help on 13 11 14.

30
COMING CLEAN

*'Let them think what they liked, but I didn't mean
to drown myself. I meant to swim till I sank –
but that's not the same thing . . .'*
– Joseph Conrad, *The Secret Sharer and Other Stories*

I knew that my family and I needed a circuit-breaker, something that would change our lives in a positive way. My mind was active during yet another long drive to work, but this time my thoughts were focused on applying for the AFP's vacant European Commander's job, which was based in London, a city I love. However, Washington DC was to be my calling because I was named the Commander of the Americas – one of our organisation's most sought-after positions. There was so much to do, but my first step was to leave Kate and Jacinta at home while I travelled to Washington for what was a non-work commitment. Twelve months before the appointment, I'd booked a return flight to Washington to compete in the 2015 World Police and Fire Games (WPFG) in Fairfax County, which was only a decent javelin throw away from where my great mate David 'Sharpie' Sharpe, the incumbent Commander of the Americas, lived.

I always looked forward to the WPFGs. I'd competed in them since 1997, and besides setting records in the shot-put and powerlifting, over the years I'd also made some great friends, and we always enjoyed catching up. The competition at these games is fierce. Sometimes countries such as India send members of their Olympic and Commonwealth track and field teams to compete in the Open events because they're also members of the police force. However, this trip had an added dimension to it for me because I'd been named Sharpie's successor one month before the games started. Even though I'd taken time off work to compete, I used this trip as an opportunity to get a glimpse of what would be expected of me.

That invisible police-issue backpack was no longer filled with pebbles – instead, they had been replaced with a boulder, and the morning I went to the athletics track to prepare for my events it dislodged itself from my shoulders and crushed me. It had been eighteen months since my GP had diagnosed my PTSD and I felt so overwhelmed by everything that was happening in my life that I found myself sitting down under a tree with a ringing and buzzing sound filling my head, my mind swamped by the many heartaches and miseries that had embedded themselves into my psyche. Tears streamed down my cheeks. I'd never sobbed so hard before. Finally, I accepted that I couldn't continue the way I was living. The energy it took for me to get through each day meant I had nothing left for my loved ones, and that was denying me the capacity to feel true happiness. I now knew suicide wasn't an option – believe me, it isn't for anyone – so for the first time it struck me that the only way I could really mend myself was to perhaps cut ties with my second family: the force.

The people who *really* knew me realised something wasn't right. Jenelle had moved to Brisbane many years before I dropped anchor in Queensland, and after one of our catch-ups she told her husband, Geoff, that my eyes appeared lifeless and cold. I didn't know she'd thought that until two years later, but what my little sister had observed was an exact summation of how I felt. Kate was frantic. I was no longer the man she'd bravely placed all her cards on the table for that day we climbed Mount Taylor, saying she wanted to have a family with me. I didn't know it, but she was phoning the people I was closest to at work and asking if I seemed all right to them. Everyone answered that I was fine and doing a great job. While Sharon and Con realised I was struggling, neither of them had any reason to suspect I'd considered ending my life as I drove to work one morning. But how could they – or anyone – have known that? I still guarded my secrets as closely as I did when I was a kid who feared being judged and humiliated in the school playground.

When Commissioner Colvin phoned to tell me I'd been given the job in Washington, he thought my reaction was odd. After our conversation ended, the commissioner told his chief of staff it had seemed strange that I didn't sound overly excited about being presented with such a prized position. What had happened was so typical of me at that time. I was initially over the moon to hear I'd been given the job, but the longer he spoke the more I began to doubt myself, wondering how I could assume such an important post when I couldn't even handle the pressures of everyday life. That voice of treason always nagged away at the back of my mind whenever anything good happened to me.

I don't remember how long I sat under the tree that day, but it was there that I surrendered to reality and finally accepted that if I wanted peace I had to make drastic changes – and sacrifices. However, I still wanted to be 'the strong man', and after I finished sobbing I again used sport as a crutch. I would have denied the suggestion at that time of my life, but sport provided me with so much emotional support and emotional strength. Looking back now, I appreciate that it was my escape. While it was increasingly hard to get them, endorphins gave me a natural high. More importantly than that, sport gave me a purpose. It helped me feel positive about myself, and provided me with a healthy focus, different to everything else. The quality of my work was deteriorating because I couldn't function in the office. As for my family life, it was only due to Kate's strength, love and faith in me that I even still *had* a family.

After I sat under that tree bawling my eyes out, I was given some reprieve from the miseries that had swamped my mind by having to focus on getting out onto the field and competing. I won two gold medals and a bronze, but when I returned to Sharpie's place, instead of wanting to celebrate, I felt hollow. I switched on my laptop, drew a deep breath and poured my heart out in a long email to Kate. I let her know that I needed help, that I was a long way from being okay. I was fed up with torturing myself – and her – through my behaviour. I was done with trying to prove I was too tough to have any weaknesses. I also told her I'd tell the AFP about my mental condition, promising that if it meant I needed to hand in my badge,

I would. In that instant I accepted that my career would most likely be the price I paid to attain the peace of mind I craved. But no matter how I looked at the situation, I couldn't kid myself that it'd be easy to let go after thirty years of service to a cause I believed in so strongly.

However, as I typed that email to Kate, feeling so burnt out, I also realised I didn't need to be scared about telling other people my story. The kid who was once so terrified of anyone knowing that his father was gay, that his mother was an alcoholic and gang members shot up heroin in his family's lounge room, had finally grown up. And because his lifetime of secrets had taken its toll, he didn't give a damn what people thought anymore, even if that meant giving up on one of the most prestigious jobs in the AFP.

Kate read my email with mixed feelings. She'd been waiting for so long to hear me acknowledge that I needed help, and it meant the world to me when she vowed to be by my side every step of the way. But she also had an emotional reaction after reading that we would need to give up on Washington. Until then, I'd thrown myself into the many facets of what my new role would entail, but due to my state of mind I no longer had any interest in the machinations of shifting my family overseas. For various reasons our departure date had already shifted a few times, and every time Kate handled the drama of finding a school for Jacinta, getting the repairs done to our home so it could be rented out, selling the car and furniture, suspending our private health insurance, cancelling the gym memberships and our utility accounts, renting out our home and booking flights. All that was Kate's job. What I failed to appreciate was that whenever the date was pushed back, she needed to yet again phone a large circle of people and make apologies for having to change the plans that she'd put in place. It was a tough job and I really wasn't much help. In fact, I'm ashamed to admit that on the rare occasions when Kate complained about the problems the changes entailed, I just told her to 'deal with it'.

Her frustration came to the fore after she'd gone to Jacinta's school the morning after reading my email to explain that our daughter would stay put. As she spoke to the school's administration officer, she broke down in tears of frustration. But what Kate discovered – as I soon would too – is that people are understanding. The administration officer arranged for Kate to see the headmistress, and it meant a lot to Kate to hear that the principal's main concern was to ensure she was okay before assuring her there'd be a position at the school for Jacinta. That incident was one of many that opened my eyes to how tough my wife's life had become. Her strength of character – and her capacity to love – still floors me. And knowing that Lordy would be by my side regardless of the outcome steeled me to front up and tell the AFP about my problems, which I knew would be the hardest thing I'd ever have to do as a cop.

Now that I'd committed myself to telling the commissioner about my problems, I came clean to Sharpie, telling him my head was a mess. 'Mate,' I said over a coffee, 'I'm fucked.' I told him I doubted that I had it in me to do the job successfully. I'd attended a few meetings with David while I was in Washington and even the casual ones were high-powered and politically charged. Being privy to that helped me realise that by becoming

Commander of the Americas I wasn't only responsible for a group of people, I was also accountable to Canberra. I was often so drained of energy I had to excuse myself at many of the things Sharpie took me to because I needed to lay down and try to sleep. That insight ate away at me until I was convinced I was incapable of doing his job. I couldn't see how I could work during the day and then back that up of an evening to meet with diplomats, ambassadors and other people of significance. It chipped away at me and I unloaded stuff to Sharpie that I'd been carrying for far too long.

Sharpie, who'd become the head of the Australian Sports Anti-Doping Authority (ASADA) when he left the AFP, tried to convince me I was just nervous and shouldn't doubt myself. That was when I confided in him that I thought I had PTSD. Sharpie is someone I'd trust with my life, but upon hearing that he looked me square in the eye and sounded like a true cop when he asked: 'Where the fuck did that come from?' As I told him my story I saw Sharpie's eyes soften and he offered words of support that I knew came from his heart. However, he urged me not to chuck the towel in because he was adamant that *we* could work through any problem. He said we could both talk to the commissioner and his deputy. Sharpie then said I could seek help from a psych, and he again urged me not to give up. He is such a positive force and, because he knew I was competing in the WPFGs later that day, advised me to get to the track, enjoy the competition and talk some more with him when I returned to his house that evening.

We phoned Canberra and spoke to 'Irish', otherwise known as Acting Deputy Commissioner for Operations, Ian McCartney.

He is a good mate of mine and his response was exactly the same as Sharpie's, albeit in a booming Irish brogue. 'Oh mate,' he said from the other side of the world, 'you don't want to be making any rash decisions. We can get through this, but I want you to know, Grant, whatever way you choose to go you will be supported. If you want to stay in Australia we'll find you a job; should you choose to go to Washington we'll do everything we can for you.' The support I was receiving was much more than I'd expected. I felt humbled.

When I spoke to Commissioner Colvin in Canberra, I again held nothing back when I discussed the state of my mental health. He was stunned when I said I wanted to step down from the job, saying I was the last person in the world he expected to suffer from PTSD. However, he wouldn't hear of my resigning my post. His view was that if, as a police force, we can't help ourselves, how can we help the rest of society? He promised to support me and said he was aware that, like other police forces, the AFP had stigmatised mental health, something that needed to stop.

What made the biggest impression on me during the conversation was that his priority was to enquire about my wellbeing and ask what help he and the AFP could provide for me and my family. He asked three pivotal questions: Was I on medication? Was I going to see a psychologist? Was I going to continue the treatment? When I answered that I would be doing all three when I returned to Australia, I was floored by the commissioner's response. He said he would prefer for one of his officers to tell him that they had problems, because it's the ones who don't acknowledge a problem who worry him.

One of the commissioner's traits that has gained him broad respect is that he believes in empowering his people. He's a leader who possesses the fortitude to take on issues that could hurt him. When the former sex discrimination commissioner Elizabeth Broderick completed her investigation into the AFP's workplace in 2016, she reported that 46 per cent of women who worked for the AFP had experienced sexual harassment, while bullying was cited as a day-to-day workplace reality for members of both sexes. It was damning, but the commissioner did not hide behind spin. Instead, he conceded that he was as much a part of the old culture, which believed women had to be twice as good to succeed. However, he declared he was spearheading cultural change in the force and his advice to all ranks was that they'd better follow his lead. I'm so proud to serve under Commissioner Colvin; he's an outstanding leader of men and women. He stands for – and demands – good values, and we're a much better force for all that he's brought to the AFP.

While only Commissioner Colvin, Acting Deputy Commissioner McCartney and Sharpie knew about my mental battle, I was pleased that none of them treated me any differently than they had before I came clean. They even called my decision to step forward 'brave'. Assistant Commissioner Dave Sharpe, Commissioner Colvin and the then Chief Operations Officer Andrew Woods set up a mental health strategy advisory group, and among their number were senior members of the AFP and some external experts. I was in Washington at the time, and as well as speaking at one of the meetings, it was Sharpie who took the initiative to do something to address the stigma of mental health in our organisation. And, as was his way, he was all systems go.

He contacted some of the leading experts in Australia who he thought could provide us with advice. Tragically, when the advisory group was preparing to launch their plan in February 2017, one of our colleagues, Detective Leading Senior Constable Susanne Jones, took her own life in our building in Melbourne.

Sue was a 53-year-old highly respected member of the AFP who excelled in her duties as a member of the Joint Organised Crime Task Force, Drug Operations, as well as other stations. Her death hit me especially hard because of what I'd tried to do on that highway in Queensland. I also felt angry – angry that officers still didn't realise they could ask for help. I decided to do something, and I sat down in front of my computer and proceeded to write a 1000-word email that told my story. When I finished, I addressed it to every member of the AFP. With one deep breath I clicked the send button, and within minutes people who had no idea of my battles were reading such things as:

I found myself sitting under a tree, alone in an athletics track in Virginia, having a crisis of confidence and sobbing for reasons I couldn't really understand. What I did know was that I was broken, and for the first time in my life I acknowledged it.

I was tired and overwhelmed, but the desire to get healthy overrode my desire to worry about what work or others for that matter would think of me.

I declared to the Commissioner my mental health issue as I wanted him to have the right to veto my deployment to Washington D.C. He too was 100 % supportive and their collective engagement with me made such a difference to my approach to getting better, something that I will be ever grateful for.

I've done some pretty tough things in my life, but acknowledging this and seeking help was by far the hardest thing I have ever done.

When Sharpie asked me to speak to the board after my email went public – the *Canberra Times* picked it up – I told them we always needed to remember the human element of our job. I also said if we were serious about ending the stigma of mental illness in the police force, we also needed to show greater respect for mentally ill people in the broader community. I noted that there had been times when someone with a problem was going off at the front desk of a station, and I'd tell people there was a 'nutter' in the house. It remains my belief that that is unreasonable language. We will never fully respect the battles those people are fighting while calling them names that make light of their problems. I advised the board not to call the end result of their work 'policy', because if cops are anything they're cynical, and the rank and file would interpret that as old-fashioned arse-covering. I also said any discussions needed to be held in an informal environment, a place where the officers could meet for a beer so the dialogue was delivered in a more personal, non-threatening way.

I received a lot of positive feedback after sending my email, but there were also a few trolls in the force who made hurtful comments. I didn't write it for them. After Susanne's death I felt it was high time we spoke about the elephant in the room. As I've said, when I came forward, the commissioner was the first of many people who said I was the last person they expected to suffer from PTSD. I think that's half the problem. We look at our colleagues – they're laughing and smiling, they attend after-work drinks – but we never ask if all is well with them, or whether the job is having a negative effect on their lives. However, the day the commissioner offered me his support, the organisation took a giant step in changing the perception that having a mental health condition means you'll be chucked on the scrap heap.

It's indisputable that we still have a long way to go in in the AFP towards destigmatising mental health. Despite one in four officers being found to suffer moderate to high psychological stress, two reports commissioned by the AFP – in 2016 and 2018 – identified that management had a poor understanding of mental health problems and that was compounded because many of us were too frightened to speak out because of the *perceived* repercussions. Great leaders such as AJ Colvin leave legacies, and among his will be that he helped change the culture for the better in so many ways. One of the most important is that he's relieved officers of the burden of carrying secrets and stressors that ultimately cripple them. But sadly, these changes came too late for many, including my dear friend Audrey.

I met Audrey Fagan when I moved to Canberra in 1994 to work in internal investigations as a young cop. She was a lovely person, very intelligent and engaging, and a great police officer who took me under her wing. She struck me as someone who could handle anything. Others shared that view too – Audrey rose quickly through the ranks. In 2005 she was not only an assistant commissioner but also the Chief Police Officer of ACT Policing – the first female to hold that rank. It was, however, a stressful tenure and by 2007 Audrey was taking the brunt of the Canberra media's incessant criticisms about the ACT force's perceived reluctance to make details of its work public. There were also complaints about Canberra's watch-house custodial procedures following a series of allegations concerning minors being held in custody without notifying their parents, the treatment of intoxicated people and those with a disability, the use of force, and property going missing. It was also suggested that Audrey was upset when a cartoon appeared in *The Canberra Times* portraying a senior police officer whose face had been replaced by a lock and key, as if to suggest the force withheld information. Audrey was a great cop. She upheld the greatest of personal and professional standards, and she would have viewed the constant negative headlines and questioning of the force as a reflection of her work. But none of us ever saw her as anything but a tremendous leader, a decent person, and, in my instance, a dear friend who I admired immensely.

The last time I saw Audrey she was in an elevator at work. I was waiting on the ground floor to go upstairs to my office and when the doors opened our eyes met. Audrey was going down to the building's underground car park, and as people left the lift I said we should meet for a coffee. Audrey said with a smile, 'Yes, coffee. Next week when I'm back. Definitely. Let's do it.' I'd find out later that she was going away for a break with her husband to Hayman Island in North Queensland. As the elevator door closed I thought to myself that that was the chirpiest I'd seen her for a long time. Whenever Audrey and I said we needed to have a coffee it was code for a chat, but there was no way I could have imagined Audrey would commit suicide that weekend in the bathroom of her hotel room in the Whitsundays. It was such a sickening, and hurtful, thing to be told. I've punished myself since, trying to work out if I missed a cry for help. I go over our conversations in my head, but there's nothing. It's now twelve years since we lost Audrey and I still ask myself why we both allowed work to get in the way of our chats. Both of us kept cancelling at the last minute, and I can't help but wonder if I might have been the person she'd have trusted enough to admit how stressful she was finding the scrutiny. I say that knowing that when I was in my own dark place I gave nothing away. Maybe we police are good at hiding pain.

I can merely guess she just couldn't see the love and affection so many people had for her. As I write of the pain I still feel for Audrey, my heart goes out to her husband, Chris, and daughter, Clair, because no one suffered like they did. And despite the AFP's decision to accept mental health problems, we have still had officers take their own lives. The pressures of daily life, compounded by a job that requires you to deal with the worst of society and the associated traumas, mean that police often suffer mental health injuries. We have taken a big step in acknowledging that our mental health does suffer; now we just need to convince our officers that they can trust us. Jim Torr, the chief executive of the AFP Association, summed the situation up better than most in the aftermath of Audrey's death when he said, 'People expect absolute perfection, and punish anything less. That might work with robots, but in the intensely human world that is policing, it takes its toll.'

31
CAPTAIN AMERICA

Encouraged by the staunch support I'd received from Commissioner Colvin, I accepted the role as Commander of the Americas. He'd suggested that I just go to Washington and if things didn't work out I could put my hand up and come home. However, I had no intention of doing that. I was determined to do the best job possible. My overriding motivation was to justify the faith he – and Sharpie, especially – had in me. I managed to make a lot of progress with my mental health in the months leading up to my departure to DC. I took anti-depressants, and the improvement was incredible. While they aren't a cure, the medication provided me with 'space' in my head that allowed me to think things through. I explained to the psychologist I was seeing in Canberra that I'd be so busy during my three-year tenure in the Americas that it would be impossible to commit myself to the level of treatment required. However, when she heard that I planned to do what was necessary for me to at least tread water, her opinion was that would be fine.

The AFP fulfilled the commissioner's promise of support. I sat down with the organisation's doctor before leaving Australia and we formulated a health plan. The idea was for me to use my first three months to settle into my new environment and then visit a doctor who'd reassess me, and check my medication and progress. I'd then do a three-monthly mental health check-up. It was great. For the first time in such a long time I felt as though everything was going to be okay. The AFP committed their psychologist's case officer to ringing me at regular intervals to ensure I went to the doctor and to find out how I was travelling. However, I knew Lordy would keep me honest in Washington in terms of attending appointments and taking my medication. Testament to the incredible level of support I received from my colleagues is that before Sharpie returned to Australia he'd made it a priority on his very long 'to-do' list to find a highly recommended psychologist for me. It was the act of a true mate.

When I left to take command of the Americas from Sharpie, my bosses in Canberra gave me the same standing order as they had when I'd departed for East Timor and Afghanistan: 'Don't fuck it up, mate.' While it was blunt and to the point, it's an edict that's always kept me on the right track. I arrived in Washington with the objective to develop a strategic footprint for Australia in what's becoming an increasingly important part of the world for us because of the drug trade. This meant looking at our responsibilities as our nation's Federal police force, how we engaged with our allies in the Americas, and how we could best position our resources and identify what risks the Americas presented to Australia. I pinpointed Mexico's organised crime as the biggest threat because they're all-pervasive.

While we'd already forged solid relationships with some countries, I wanted to explore unique and different options in new territories. The United States was already represented by each of its law enforcement agencies in Canberra, so I was keen to form partnerships with non-traditional policing partners to help us with both capability and capacity. I wanted to gain ideas of how we could do things more effectively. We started to work with academic institutions – the Brookings Institution, the Center for Strategic and International Studies, the Milken Institute School of Public Health of the George Washington University – to assist with what we were trying to achieve under Commissioner Colvin's stewardship.

The commissioner pinpointed that what separated the AFP from the state and territory police forces was that we owned the international space. In other words, we're the only Australian police force with the authority to operate in an-offshore capacity. The other forces in our nation can liaise with international police, but the AFP is the force with the legislated operational authority to act on any police matter that impacts upon Australia's interest on the international stage. We've excelled in that role. Our people have done brilliant work in Afghanistan, East Timor and the Ukraine when MH17 was shot down by rebels, in investigating the Bali bombings and on many other missions, including the Solomon Islands, Nauru, Papua New Guinea, Namibia, Somalia, Mozambique and Thailand.

I made it a priority to strengthen or build relationships in Central America, South America, parts of the Caribbean and Cuba. Adding to a tough slog was that I'd only stay with Kate and Jacinta at our home near Georgetown for an average of five days a month. As you'd appreciate, that was tough on Kate. She was almost living the life of a single mother on the other side of the world, and while she soldiered on again, I know it was at times a difficult and lonely existence for her. However, I had tunnel vision about doing the best job possible. In my mind I had a lot to prove after the commissioner backed me when others might have looked the other way, and I was straight into the challenge from the moment we landed. I was vigilant in following the mental health plan that had been mapped out for me by the AFP's doctors, and that allowed me to be the most productive I'd been since I'd returned from my year in Afghanistan.

It was a busy time, and I was fortunate to be in charge of a great crew. Our staff consisted of a cybercrime expert, an officer who was dedicated to counter-terrorism, a drugs and organised crime specialist, and we also had someone assigned to the National Center for Missing and Exploited Children. We also assisted US law enforcement agencies in dealing with their Aussie counterparts if an American citizen was in trouble, and we'd help them with their investigations when an Australian citizen was either the victim of a crime during their stay in America or accused of committing one.

I started the ball rolling on some long-term initiatives, including having an AFP officer attached to the FBI-run Terrorist Explosive Device Analytical Center (TEDAC) in Alabama. It was formed in 2003, and its charter is to fully examine and exploit all terrorist improvised explosive devices (IEDs) that US and coalition forces have seized in places such as Iraq and Afghanistan. Their people learn everything they can about the IEDs, and they not only link the device to its maker but they also find ways to nullify the IEDs' effectiveness by learning how to disarm them. I also laid the foundations to have an AFP officer attached the US Coast Guard. Apart from being one of the US's five armed services, it is also a law enforcement agency.

It was a thrill to lecture at the US National Defense University in Washington DC. While the university obviously has a strong military presence, law enforcement officials (aka 'select inter-agency civilians') also attend there for an intensive one-year study program. The nature of my work in Afghanistan appealed to the university's administration, and among the subjects I discussed was Australia's gun laws. Some of the people in attendance at that lecture rued the fact that the US would never follow Australia's lead in that regard. Conversely, there were others who thought we were downright crazy to restrict gun ownership.

It was also my privilege to work with two tremendous ambassadors in Washington: the former Labor opposition leader Kim Beazley and the LNP's former treasurer Joe Hockey. I'm apolitical, so I tend to judge politicians by the quality of person they are. Both Beazley and Hockey impressed me as genuine political heavyweights. Despite approaching the role very differently, they each represented Australia's interests with dignity and enthusiasm. Beazley had already served as Australia's ambassador to the United States for six years when I arrived in Washington, and he was the ideal representative for our nation because he knew everyone on Capitol Hill and was universally respected. Foreign heads of state, dignitaries and the media all regarded him as a warm and engaging character. He boasted a vast knowledge of the American Civil War and would regale his dinner guests with an endless array of enthralling stories.

Hockey was very entrepreneurial. He'd do such things as recruit the two-time British Open winner Greg Norman to play golf with VIPs, and recruit tennis legends to spend time on the court with them for the same reason. It was a highly effective form of soft diplomacy. He was interested in my work, and apart from inviting the AFP to use his residence whenever it was needed, I'll never forget his reaction when he accompanied me to the National Center for Missing and Exploited Children (NCMEC) in Virginia. He was visibly shocked to see the prevalence of child exploitation, which ranged from abduction to trafficking children for sex. He was horrified to see the role computers play in robbing children of their innocence. In 2016 the NCMEC's Cyber Tipline received 8.2 million reports, which included child sex abuse images, 'sextortion' or online enticement, child sex trafficking and child sexual molestation. After we finished our tour Hockey hit his head on the desk in frustration, and after describing what he'd discovered as 'despicable' said much more needed to be done to address this crime.

I continued my treatment, seeing a psychiatrist who was recommended by Comcare (the Commonwealth's workers' compensation scheme). She was good, but very formal. The first time I met her I invited her to call me 'Grant', but she insisted I call her 'Doctor'. It wasn't what I expected, but I respected that. My psychologist was the opposite. She was lovely, viewing me as an interesting case because she hadn't worked with a police officer before. She learnt a number of things through our sessions, including a police officer's constant state of hypervigilance. It was obvious my mental conditioning threw her. When we went out on a 'field trip' to get a cup of coffee at a Starbucks in a less than salubrious part of town, she took note as I made a point of getting the seat against the back wall. When she asked why I *had* to sit there, I explained that it provided me with a clear view of what was going on out on the street. It also allowed me to see who was coming towards us, and meant no one would be able come at me from behind. It rattled her to see that while I could engage in meaningful conversation, my eyes were always observing what was happening around us. That's what life as a cop does to you.

I was busy in Washington – always on the go – but I lived up to the pledge that I had made to my psychologist in Canberra, and made sure I did enough to at least tread water. Seeing the psychiatrist in Washington helped, as did the anti-depressants. However, I think the best tonic for me was knowing the AFP had my back. I wasn't hiding anything, and the weight of the world was off my shoulders. Allied with that, I was channelling my energies into my mission, and my confidence was back up because I was doing a good job. While I was always wary of what might happen in terms of my mental health, I was so different to the man who had been in charge of aviation in Queensland.

The drug trade has made it essential for Australia to have strong relationships with governments throughout the Americas. One country that is critical to cutting the cartels' pipeline is Mexico, especially since the UN Office on Drugs and Crime identified it as one of the top ten embarkation points (by weight) for amphetamine-type stimulants – a shift from the penchant of its criminal gangs for smuggling cocaine. The Cartel Jalisco Nueva Generacion (CJNC) – regarded as the most violent criminal group in Mexico – is up to their necks in a trade that's doing as much damage to Australian society as it is to the rest of the world. Mexico's war on drugs has been bloody, with 234,966 people killed between 2008 and 2017 alone. And many police have sacrificed their lives.

I was surprised that, despite the global influence of Mexico's gangs, some of my American colleagues maintained the same opinion of them as they did when I worked out of LA in the 1990s, dismissing them as wannabe gangsters. My research suggested they were anything but. They're a highly organised, lethal machine that's formed alliances with criminal gangs in many countries, including outlaw motorbike gangs in Australia.

My approach to building on the relationships I'd made in Mexico in the 1990s was the same as when I was in Timor-Leste and then Afghanistan: you must be sincere. You also need to be honourable, and the foundation you build the relationship upon has to be one of honour, trust, genuine engagement and commitment. America buys their support by splashing around millions of dollars, and while they eventually get what they're after, it's given to them begrudgingly by the locals. The Australian agents who are working in the AFP's bureau in Mexico City are brilliant police officers who've worked tirelessly to forge strong relationships with the local law enforcement agencies. They've spent quality time doing everything from helping train their officers to identifying people to send on courses that Australia either funds or contributes to. They also speak the language fluently and have hosted their Mexican peers at their homes. It's yet another example of the importance of respecting the personal touch to foster trust. The relationships built with nations such as Mexico must be tangible and long-term to get results.

During my time in Washington I made a point of reconnecting with the Mexicans I'd befriended twenty years earlier. I wanted to build on the foundation I'd established as a young cop. I considered it a great day for the AFP when Michael Keenan, the Minister Assisting the Prime Minister on Counter-Terrorism, opened our post in Mexico City in 2017 because it signified a solid commitment to our partners that we wanted to help them. The post is run by Senior Liaison Officer Conrad Jensen, a very experienced and exceptional officer, and it is from that office that we share our intelligence on the organised crime threat with the Mexican authorities.

When we opened the office in 2017, we took our official delegation to pay our respects to the local police who'd fallen in the line of duty. At the time the city was building its fourth memorial wall, testament to their officers' commitment to the fight. We were dressed in our ceremonial uniforms as we laid a wreath and offered a prayer for the fallen. This is something I try to do in all of the countries I visit on behalf of the AFP. As someone who to this day is proud to be a cop, I need to honour those in the blue family who've made the ultimate sacrifice performing their duty.

The Mexican Federal Police Commissioner, Manelich Castilla Craviotto, was so moved by our gesture that he wiped his diary clear of all meetings that day to accompany us. And he had us choppered about the city in one of his air wing's Black Hawk helicopters to ensure we weren't delayed by the city's notorious traffic jams. Commissioner Craviotto is a man committed to winning the war against the cartels. As he admitted in an interview with Australia's *60 Minutes* program, it was true his officers felt fear: 'Every policeman feels fear. It is fear that allows us to be alert. The right fear is an ally to police work, and of course we are afraid. But our conviction in the face of this problem is much greater. Fear will never be greater than our conviction.' As an ally, I think all Australians should be grateful for that approach.

When news of the treatment we received in Mexico reached the Americans they were stunned. They wanted to know how we did it, but it was only a matter of showing genuine respect. While the United States is an old and valued friend of Australia, I found it interesting to learn how their neighbours viewed them. Most were wary of the US. They'd say Australia listens, but Americans 'talk and tell'. When they said that, it sounded as though they felt they were bullied. By simply listening, I learnt what was happening in their jurisdictions, and that allowed for me to ascertain how we could best provide support.

In early 2019, the threat Mexican cartels currently pose to Australia was highlighted when a AU$1.29 billion haul of ice seized in the US was also the largest seizure of meth bound for the Australian market. It was estimated the drugs would've led to more than 17 million drug deals. AFP Assistant Commissioner Bruce Hill hit the nail on the head when he said the cartel responsible was 'powerful and violent'.

When Guatemala opened an embassy in Australia in 2016, one of their first requests to our government was engagement with the AFP. Australia's Foreign Minister Julie Bishop was happy to oblige, and I was instructed by her office through Deputy Commissioner of Operations Leanne Close to travel to Guatemala City. I visited there twice. On my first trip I spent the day listening to their commandant and his chiefs list the many problems they had: not enough police cars, guns or handcuffs, and they also lacked proper marine capability, IT infrastructure, training and leadership. However, despite those handicaps, they were proud of their efforts and had somehow reduced the murder rate from over 500 people a month to 300. While it was a phenomenal achievement, it also highlighted how cheap life is in Guatemala.

Under the Howard regimen we had the Law Enforcement Cooperation Program. They were funds that allowed for us to promote goodwill, but due to the government's policy in 2017–18 to cut our budget, the AFP just didn't have the ability to financially assist the Guatemalans. I advised them it was possible to help via online training, something we'd done very well in East Timor when we partnered with the United Nations Office of Drug Control. Many East Timorese were illiterate, and when we realised Guatemala had the same problem, we suggested developing an online training component to teach such procedures as stopping and searching a car. The process is explained in their language and the beauty of this option is that it means they can learn police procedures with the click of a computer button.

Another request that surprised me occurred when our counter-terrorism expert attended the Caribbean Chiefs of

Police Conference. He was approached by the chief of Trinidad and Tobago for help. Most Australians would know of this tiny Caribbean country for producing cricketing superstar Brian Lara, and perhaps Dwight Yorke, who played football in the English Premier League and in the A-League for Sydney FC. However, it also has – per head – the world's highest number of foreign fighters returning from fighting for ISIS on Middle Eastern battlefields, and the authorities were at their wit's end trying to work out what to do. They were frustrated that their request for help from the Americans fell upon deaf ears. As the AFP's Commander of the Americas, I was on the Counter-Terrorism Committee for the International Association for Chiefs of Police, so I was in a position to act as their mouthpiece. When I discussed Trinidad and Tobago's plight with my contacts in the US Department of State, we had arguments because they couldn't grasp the seriousness of what was happening on their own doorstep. It didn't register with them that it was a concern.

To demonstrate how serious the problem was, in February 2019 the Trinidad and Tobago government shared statistics that detailed 400 of their men, women and children had undergone training or indoctrination with ISIS. When I was in the Americas there was a theory that the reason many Trinidadians joined ISIS was because it was similar to joining a gang – it offered recruits a sense of community as well as a source of income. However, the tone seems to have changed dramatically because I've since read of fears that Trinidad and Tobago's affected citizens could help ISIS infiltrate the Caribbean.

We couldn't believe the numbers they were dealing with, so I sent our counter-terrorism officer to the capital, Port of Spain, to see how he could help. I also thought we could learn from the Trinidad and Tobago experience because Australia also has ISIS veterans returning from the frontline. I saw the issues as something we could work on with the Canadians and British, and they were happy to offer their expertise and assistance. It was a good result and the Trinidad and Tobago authorities have expressed gratitude that the AFP took the time to not only acknowledge their problem but to help them.

Australia doesn't have a mission in Cuba but I visited the one-time hardline Communist country after Fidel Castro's death in 2016, when it opened its doors to the rest of the world. It was expected that Australians would be among the tourists who flocked there and I wanted to learn about the landscape from a police perspective. It was an important visit because while Australia didn't have a diplomatic relationship with Cuba, a lot of our citizens visit the country. The Canadians had maintained ties with Cuba throughout the crisis, and through my contacts in the Royal Canadian Mounted Police I was welcomed there by the authorities in Havana. There were two matters on my agenda: the cocaine trade and the exploitation of children and women.

What struck me was that the Cubans weren't prepared for change; they didn't have the capability to monitor the huge number of foreigners who would visit their small country. When they realised I'd worked on the police side of aviation, they said they wanted Australia's help in developing their border security. They knew Australia had developed the SmartGate technology, which uses facial recognition to help Border Force verify a traveller's identity against the data stored in the chip in their biometric passport. It also checks their bona fides against the immigration database.

Cuba seemed to be a safe country, but a lot of the work I did with Havana concerned the exploitation of children, something the Cubans were keen for help with because it had become such a serious problem. Cuba's press hadn't given the subject any exposure, so there was an impression that the problem didn't exist. However, as I learnt, the locals despise child exploitation and there'd been occasions when the police needed to save perpetrators from being lynched by angry mobs.

One of my most enjoyable experiences in the Americas was celebrating the 100 years of mateship between the Australian and US military, a relationship forged during the First World War. My contribution on behalf of the AFP was to convince one of my favourite singers, Amber Lawrence, to write and perform the event's theme song, 'The 100-Year Handshake', which she sang at the official ceremony to celebrate the Battle of Hamel on board the USS *Intrepid*, with President Donald Trump and then Prime Minister Malcolm Turnbull in attendance. I was aware of the centenary celebrations from talking to Joe Hockey, and it struck me that we needed a theme song, so I took the initiative to get one. I chose Amber to write and perform the song because, besides her talent, she's also supported the nation's troops by performing for them in East Timor and the Sinai. She also wrote a song about a veteran called 'Man Across the Street'. It's very moving and gained her a nomination for Best Female Artist of the Year at the 2013

Golden Guitar Awards in Tamworth, so I had no doubt she was the person for the job.

It's funny how fate works because I bumped into Amber when I was returning to Washington from Sydney after attending a commanders' meeting. I felt star struck when I saw her in the lounge at Mascot Airport. She was with her husband, Martin, and her mother, and I have no idea what she thought when I introduced myself as a massive fan. The look on her face was a mixture of fear and confusion while I rambled on about the possibility of her writing a song for the centenary celebrations. Her flight was called and she had to rush off, but, a few days later I was pleasantly surprised to receive a message from her via Facebook asking for more information. We spent a lot of time talking about the significance of the song. The only hiccup was that the Americans did not like the term 'Yankees', which appeared in the original draft, because it has connotations to the Civil War – instead, the word was shortened to 'Yanks'. When the big moment came for Amber to sing, I was emotional – she belted it out of the park!

Amber and Martin came to Washington and I took them on a tour of DC. The best memory I have from that day is of Jacinta, who took the day off school and sat in the back of the car talking and laughing with one of Australia's most pre-eminent country-and-western singers as they listened to songs on an iPad. Lordy and I were thrilled that Amber used this experience as inspiration for another song, 'All the Kids in the Back'.

While the centenary celebrations in New York were a highlight, I was to get a stark reminder of the human cost of Australia and America's relationship when I attended the return of a US Air Force C-17 Globemaster from Afghanistan. I'd attended too many ramp ceremonies in Afghanistan, the solemn memorial service that's held at the airport for military personnel who are killed while serving in a hostile land, before an honour guard carries their coffin onto the plane for the final journey home. However, when a close friend, US Marshal Mike Prout, told me that one of the six officers in the US Air Force Office of Special Investigations (AFOSI) returning from Afghanistan that week was a member of the NYPD, I felt the need to be there as a sign of respect to both the AFOSI and NYPD. The six had been killed when a Taliban suicide bomber targeted their patrol outside the Bagram Air Base by ploughing a motorcycle laden with explosives into them.

I expected there'd be a good number of law enforcement officers there to salute the fallen soldiers, but the night their C-17 Globemaster landed amid the airfield's bright lights was a miserable one – cold and wet – and apart from a contingent of fifty New York Police Department officers there to raise arms for their deceased comrade, there were only marshals for the others, which was tough to witness. As I stood to attention on the tarmac I felt torn. It seemed wrong that these heroes weren't being afforded the 'welcome home' they deserved. The repatriation of each officer had been structured to give each family their due courtesy, and the coffins were carried from the aircraft one at a time. As they were carried off, I stood in the downpour dressed in my full ceremonial uniform, lost in thought about the sacrifice each hero – and too many others in Australia and other nations – had made.

The US Secretary of Defense Ash Carter was at the airfield to offer his condolences to the families. I was honoured that he introduced himself to me. He was shocked to see an Australian police officer there and wanted to know whether I'd come all the way from Down Under to attend the ceremony. When I explained to him that I was based in Washington but had served in Afghanistan, he shook my hand warmly, and after introducing me to his wife he handed me a challenge coin, which is a military token offered as a sign of friendship and respect. I treasure it as a reminder of the night six heroes returned home. I stayed there the whole night paying my respects, and it clearly meant a lot to the USAF personnel. Mike told me that the likes of Brigadier General Keith Givens – and his was a presidential appointment – was one who often spoke about the night an Aussie stood at attention out in the rain. We had a similar experience when four of us, including the commissioner, attended the funeral of a female police officer who had been assassinated in New York City. The NYPD officers broke ranks to hug us as a sign of thanks. I sent officers to other funerals in Las Vegas and Dallas following the devastating shooting sprees that resulted in mass casualties, as a sign of respect for our fellow officers.

When I left Dover Air Force Base in Delaware, a number of thoughts flooded my mind. One was whether I could return to the strongman sphere and pull a 53-metre long, 190-tonne (or 344,825 pounds) C-17 Globemaster to honour the fallen and at the same time raise awareness for the mental injuries first responders suffer. I was 55 at the time, and the last time I'd tested myself was in 1997 when I pulled a bearcat and emergency truck that were hitched together. While I wondered whether I could do it, the will was definitely there. I committed to doing the feat at the Dover Air Force base and it was perhaps the most nervous I'd ever been about an event. I'd been out of the game for a long time, but as I stood there with the media, the might of the USAF and the crowd, my hope that I could move the thing was fulfilled when I pulled it 5 metres. It was a big effort, and so many thoughts forced me to push myself – Kate's love and strength being one. And while my body made me pay for it over the days that followed, I was pleased that my efforts had highlighted the fact that even though I was physically strong, I still needed help when the pressures of life started to crush me. And that's a message I expect to champion for many years.

EPILOGUE

I gave my posting in Washington my all, and to perform my duty I travelled to Toronto, Ottawa and Edmonton in Canada on a number of occasions. I also went to Argentina, Dubai, Great Britain, The Netherlands, Mexico, Brazil, Colombia, Panama, Cuba and Guatemala. In America I travelled to California, Texas, New York City, Las Vegas, Los Angeles, San Francisco, San Diego, Chicago, Miami, Key West, Tampa, Arizona, Boston, Pittsburgh, Delaware, Quantico in Virginia, Tennessee and Kentucky, and I also travelled back to Australia on half a dozen occasions. It was rewarding work, but I know the price Lordy and Jacinta paid for it was loneliness because I was often away. However, we managed to share some memorable experiences, including our road trips to Lake Placid, Toronto and Niagara Falls, which was especially brilliant. We went there in winter and, while it was bitterly cold, seeing the falls remains our most enduring memory from our time over there. I booked a hotel room that overlooked the falls and the view was spectacular. The three of us were so enthralled by nature's majesty and sheer power that we'd stare silently for hours, in awe. We all gained an appreciation for the reasons why the mighty falls have inspired explorers, adventurers, artists, poets and filmmakers.

My trips with Kate and Jacinta also represented a welcome change in me. I was again engaged with my family. I threw myself into the lives of my beautiful wife and precious daughters. I was no longer the mute, grumpy cop who swilled grog and popped painkillers as he watched war documentaries to fill his mind with something other than the terrible thoughts that haunted him after a demanding year in Kabul.

Another privilege was being invited to attend the Crocodile Hunter Steve Irwin's posthumous star being embedded on the Hollywood Walk of Fame. I was a huge admirer of Steve. The ceremony for the unveiling of his five-pointed terrazzo and brass star near the corner of Hollywood Boulevard and Vine Street was a momentous occasion, and a worthy celebration of the life of the Wildlife Warrior. People carried plastic blow-up crocs and yelled 'Crikey' in tribute to the lovable Aussie who died in 2006 after being pierced in the heart by a stingray barb while filming a documentary. A fan with 'Crikey' tattooed on her right forearm and who'd named one of her twins 'Irwin' left her home in San Diego at 2 am to pay her respects. Mostly I was moved by the dignity of Steve's widow, Terri, and his children, Bindi and Bob. They articulated their love for him so brilliantly. Since that day, Kate and I have forged a treasured friendship with Terri. She has had a huge impact on Jacinta, and I'm confident my daughter will one day devote her life to working as a Wildlife Warrior, if her love for animals is any guide.

Terri was one of the many people who were kind enough to reach out to me after I appeared on ABC's *Australian Story*. I had mixed emotions about doing the show because, while I'd revealed the extent of my mental battle in the email I sent to the entire AFP organisation, I knew it'd be tough to appear on a television program that had prised reveals from such people as the premiership-winning rugby league coach Wayne Bennett, Australia's first female Prime Minister Julia Gillard, the entertainer Red Symons and a survivor of the Holocaust, Sabina Wolanski. I realised I'd need to dredge up elements of my life I really didn't want to revisit – Mum, Dad and Pa among them. What convinced me in the end were two things. First, the people at *Australian Story* reaffirmed that it would be filmed in the first person, meaning I would tell my story. Second, I thought it might help the lives of some people who were struggling. Vanessa Gorman, the producer who oversaw my episode, was fantastic to deal with. She is a person of great integrity and empathy. When she finished hearing my yarn she was one of many people who helped me realise that what I'd long perceived as weaknesses in some aspects of my life were actually strengths. That was a breakthrough moment for me and Lordy. The program forced me to confront many of my demons, but what made the entire exercise worthwhile was receiving the feedback that someone who had contemplated committing suicide didn't go through with it after watching the program.

When I handed my command of the Americas over to Commander Xenia Cotter I was functioning, but not on all cylinders. It had been a tough three years, and while I loved my work over there, I was relieved to return to Australia. I decided to use my twelve months of long-service leave to devote my energies to my family. However, it concerned Kate and me that the euphoria I experienced from doing *Australian Story*, as well as the high I felt from succeeding in my role as Commander of the Americas, and the love I experienced from re-engaging with my family, dissipated not long after returning to Queensland. I experienced many 'dead' days, when I didn't have the energy or motivation needed to make the most of the time I'd planned to enjoy with Kate and Jacinta. Instead, I focused on other things, particularly reports of police officers who'd committed suicide and the way my officers who served in Afghanistan were – in my view – neglected by the AFP's superiors. I'd get angry and my mind would go into overdrive. I would seethe, asking Lordy why the system failed cops.

So Kate decided her Christmas present to me in 2018 would be to send me on a retreat. I welcomed the idea, but when she spoke about it I realised the one she had in mind wasn't just for me. It was group therapy, akin to holding hands and singing 'Kumbaya'. I appreciate that group retreats can help some people, but I knew I needed something else. We started googling health retreats in Queensland and found a website for the Goodsky Mental Health Retreat on the Sunshine Coast. The home page asked potential clients 'Do you have these tendencies?', and when I went through the list of thirteen traits I ticked all but one box. Their list included all the things I was angry about, including the subjects that I found other doctors wouldn't discuss, and that included the impact the inflammation in my body was having on my state of mind. Goodsky was appealing because it was a holistic program that addressed *me*: the chronic inflammation, the sleeplessness, the reliance on medication. I thought, *Hallelujah! I've found where I need to go.*

Their program was groundbreaking because it looked beyond the signs and symptoms of PTSD, depression and anxiety. Instead, it focused on the treatment of the major elements that were crucial to recovery. These include an individual's biological make-up: microbiome, chronic infection, hormones and genetics. I'd suffered some terrible diseases as a result of my policing career: tick paralysis, chikungunya virus, dengue fever, blastocystis, sleep apnoea, chronic inflammation, fibromyalgia and schistosomiasis.

Indeed, one of the biggest things I took from my stay at Goodsky was how the bacteria in the gut – microbes – can impact on the brain if their composition changes. I learnt that stress hormones can affect bacterial growth and compromise the integrity of the intestinal lining. This has a knock-on effect: those bacteria and toxins flood into the bloodstream, which can cause inflammation, a situation that studies around the world have found plays a role in several psychiatric disorders. It explained a lot, especially when I thought of the illnesses I'd suffered as a result of my service. Armed with this knowledge, I remembered the time I couldn't even pick up a coffee cup or open a door because my inflammation was so bad. I have no doubt those illnesses contributed to the deterioration of my mental health. The Goodsky course also took into consideration other contributors to an individual's mental and emotional health, including long-term stress, adverse childhood events, trauma and self-esteem issues. It also examined lifestyle factors, including low nutrition, insufficient sleep, lack of movement and connection. I swear, this program could have been tailored for me.

In the decade I'd spent speaking to medical specialists and practitioners, I'd insisted my problems were somehow interlinked, but as compelling as my case was, none of them agreed. It wasn't until my fortnight on the Sunshine Coast that I discovered that unless the issues I spoke to those other doctors about are identified and properly treated, a person will likely experience depression and anxiety, chronic inflammation, pain, adrenal fatigue, exhaustion, hormonal imbalance, digestive issues, insomnia, lowered immunity, and bacterial and other imbalances.

What I liked most about the course is that patients aren't lumped into a group, and there were occasions when I received up to fourteen hours a day worth of personal treatment, all monitored by trained medical personnel who would punch data and their observations into a computer to formulate the best treatment for my problems. It encompassed mind, body and spirit. One aspect of the course I really loved was the equine therapy, which allowed me to understand and connect with perhaps the most intuitive animal on the planet: horses. As 'prey' animals, horses have learnt to assess any creature that crosses their path and, depending on their assessment, they'll either stay or they'll flee. My horse was named Nelson, and he could quite easily have been my equine spirit. He had competed in equestrian as a younger stallion, and just as my sporting pursuits had left me with a badly damaged hip, Nelson suffered with the same ailment. Nelson taught me that, unlike humans, horses have retained the instinct to quickly let go of any stress. If they're spooked they might run for miles, but once they've outrun the danger they don't hang on to the anxiety or fright. They let it pass, like a breeze. Sometimes, when I look at the photographs that were taken of me and Nelson during my stay I feel a sense of calm. That feeling is his gift to me.

Now I follow a stringent program to control my PTSD, which includes:

- following a substantial supplementation program to help re-establish the gut microbiome and neurotransmitters. These noxious elements will eventually be obliterated and then replaced with new microbiome and neurotransmitters through nutrition.
- a recalibrated diet to assist with rebalancing the gut, which means I eat more vegetables and steer clear of caffeine and alcohol
- regular psychotherapy sessions
- continued engagement with a dietician and a naturopath
- a recalibrated exercise program
- undertaking therapy to improve the quality of my sleep and using technology to support it
- mindfulness and meditation
- re-engaging with my family and friends.

While I was optimistic about what the Goodsky program could do for me, it helped that I made the conscious decision to throw myself into it. The first few months of the program were exhausting, and I was grateful to have done the course when I didn't have any AFP commitments. Kate was included in everything I did, although there were times when I was so exhausted during the course all I could do was text, 'Love you. Good night,' when she messaged to find out how I was. Her support, as always, played a major part in where I am today. Another activity that helped underpin the results I enjoyed through Goodsky was writing this book because, while I've revisited a lot of things I didn't want to, it allowed me to understand how I'd reached my lowest ebb. When I returned home to Kate and Jacinta from what I call two 'super-charged' weeks of treatment, it was the best I had felt in years.

I'd finally returned home to my family.

For almost fifty years my life was a closed book. I hid so many things that I was ashamed of: a homosexual father, a mother who turned to alcoholism and welcomed drug-addicted gang members into our home, and the grandfather I loved more than anyone else who killed himself. For most of my childhood – and the years that followed – I was worried people would judge me based on those things. I didn't want to be known as the 'poof's son', the kid with a mother who some would judge harshly and the boy whose Pa committed suicide. I unnecessarily tormented myself for years, worrying that people would discover my secrets. I saw elements of my family life as weaknesses that could be used against me. I also fought very hard to suppress the old thought that in some way my family background made me less worthy than the other children Jenelle and I went to school with. It didn't.

As someone who has spent over thirty years in a profession that deals with facts and evidence, this is what I now realise about myself and my background: I am the product of a gay father, an alcoholic mother and the grandfather who took his own life. However, I've realised that while each of them had their flaws – who doesn't? – they were essentially good people.

And I know they loved me. I didn't appreciate until I grew older and wiser that each of them played their part in fostering a great strength in me. Yes, physically I grew into a giant who could pull a steam train, but of greater significance is that having to deal with the abnormalities of my family allowed me to develop an inner strength that galvanised me to become a member of the Australian Federal Police Force. That allowed me to deal with the worst of society and survive some tough tests. However, I do acknowledge that after enduring years of trauma I reached a breaking point that almost led to my self-destruction.

I hope my book empowers people to realise the wisdom in letting go of whatever their baggage may be. The title of this book is *The Strong Man*, but ultimately I found an unexpected strength from leaping into the great unknown and trusting people with the truth about . . . well, who I am. That has enriched my life because I saw people such as Assistant Commissioner David Sharpe and Commissioner Andrew Colvin rise to their very best as human beings. My fear of being thrown on the scrap heap wasn't ever an option for them. Instead, they offered me hope and purpose through keeping faith in me. Kate, Emilee and Jacinta have humbled me by teaching me the strength that exists in unconditional love and loyalty. Each of them were my guiding lights in the darkest times of my life. Especially Lordy.

I'll sign off with a message to my brothers and sisters in the police family. You are a rare breed, and by following a calling that by its very nature will expose you to the worst of society, I am sorry to say you're guaranteed some terrible days. However, take my tip: keep your eyes open for the good about you, because it is there. It might be in your wife or husband, your kids or your pet, but there is goodness about you, and you need to cling to it. As for that bloody invisible backpack you're handed on graduation day, it's a pain in the arse. However, you don't have to let it break your back by continuing to carry every pebble you'll collect. Try to take it off occasionally. Readjust the straps and, most importantly, *trust* the people around you to help lighten the load when it gets too hard to keep moving forward.

It might just save your life.

KATE'S STORY

Anyone with a partner who is suffering from post-traumatic stress disorder will appreciate it when I say being the 'other person' impacted is debilitating. It's a one-way ticket to an exhausting and heartbreaking existence where everything you hold dear is challenged.

Through no fault of your own, your life becomes an emotional roller-coaster ride where you're pushed to the limit. It's relentless and brutal, although I did find occasional respite when I briefly saw the man I'd married before he disappeared – again – into the depths of depression and PTSD.

When I'm desperate for information I'll google my queries – after all, the internet has the answers to everything, right? I tried what seemed a million ways to ask how the partner of someone with PTSD could help their own situation. While I was bombarded with pages of information, all of it related to the patient and not the carer. 'Come on, Google, help *me*!' I didn't need any more information on how to help Grant.

When I realised there was nothing I could access for practical help I felt despondent. What made my particular situation harder was I couldn't talk to anyone – outside of the strict confidence of my mother and best friend, Cathy – given that Grant was terrified his career would be over if his 'secret' was exposed.

It was a tough time. While I realise some people with PTSD can lash out physically and verbally, I didn't have that problem because Grant and I don't argue – not even during the worst of his struggles.

However, I can't describe the hurt I felt to have my husband sitting two feet away from me after he returned from Afghanistan and knowing he wasn't really 'with' me and our daughter, Jacinta. What added to my hurt was that Grant had so much energy for his police work and the long line of outsiders who wanted his help. I'd even ask, 'Why do those people get the best of you, but we get nothing?'

His coldness was so unbearable there were many times when, as much as I clung to the countless reasons why I loved Grant, it could've been easy to just walk away. But I didn't want that. I did everything possible to fight for 'us'. I'd look at Jacinta and think how she deserved better from her parents. She was the reason why I dug in for our family. I also clung to the good days we had – and hoped the time would come when we had more good days than bad weeks.

Grant couldn't understand that. He had the notion that everything was glowing. He was at home, after all. He believed his physical presence was enough. He was unable to realise he wasn't emotionally present. There were days when I wondered whether Jacinta and I mattered to him. And, while I hate to say this, there were countless occasions when he was downright selfish – a point Grant has acknowledged throughout the writing of this book, and now to me.

Keeping your identity as the partner of someone battling PTSD is tough. The first time I ever heard Grant reveal he'd come close to committing suicide was when he spoke about it on ABC's *Australian Story* in 2017. My anxiety levels escalated, and I started to again tippy-toe around because I didn't want to put Grant under pressure. I feared saying something that could cause him to do something dreadful to himself. I only became aware of the specifics of that terrible moment by reading a draft of *The Strong Man*: the undoing of his seatbelt, speeding the car up, looking towards the horizon at the spot where he intended to end his life . . . I felt ill. But, I was also terrified. If I couldn't pick up on any of that the first time, how could I if it happened again?

After living for years with a partner who suffers from PTSD, I've started having my own psych sessions through *Soldier On Australia* (expanded from the military to also care for members of the AFP, Border Force, Department of Foreign Affairs and Trade as well as other security agencies) to help me deal with the impact the battle has had on me. And they're helping.

The PTSD epidemic will continue to be an issue for as long as the government continues to commit troops – and now, police – to war zones. But on the home front, we need to acknowledge that there are first responders who've had careers in excess of thirty years, and they've seen terrible sights in their roles as paramedics, fire fighters, police, prison officers and SES workers. As a society we can't believe these people really turn up to work unaffected by the sights and sounds that cause them to have horrific nightmares.

The government has committed itself to protecting children from illnesses with vaccinations. It's called 'preventative medicine'.

It needs to show the same care for those in service occupations by initiating preventative programs that teach first responders and military personnel mechanisms that will help them cope with the traumas they'll endure.

Finally, I'd like to note the importance of the commitment AFP Commissioner Andrew Colvin and his peers made to Grant when he came forward to say he had a problem. By accepting PTSD is a direct result of the work police officers do, AJ Colvin has proven how far compassion, support and the police virtue of 'having your back' can go. I would like to thank AJ, and friends such as Chief of Staff Chris Black, David Sharpe and Megan Fox (who went beyond the call of duty to help Grant and me), because without their support, acknowledgement and encouragement . . . we wouldn't be here today.

By ensuring Grant remained a functioning member of the AFP, AJ not only provided my husband with hope, but he also instilled the belief he hadn't lost his whole identity to some terrible demons.

Kate 'Lordy' Lord
2019

ACKNOWLEDGEMENTS

Writing *The Strong Man* has been a cathartic experience because I've confronted many aspects of my life that would've been easier to leave untouched. There are stories within this book that hurt to revisit, but I hope they help anyone who is going through a challenging time to realise they aren't alone. For so many of us, 'abnormal is normal'.

My childhood was tougher than most, but one benefit from telling my story is realising that my sister, Jenelle, and I were well loved and cared for by our parents, despite the many issues that plagued our childhoods.

I am forever indebted to author Daniel Lane – whom I knew a lifetime ago at East Hills – for the countless hours of interviews, as well as the long days and late nights that were needed to produce this book. I know Daniel is as proud of the end result as I am.

I thank Simon & Schuster Australia, especially Roberta Ivers, for having the faith to tell my story. The trust I placed in Roberta and her staff was well placed. I'd like to single out Janet Hutchinson for her superb job of editing my manuscript.

While this book details my career as a proud member of the Australian Federal Police, the sacrifices and pain I detail are applicable to officers in any law enforcement agency who take the oath to serve and protect their communities. Only those who do our job (and their families) can truly appreciate the toll it takes.

I would like to express my gratitude to Commissioner Andrew Colvin for writing the foreword for *The Strong Man*. The commissioner's willingness to do this is a personal honour because I've long been inspired by his integrity, the courage of his convictions and the empathy he's shown his officers. Thank you, Sir.

My experiences have led to me committing myself to promoting throughout the police community the importance of mental health and welfare. I therefore thank the following people for the help they provided me in designing and implementing two AFP Global Mental Health Conferences. These distinguished people made themselves available for a senior executive from the AFP to meet with them in order to learn best practices for treating the issue of mental health in law enforcement. I acknowledge: Professor Richard Southby, Distinguished Professor of Global Health and Executive Dean Emeritus, Milken Institute School of Public Health, The George Washington University; Professor Nick Crofts AM, Director, Centre for Law Enforcement and Public Health, Honorary Professorial Fellow, University of Melbourne; Dr Katy Kamkar, Psychologist CAMH and director of Badge of Life Canada; Sergeant Bill Rusk (Ret), Badge of Life Canada; Lynne Rusk, former police officer at Badge of Life Canada; Detective Jeff Thompson (PhD), NYPD; Sergeant Stephen Bishopp (PhD), Dallas PD; Chief Constable Andy Rhodes, Lancashire police

(UK); Dr Ian Hesketh, Lancashire Police (Ret) and UK Policing College; Director Andy Traver, NCIS; Executive Director AFOSI, Jeff Specht (Ret); Executive Director Peter Edge (Ret), US Immigration and Customs Enforcement; David Bowdich, Deputy Director FBI; Allan Sparkes, Deputy Commissioner NSW Mental Health Commission (NSW Police Ret), International Association of Chiefs of Police, Canadian Association of Chiefs of Police; Dr Greg Anderson, the Dean, Office of the Applied Research & Graduate Studies at the Justice Institute of British Columbia (JIBC), and the Associate Director, Police Services for the Canadian Institute for Public Safety Research and Treatment.

Grant Edwards
May 2019

ABOUT THE AUTHOR

Sydney-born Grant Edwards is a senior officer in the Australian Federal Police.

During his thirty-four-year career, Commander Edwards has served his nation in dozens of foreign countries. In 2008, he was sent to East Timor to command all AFP personnel after the tiny nation gained its independence from Indonesia. In 2012, Edwards was Deputy Commander of the International Police Coordination Board in war-torn Afghanistan.

Two years later, Edwards was selected for one of the AFP's most coveted roles – Commander of the Americas – where he was based in Washington D.C. While there, he formed a strong alliance with Mexico's federal law enforcement agency to combat the cartels that are flooding Australia with shipments of drugs, including ice.

He has enjoyed a varied – and outstanding – police career, working in a number of portfolios, including child exploitation, human trafficking, cybercrime, aviation, surveillance and the drug squad.

Edwards has also excelled in sport. Besides securing the title as Australia's Strongest Man, he was also a champion power-lifter, member of the Australian bobsleigh team, one of the first Aussies to receive an American Football scholarship at the University of Hawaii, and he won a bronze medal for shot-put at an international tournament.

He muscled his way into the Guinness World Records after pulling a nineteenth-century 201-tonne steam train engine for a world record 36.8 metres. Over the years he's stunned people all around the globe with his ability to single-handedly pull heavy machinery, including a RAAF Hercules, a tram, and even the HMS *Bounty*.

Edwards in happily married and is the proud father of two daughters. *The Strong Man* is his first book.